THE FAR EASTERN CRISIS

Recollections and Observations

THE FAR EASTERN CRISIS

CRISIS

Recollections and Observations

BY

Henry L. Stimson

NEW YORK
Howard Fertig
1974

Library of Congress Cataloging in Publication Data
Stimson, Henry Lewis, 1867-1950.
The Far Eastern crisis.
Reprint of the 1st ed. published for the Council on
Foreign Relations by Harper, New York.
1. Eastern question (Far East) 2. Manchuria.
3. Japanese in Manchuria. I. Council on Foreign
Relations. II. Title.
DS783.7.S8 1974   951'.8'04   70-80593

Printed in the United States of America
by Noble Offset Printers, Inc.

To

M. W. S.

CONTENTS

MAPS

FOREWORD

THE assault upon the Chinese government in Manchuria by the Japanese army in September, 1931, was the first major blow at the new system of war limitation and prevention built up by the nations which had suffered in the Great War. More and more it is becoming recognized as a critical event in world history. The military successes of the aggressor at that time have already lent encouragement to further attempts against that system by other discontented and autocratic governments. On the other hand, the lessons to be learned from the experiences of those who then labored for coöperation in support of peaceful methods for the solution of international controversies have been neither thoroughly recorded nor studied.

While possessing neither the time nor the talents of an historian, I was in a unique position to witness the efforts and understand the purposes of one of the governments engaged in those efforts. In this book I have not attempted a revelation of hitherto unpublished facts. But the sequence of cause and effect, as well as the governmental purposes which underlay the facts, I believe, have not been adequately recorded, and my effort is to make them clear.

We are living today in a new and interdependent world with rapidly developing problems involving peace or war. The Covenant of the League of Nations, the Pact of Paris and the so-called Nine Power Treaty relating to the Far East, represent perhaps the three chief contractual efforts which have been made since

xii   FOREWORD

the Great War to assist in the solution of those problems. To two of those treaties the United States is a
prominent party; to the League Covenant, although a
proponent, we are not a party. Nevertheless that
League today remains the medium by which the great
majority of the governments of the world seek to limit
and prevent a general war and our relations to it in such
a matter are therefore of vital concern both to it and to
us. The development of effective methods of coöperation between it and us is an underlying international
problem of the most urgent importance in the world
today. It pressed upon us in regard to Manchuria in
1931; it pressed upon us in regard to Ethiopia in 1935;
it has not yet been adequately solved. The urgent pressure of this problem is my reason for writing of a matter
concerning which otherwise I might appropriately
have remained silent.

THE FAR EASTERN CRISIS

Recollections and Observations

PART ONE

BACKGROUNDS OF AMERICAN
POLICY IN THE FAR EAST

BACKGROUNDS OF AMERICAN POLICY IN THE FAR EAST

ON DIPLOMATIC DAY at the State Department, September 17, 1931, the Japanese Ambassador at Washington, Mr. Katsuji Debuchi, called upon me and told me that he was about to return to Japan on his triennial leave. He said that he expected to be gone until February and trusted that there would be no important matters between our two countries which might be inconvenienced by his absence. We discussed the relations of the two countries and we agreed that they seemed to be more tranquil than for many years past. Mr. Debuchi said he recently had been on a long trip throughout the United States and had found everywhere more marked evidences of friendliness towards his own country than he had ever before noted during his long stay as Ambassador.

I replied that that corresponded to my own observation; that American opinion towards Japan had become so kindly that I was encouraged to hope that before I left office I might be able to take up for successful solution the long standing source of irritation arising out of our immigration laws of nearly ten years before, and to put them upon a basis which, while conforming to our own requirements, might be not offensive to the sensibilities of the Japanese people. He expressed his strong concurrence in my hope and, after our mutual expressions of satisfaction on the situation, he departed saying that on the following week he would return to make his formal adieu.

Mr. Debuchi had been a hard-working and efficient Ambassador. During the two years and a half which had elapsed since I had assumed my post in the Department, we had occasion to handle difficult problems together and he had been earnest and effective in his efforts at promoting mutual understanding in Far Eastern matters. His two sons were being educated in Princeton University and in telling me of them he had said to me, "You see, I have given hostages for the good will of your country." I looked forward even to his temporary absence with regret.

Within forty-eight hours of our conversation cables were pouring into the Department from the Far East filled with such ominous news from Manchuria that I shortly sent for the Ambassador and requested him, in the face of the serious problem thus presented to us, to give up his proposed vacation and remain at his post. He told me that he had already canceled his passage.

At the State Department it did not seem a very propitious moment to take on the burdens of a new international crisis in the Far East. Our painful attention had been concentrated elsewhere for many months. In the spring of 1931 the long economic depression had reached catastrophic proportions in Europe. The fall of the national bank of Austria, known as the Credit Anstalt, had produced repercussions in Germany which threatened the economic stability of all Central Europe and had finally led President Hoover to propose the one-year moratorium in the payment of international debts as an effort to ward off the calamity of a world-wide financial crash. I had spent a portion of the summer in attendance at the Seven Power Financial Conference in London, as well as in visits to Paris and Berlin devoted to efforts towards the same end. While there I had witnessed the beginning of the runs upon the Bank of England, and on September 18th, the very day—almost the very hour—of the outbreak in Manchuria, I was receiving word from the British chargé that Great Britain could no longer maintain the gold standard. It seemed as though from the Occident to the Orient, politically and economically, the world was rocking.

The impact of the European financial crisis was already shaking the stability of our own banking structure in America. Some two billion dollars of investments from every portion of the United States had been poured into Central Europe and, when these were threatened after two years of local panic and depression, the effect upon our banks was ominous. The rate of bank failures throughout the country rapidly increased and soon reached proportions which seemed to threaten the entire credit system of the nation. The condition was so much worse than in any previous crisis within the experience of living men, that the usual leadership from private finance and industry, on which the country had been accustomed to rely in times past, failed utterly to meet the situation. The chief responsibility fell upon the President of the United States and throughout the autumn Mr. Hoover was absorbed with the burden of organizing those great measures of reconstruction upon which the country has leaned ever since. Under such circumstances the margin of his time and initiative which was left for dealing with a new crisis on the opposite side of the world necessarily was reduced to a minimum. If anyone had planned the Manchurian outbreak with a view to freedom from interference from the rest of the world, his time was well chosen.

It was fortunate, under these circumstances, that the American government had in its key positions at the time of the crisis men who were not altogether inexperienced in Far Eastern history and policies. The President himself had spent several years in the Far East and had had the unique experience of being in Tientsin during the Boxer Rebellion and the siege of that city by the rebels. I had made several brief trips to China and Japan and as Governor General of the Philippines had witnessed and studied the politics of the Far East from a position of official responsibility. The man who was Premier of Japan in September, 1931, had been my colleague in the London Naval Conference of 1930.

The State Department was supported both in the field and at home by a group of unusually experienced men. The Ambassador to Japan, Mr. Forbes, had held for eight years official posts in the Philippines, including four years as Governor General. The embassy at Tokyo was manned by a staff of long experience. The Minister to China, Mr. Nelson T. Johnson, was a career diplomat and a recognized expert in Chinese matters. In the State Department at Washington the Under Secretary, Mr. Castle, had been Ambassador to Japan; and the chief of the Far Eastern Division, Dr. Stanley K. Hornbeck, combined long personal experience in the Far East with careful and accurate study of Oriental problems and history. At various critical posts in China we were represented by Consul Generals of unusual experience in the persons of Mr. Hanson, the Consul General at Harbin; Mr. Cunningham, the Consul General at Shanghai; and Mr. Peck, the Consul General at Nanking.

I mention these matters only because it has become rather the fashion among our people to regard their diplomats and foreign representatives as so much less experienced in their professions than the men from other nations with whom they have to deal, as to place the interests of this country at a disadvantage in its relations with other nations. Americans who thus depreciate their government's foreign servants do not realize what a transformation in such matters has taken place during the past thirty years since the American foreign service has been lifted out of party politics and placed upon the basis of a permanent life career for its members. As a matter of fact, throughout this crisis in Manchuria of which I am writing, the American government was served so efficiently by its agents and representatives, as well as by the initiative and energy of the American press correspondents on the ground, that we were habitually placed in the position of having in our hands earlier and more accurate information than almost any other country. This soon became so well known as to be commented on in the meetings of the League of Nations, whose officials asked me to assist them in checking up their less accurate reports concerning the confused events which were crowding in upon us.

It does not come within the scope of this sketch of American policy to attempt either a detailed history of facts or an analytical study of the forces and events in the Far East. In touching upon these matters I am confining myself to such descriptions as will serve to explain our purposes in Washington and to make clear the background upon which we were acting.

To the American government Japan was a friendly, powerful, and sensitive neighbor which within the short space of a single human lifetime had emerged from the isolation of feudal military autocracy into a modern industrialized state. Under the guidance of a very far-sighted group of elder statesmen she had assimilated with extraordinary rapidity the material elements of a Western civilization. Her energetic and intelligent people had made gigantic strides in the technical arts, in manufactories, and in commerce. This industrial development was also gradually resulting in liberalism in social and political ideas. Japan had adopted a constitution with parliamentary features and she had been extending the suffrage among her people. But for seven centuries prior to 1850 her administrative and privileged class had been the soldier, while the bread-winner and business man were relegated to a rôle of inferiority.

This long inheritance in the case of a people as keenly patriotic as the Japanese had borne fruits which were not easily dislodged by the theories of modern popular sovereignty. For many years after a Cabinet was introduced, its leaders were military men. The theory that the civilian government as the representatives of the entire people should command the loyalty of the army and the navy had not been generally accepted by the Japanese nation. The chiefs of those military services, instead of being subordinate to the Cabinet, had direct and independent access to the Emperor as the head of the state. The Western school of democratic thought was making progress, but that progress was slow and never fully shared by large elements of the population. In 1930 ratification of the Naval Treaty with Britain and the United States was opposed by Admiral Kato, the head of the naval staff. When the Emperor ratified that treaty on the advice of Premier Yuko Hamaguchi, the civilian head of the government, over this naval protest, this step in the

direction of modern constitutionalism caused deep resentment and was probably influential in producing
some of the violent reactionary consequences which
followed. Mr. Hamaguchi was soon afterwards assas-
sinated by a military fanatic, and secret organizations
were formed which were destined to have a baleful influence upon the course of Japanese history.

But in September, 1931, the statesmen in office still
belonged to the moderate or constitutional school and
were those who had been in the lead of the movement
towards Western ideas. Mr. Hamaguchi had been succeeded as Premier by Mr. Reijiro Wakatsuki, who had
headed the Japanese delegation at the London Naval
Conference. The Foreign Office was presided over by
Baron Kijuro Shidehara, well known for his enlightened and liberal policies in foreign affairs and particularly towards China. Mr. Inouye, the Finance
Minister, had brought Japanese credit and finance to
a condition of soundness which was recognized throughout the financial world. General manhood suffrage had
been adopted for the election of the members of the
lower house of the Diet and the first election thereunder had been held in February, 1928.[1]

In short, to the windows of the State Department our
Japanese neighbors across the North Pacific appeared
as a proud, sensitive, and ambitious people, intensely
patriotic, with a tradition of original friendliness
towards the United States, though it had been recently
marred by what they considered the insulting form
adopted by our Congress in its immigration laws. Their

[1] During that election day I happened to be personally present in Tokyo
as the guest of the Premier, General Baron Giichi Tanaka, and in my
conversations with him and his colleagues received an interesting impression
of the progress in liberalism which was being effected by the industrialization
of the large cities of Japan as contrasted with the conservatism of the small
farmers and peasants.

basic inheritance of the virtues and weaknesses of militarism had been only partially modified by the developing economic and social conditions of the industrial revolution and the ideas of Western democracy which had come with it, and their government still reflected these two elements, as yet imperfectly blended and each striving for mastery.

Furthermore, Japan's modern army had been trained by German instructors in the ideas and theories of the German General Staff. It had fought three brief and successful wars. Instead of suffering, as had the European nations, from the World War, Japan had greatly profited. Although she had joined with those European nations in the post-war multilateral treaties[2] which had been the fruit of the Occidental suffering from war and were intended to curb and prevent war's recurrence, all of her historic traditions as well as her recent experiences made it extremely unlikely that these treaties, with their peaceful objectives, represented to her the earnest hopes and purposes which they did to the West.

There were also other friendly neighbors in the Far East besides the Japanese whose interests and problems necessarily affected the policies of the American government at least as vitally as did those of Japan. In shaping our policy towards the events which were taking place in Manchuria, we could not lose sight of the problems and interests of China. Indeed, in the long view of history, in estimating future probabilities by centuries rather than by decades, it was self-evident that the eventual trans-Pacific relations of the United States would be enormously, if not predominantly, affected by

[2] The Covenant of the League of Nations, the so-called Nine Power Treaty and the Pact of Paris. These documents are printed in full as Appendices I, II, and III.

the future development of the 450 millions of Chinese people dwelling on the mainland behind the islands of Japan. For four thousand years China had continuously and tenaciously developed and maintained her entity and peculiar culture. Often assailed and sometimes conquered by enemies, she had in the end outlasted or absorbed her conquerors and had succeeded in maintaining a civilization which outdated that of the Western nations of the globe.

When the technical inventions of the nineteenth century diminished distance and brought the Far East within easy reach of the rest of the world, it was inevitable that China's previous isolation would be destroyed and her habits and civilization vitally affected by those of the rest of the world. She had not yielded easily; she had not shown the facile cleverness displayed by Japan in assimilating Western science and technique and in adopting Western standards. On the contrary, she had for a long time stubbornly opposed all such changes and had yielded only to force in her relations with the Western world.

But in the early years of the twentieth century the inevitable had arrived and the modernization of China had begun. For nearly three decades prior to the events which I am discussing, she had been a nation in flux, absorbed in the effort to evolve administrative and governmental changes which would be adequate to meet the problems of the modern world. Her problems of assimilation and transformation were infinitely more difficult than those of Japan, owing to the size of her territory, her defective administration and finance, and the tendency of her people to think in terms of family and locality rather than of national unity.

But unmistakable evidences of transformation were manifesting themselves. The great sluggish population,

which in 1895 did not realize that it was at war with
Japan except in two or three of the provinces immediately affected by the operations, had achieved by 1925
such an increased sense of unity that the shooting of a
few students by the international police at Shanghai
caused an instantaneous quiver of nationalistic feeling
through virtually the entire country. It reacted in immediate reprisals against the commerce of those nations
which China deemed to be responsible for the incident.
The old dynastic government had fallen. The Western
theories sponsored by the followers of Sun Yat-sen had
triumphed over the more conservative military leaders
of northern China; and a government, republican in
form, had been established at Nanking.

No one could be wise enough to foresee what would
be the ultimate result of the great changes which were
taking place. We could only be certain that the character of those results would powerfully influence for
good or for evil the entire world. We could only foresee that the future stability and peace of every continent
of the earth would be adversely affected if the hundreds
of millions of hitherto industrious and peace-loving
people of China should in their awakening to modern
life be transformed into an aggressive power, fired by
the memories of wrongs done to them by other nations
and dominated by the theories of selfish military exploitation which most of the nations of the Western
world since the Great War had been endeavoring to
renounce.

Fortunately, an intelligent realization of these issues
had guided for over thirty years the policy of the
American government towards China. That policy,
enunciated first as the Open Door policy of John Hay
and afterwards carried to successful fruition in the
Washington Treaties of 1922, had been one of those

rare instances where a nation had recognized that far-sighted self-interest was dependent upon justice and fair play towards a neighbor. Breaking into a situation where the selfish attempts of the European powers to carve out spheres of self-interest at the expense of China had resulted in the chaos of the Boxer Rebellion, John Hay checked that chaos by enunciating the theory of equality of commercial opportunity for all nations in dealing with China and predicated such equality upon the preservation of China's territorial and administrative integrity.

These principles were not entirely new in the foreign policy of the United States. In substance they had been American principles for many years in shaping our commercial intercourse with other nations. But in the case of China they were invoked to save a situation which at the close of the last century not only threatened the future development and sovereignty of that great Asiatic people, but also threatened to create dangerous and increasing rivalries between the other nations of the world. When in 1922 these principles of the Open Door policy were successfully embodied in the formal covenants of the Nine Power Treaty at the Washington Conference, the American government had carried through in a most critical and vital portion of the world an example of the best kind of international diplomacy—a policy of enlightened self-interest, as contrasted with self-seeking aggression.

In doing so it had at the same time laid the foundations for the development of a good will on the part of the Chinese people towards this country which bade fair to be of permanent and real value to the United States. In this respect it served to crown the results of other American actions towards China, both official and unofficial. For many years China had received from this country the religious, educational, and medical benefits of the greatest private missionary effort which had ever been made by the people of one country towards those of another. Also the American government had been the first of the nations to return to the people of China for educational purposes the indemnity payments which America had received for the injury done to its citizens in the Boxer Rebellion. And last but not least, China had witnessed for thirty years close to its shores in the Philippine Islands, the successful efforts of the American government to educate an Oriental people in the practices of Western political freedom and social organization.

All of these things had combined to give to America a standing in Chinese eyes which was different from that held by any other country. During my stay in the Philippines I had on more than one occasion exceptional opportunities to witness how real that feeling was. Of course no one could tell how long it would survive the vicissitudes of international life, and since then unfortunate incidents have already occurred to mar Chinese confidence in American purposes.[3] But at least in facing the tremendous possibilities which were opened for future generations by the modernization of China, the American government had made a start which augured well for that future. It had created an atmosphere full of possibilities for good. So, in shaping our action and policies towards the events which were now breaking out in Manchuria, this existing confidence of China in American fair play and good faith constituted a factor which could not lightly be jeopardized.

Manchuria, where the interests of China and Japan

[3] For example, the American Silver Purchase Act of 1934 has disrupted China's finance and brought great commercial loss to that country.

had now come into armed conflict, was the least static portion of the area of China. Geographically, it was the focal spot where three large nations came within strik-

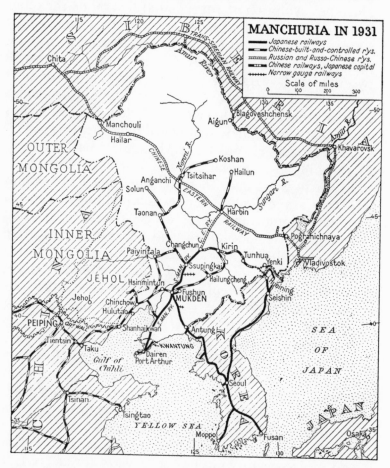

ing distance of one another—China, Japan, and Russia. It possessed almost a vital interest for each of them, and during the past forty years it had been the scene of rapid oscillations of political, racial, and economic action.

Although the Manchus were racially akin to the
Chinese and had actually ruled China for the three
hundred years from the overthrow of the Ming dynasty
until the revolution of 1911, and although, on the other
hand, Manchuria had been also largely colonized by
Chinese settlers from the south and had been in large
part subject to their purely Chinese culture for some
two thousand years, yet large portions of it remained
undeveloped and scantily populated until the beginning of the twentieth century. When the Manchus
conquered China, their southward movement was char-
acterized by an exodus from Manchuria itself, greatly
diminishing its population, and this condition lasted
until thirty years ago. In 1904, when the Russian and
Japanese armies fought for its domination, it was still
an almost untenanted frontier country, and its vast
plains of fertile unoccupied land left it open as a prize
for whoever should first effectively colonize it. Its area
is as large as Germany and France combined, and a
large proportion thereof is suitable for agriculture. Its
mountainous regions are rich in timber and minerals,
especially coal.

For many years the eyes of Japan had rested with
apprehension on the mainland lying towards the west,
and with the growth of Russian power in Siberia her
apprehension increased. To the Japanese military leaders the peninsula of Korea, running southward from
Manchuria, had been "a dagger aimed at the heart of
Japan." Behind it lay the threat of the powerful Russian Empire steadily pushing southward for an ice-free
harbor on the Pacific Ocean and the ultimate domination of that portion of the world.

The Sino-Japanese War of 1895 was Japan's first
battle to ward off such a menace. By ending the titular
sovereignty of China over Korea, it left Japan a free

hand in that country and by successive steps she ultimately took possession of and annexed it in 1910. It
also gave her for a brief period Port Arthur and a foot-
hold on the Manchurian hinterland, but Russia, with
the aid of France and Germany, intervened and forced
Japan temporarily to release these Manchurian acquisi-
tions. When Russia pushed on and seized them for
herself, Japan, summoning the limit of her resources,
had fought Russia for what she deemed to be her very
life's existence; had won back Port Arthur and the
Liaotung peninsula, and had succeeded to Russia's
rights in southern Manchuria.

To every Japanese this was a war for freedom and
safety. These rights in Manchuria were called the "life
line" of Japan's national defense. Her victory cost the
lives of 100,000 Japanese soldiers and two billion yen
in gold, and left in Japanese minds a determination that
such sacrifices should not have been made in vain.
Russia was driven back into northern Manchuria and
her rights there were reduced to her interests in the
Chinese Eastern Railway, which, running across the
north of that country, afforded a short cut in a great
loop of the Trans-Siberian Railway.

But singularly enough, though they had this deep
patriotic spirit to stir them and a steadily growing
population behind them to press them on, and though
the door of this new empty country was now wide open
to them, the Japanese people failed to press in and
colonize Manchuria. During the thirty years since the
close of the Russian war only about 230,000 Japanese
have settled in Manchuria, and they are mainly concentrated along the South Manchuria Railway and on
the Liaotung peninsula. Although the agricultural land
of Manchuria has been regarded as necessary for the
food supply of Japan, Japanese farmers have been un-

willing to go in and till it, and the bulk of the Japanese immigrants have been not producers, but persons connected with the administration of the railway and the towns which it has built up. Overcrowded Japan has been unwilling or unable to spread out westerly into this great open country.

On the other hand, the same period has witnessed a very different effort by China. The Chinese have come to look upon Manchuria as their first line of defense—a sort of buffer against the adjoining territories of Japan and Russia and an outpost against the penetration of these foreign influences into China. They also have awakened to its economic importance. They have long called it "the granary" of China, and of more recent years have regarded it as a region furnishing seasonal employment to farmers and laborers from neighboring Chinese provinces. But while the Japanese interest has mainly confined itself to the efforts of military leaders to develop its strategic strength and to the efforts of railway administrators and capitalists to exploit its opportunities for railway and industrial development, and while the Japanese people as a whole have kept aloof, Chinese farmers have moved in and occupied the soil. The last thirty years have witnessed one of the greatest popular migrations of world history. Nearly thirty millions of people are said to have poured northeastward from the crowded Chinese provinces of Shantung and Hopei and have occupied Manchuria. "Manchuria is now unalterably Chinese," was the verdict of the Lytton Commission in 1932. The Treaty of Portsmouth, which closed the Russo-Japanese War in 1905, at the same time reaffirmed the legal sovereignty of China over Manchuria. Since then the Chinese people themselves have transformed that legal title into an actual fact.

Due weight has not been given in current discussions
to the inevitable consequences of this great Chinese
migration into Manchuria. Titular sovereignty, like a
legal title when not backed by possession, may be overthrown or whittled away. But a population of thirty
million human beings, tenacious of their racial culture and stubborn in the assertion of their individual
rights, cannot permanently be ignored. Particularly is
that the case when the country which they occupy is
not an isolated region, but lies adjacent to another
country occupied by four hundred million more of the
same race, now slowly but with ever accelerating speed
developing a consciousness of national unity.

The development of Manchuria which has ensued
since 1905 has been indebted to both the Japanese and
Chinese peoples, each contributing in its own way; and
in providing for their respective needs Manchuria has
proved the usefulness of their partnership. Without the
benefit of Japanese capital and manufactures Manchuria could not have attracted and absorbed such a
large farming population. Without the flood of Chinese
farmers and laborers Manchuria could not have developed so rapidly and thus provided Japan with a market
for her exports as well as with supplies of food and
other raw materials. This mutual economic interdependence reveals how lamentable it is that conflicts
should arise to mar and destroy such a working partnership. Yet under the facts as they existed and in the
light of actions and reactions by which humanity is
habitually influenced and governed, it was inevitable
that such misunderstandings and controversies should
come about.

Manchuria was actually and legally a part of China.
But the people of Japan felt in it such an interest, historical, sentimental, and political, and were fortified in

their interest by such exceptional rights and claims, that a conflict between these claims and the sovereignty of China was practically inevitable. This danger was also accentuated by the fact that many of these rights, while always asserted with emphasis, were defined in very general terms and were not attested by documentary evidence which was unchallenged. Some of the treaties upon which Japanese claims rested were strenuously asserted by China to be either unauthentic or to have been executed under duress.

Whatever their authenticity, Japan under cover of these treaties was actually occupying a very unusual position in Manchuria. She governed the leased territory of the Liaotung peninsula with practically full powers of sovereignty. Throughout a zone which bordered the South Manchuria Railway she exercised powers of administration and police based upon the armed forces which she was permitted to maintain. These areas included towns and portions of large cities like Mukden and Changchun. In all these areas she controlled taxation, education, the police, and public utilities. In effect she maintained at least three varieties of armed forces—the Kwantung Army in the leased territory, the railway guards in the railway areas, and consular police throughout the various districts.

The Lytton Commission thus summed up the anomalous situation:

> This summary of the long list of Japan's rights shows clearly the exceptional character of the political, economic, and legal relation created between that country and China in Manchuria. There is probably nowhere in the world an exact parallel to this situation, no example of a country enjoying in the territory

of a neighboring state such extensive economic and administrative privileges. A situation of this kind could possibly be maintained without leading to incessant complications and disputes if it were freely desired or accepted on both sides and if it were the sign and embodiment of a well-considered policy of close collaboration in the economic and in the political sphere. But in the absence of those conditions it could only lead to friction and conflict.[4]

Somewhat such relations have been maintained in other portions of the world by powerful and advanced nations over populations of an entirely different race or civilization and of backward political and social culture. Even in such cases the march of history is demonstrating that such relations are transitory. No such disparity, however, was recognized here. The individual Chinese had for countless centuries considered himself at least the equal of the Japanese in capacity, culture, and race. The standing of his nation he has regarded as greatly higher than that of his neighbor. Indeed, for centuries the Chinese had maintained an unshakable feeling of superiority over all other races. Only the quickness with which Japan had imitated and adopted the externals of a Western civilization, which China for nearly a century had sincerely despised and rejected, had recently given to Japan a superiority in administrative capacity and military power.

Now, however, the awakening of China had begun in earnest and this awakening was certain to bring

[4] *Report of the Commission of Enquiry.* League of Nations Publication No. C.663. M.330, 1932. VII, Chap. III, Part 1. (Referred to hereafter as the Lytton Report.)

pressure upon these anomalous relations in Manchuria. The Imperial government of China was overthrown in 1912. For nearly two decades thereafter China was involved in a chaotic civil war between provincial leaders without apparent principle except the desire for power and loot. But under the leadership of Sun Yat-sen a Nationalist party, professing constitutional principles, emerged in the south at Canton and this party gradually won its way northward. At first it was aided by Communist emissaries from Russia, but it subsequently threw off this influence, quarreled with Russia and fought strenuously to put down the communism which had become established in several provinces. At last in 1928 this Nationalist movement succeeded in producing in China a nominal unity and a measure of actual unity and established a central government at Nanking under the presidency of General Chiang Kai-shek.

This period of struggle in China is often looked upon by outside observers as mere chaos. They are wrong. It has the inevitable roughness of the transition period during which this great people is pushing its way from its ancient patriarchal system into the modern nationalism of the present world.[5] In the process Chinese nationalism assumed the bitterness of an anti-foreign spirit. This also is not extraordinary when we recall the foreign encroachments of leased territories,

[5] The Washington Conference met at a most discouraging portion of this period of transition when conditions in China were more chaotic than they are today. It is one of the best tributes to the leadership of that conference that the leaders of all countries there assembled were not affected by the discouraging features, but recognized that they were inevitable symptoms of an encouraging evolution in China which should be sympathized with and protected. The principles of the Nine Power Treaty then adopted at Washington, which were agreed to by all governments interested in the Far East, including the then moderate government of Japan, symbolized this far-seeing and intelligent spirit.

concessions, and extraterritorial rights against which
the Chinese were forced to struggle for emancipation.
What is more relevant to our present study, they were
developing during this period a power of coördinated
action which they had never before possessed and a system of tactics which was peculiar to themselves. The
persistence which the Chinese have always shown as individuals was demonstrated here. The thing that was
new was the gradual acquisition of the power of co-
ordinated effort, extended over a greater and greater
territory and through ever-increasing masses of population. Instead of being dismayed by the chaos of China
during this period of transition, her friends should be
rather encouraged by the progress which she has made
in acquiring powers which were not only novel, but
were developed in the face of almost unique difficulties
in communication and transportation.

It was inevitable that this new spirit in the rest of
China should spread into Manchuria. It was equally
inevitable that in Manchuria it should produce repercussions in the unstable balance between the underlying
Chinese population and the super-imposed Japanese
privileges. The growth of national spirit in Manchuria
and the increasing sense of kinship felt by the people of
that portion of China with their countrymen in the
south can be easily traced in the conduct of their rulers.

When the revolution against the empire broke out
in 1911, the Manchurian authorities at first sought to
resist the advance of the revolutionary troops. Afterwards, throughout the broken period of civil war in
China, Chang Tso-lin, who was becoming the virtual
dictator of Manchuria, acted with great independence
towards the various factions which were in power in
China, sometimes siding with one and sometimes with
another. This was true of his attitude towards Sun

Yat-sen and the Nationalists during the early years when they were fighting their way into power. He sometimes worked with them and sometimes against them. He did not approve of Dr. Sun's constitution, but did approve of the unification of China which Sun and his followers were gradually accomplishing. He several times acted under Japanese advice and with Japanese aid against threats of invasion from one or the other military commanders in the south. But as the unification of China proceeded and the Nationalist government became established in Nanking, he gradually swung away from any association with Japan and showed an increasing unwillingness to allow her to profit from the privileges she possessed under the various treaties and agreements. He resented and disregarded the Japanese advice to keep out of the factional strife in China and concentrate his energy on the development of Manchuria. Even though he was often fighting with one or the other of the Chinese factions further south and several times invaded China proper with his armies, he did not do it as if it were a foreign country, but merely as one of the participants in a Chinese civil war.[6] When in June, 1928, he was killed by an explosion which wrecked his railway train near Mukden, his estrangement from Japan had become such that his followers strongly believed his death to be due to Japanese influence.

His son, Chang Hsueh-liang, who succeeded him as the ruler of Manchuria, swung still further away from Japan and within a few months, in December, 1928, contrary to the desires of Japan, declared his allegiance to the Nationalist government at Nanking and accepted the national flag as his. He was made Commander-in-chief of the northeastern frontier army and confirmed

[6] Lytton Report, Chap. II, Part 2.

as chief of the administration of Manchuria with the addition of Jehol, a part of Inner Mongolia.

This official recognition of the Nationalist government at Nanking by the rulers of Manchuria stimulated the growth of nationalism and anti-Japanese feeling throughout Manchuria. A "forward policy" to relieve Manchuria of the superimposed rights of foreigners had been begun by Marshal Chang Tso-lin. It was greatly accelerated under his son. His declaration of allegiance to Nanking opened the door to well-organized and systematic propaganda by the Kuomintang, the party of the Nationalist government, which had long been prosecuting a campaign throughout China for "the recovery of lost sovereign rights, the abolition of unequal treaties and the wickedness of imperialism." Such propaganda naturally created an unusually strong impression in Manchuria, where the reality of foreign interests in the shape of foreign courts, police, guards, and soldiers on Chinese soil was very apparent.

In 1929 the Chinese government came to an open quarrel with Russia over the Russian rights in the Chinese Eastern Railway in north Manchuria. Although in this they were unsuccessful, the agitation in south Manchuria against the Japanese continued with growing intensity. Systematic pressure was brought to make the position of Japanese and Korean residents uncomfortable; conferences were held of "Peoples' Foreign Policy Associations" to discuss the liquidation of the Japanese rights in Manchuria, including the recovery by China of the South Manchuria Railway, and a growing and dangerous tension gradually developed.

Thus the rise of national feeling in China, which for several years had resulted in increasing efforts by the

Chinese government to terminate the exceptional privileges of foreigners throughout the rest of the republic, was similarly manifested with increasing vigor in Manchuria. It was not an evidence of Chinese chaos. On the contrary, it was evidence of the increasing growth of a spirit of united nationalism in a people who had not previously possessed that feeling.

This tension was flavored with economic as well as political rivalry between Chinese and Japanese interests in that province. As the Chinese population increased, Chinese capital built additional railway lines, tapping rich agricultural portions of the province. These came into sharp competition with the interests of the South Manchuria Railway. The Japanese claimed that this new construction was in violation of the treaties between the two nations. The Chinese denied it, and the increasing prosperity of the Chinese lines at the expense of the earlier Japanese road greatly heightened the feeling of tension. By the summer of 1931 a number of incidents had occurred marking the continued growth of this political and economic animosity, some of which had been reported in the cables which the State Department was receiving from the Far East. It is not necessary to review them here. They were none of them of such gravity that they could not have been peacefully handled between governments whose relations were normal. But in Manchuria, as we can see now, they reflected a growing pressure between two rival nationalities which was certain sooner or later to break into flame.

When we come to examine the policy of the Japanese government towards this situation in Manchuria, we find a subject which is not free from complexity. On the one hand, there had been no apparent division among the Japanese people themselves or their parties or statesmen as to the importance of Japan's privileges in Manchuria. Ever since the close of the Russian War patriotic sentiment, the supposed exigencies of national defense and economic interest have all combined in support of a feeling that Japan possesses some very important special rights and interests in Manchuria differing from those possessed by any other nation. But exactly what that interest is—whether political and sovereign or merely economic and contractual—has not yet been made clear. Japanese statesmen have at various times sought to obtain from Russia, France, Great Britain, and the United States an international recognition of this "special interest" in Manchuria, but they have not defined it and their efforts have not met with permanent success. On the contrary, by joining in 1922 with the other signatories of the Nine Power Treaty, Japan would seem by the clearest language to have formally abrogated any claim to an interest which would impair "the sovereignty, the independence, and the territorial and administrative integrity" of China.

While, as I have said, there has been no cleavage in the Japanese feeling as to the existence and importance of this interest in Manchuria, whatever it is, there has been a very deep and fundamental cleavage in Japanese political thought as to the *method* by which that interest should be supported and enforced. This cleavage has in general corresponded with the alignment in Japan, to which I have already alluded, between those leaders who were following the ideals of constitutional and popular government on the one hand, and the conservative and military leaders on the other. The different policies which have resulted from this cleavage have come to be called, respectively, the "friendship" policy and the "positive" policy towards China. Historically, these names did not develop until about the time of the Washington Conference in 1921.

The friendship policy is associated with the name of Japan's great Foreign Minister, Baron Shidehara, and, in his words, was to be founded "on the basis of good will and neighborliness" towards China. The chief exponent of the positive policy was General Baron Tanaka. That policy rests ultimately upon military force, and its character was made clear by the frank declaration that "if disturbances spread to Manchuria and Mongolia and as a result peace and order are disrupted, thereby menacing our special position and rights and interests in these regions," Japan would "defend them, no matter whence the menace comes." Thus the latter policy assumed that Japan would take upon herself the task of forcibly preserving peace and order in Manchuria. It would thus seem to assume that Japan's rights are political and sovereign, whereas Shidehara had defined them as economic and contractual.

In short, while Japan's popular support of her privileges in Manchuria has always been strong and unanimous, their nature has never been clearly defined or internationally recognized, and the methods by which they should be asserted in the coming contest with China was an issue reaching down into the depths of the evolution towards constitutional government which was still in process of development in Japan itself.

PART TWO

EFFORTS AT CONCILIATION IN THE
MANCHURIAN CRISIS

EFFORTS AT CONCILIATION IN THE MANCHURIAN CRISIS

I

THE CLASH

ON THE morning of September 19, 1931, the world awoke to find that armed hostilities had broken out in Manchuria and that during the night Japanese forces had occupied not only the city of Mukden, but other cities in South Manchuria.

Of course we had known in the Department of the strained relations in Manchuria arising out of the rivalry of the two nations there and the acute controversies between the Chinese based upon their titular sovereignty and their enormous population on the one side, and the interests of Japan arising out of her claimed treaty rights along the South Manchuria Railway on the other. There had been preliminary warnings of possible trouble during the summer. A Japanese army captain, Nakamura, had disappeared and had then been found murdered. The Japanese army were resentful and were agitating for forcible action in reprisal. Investigations were going on and there was reported to be a very sharp division between the army authorities and the Foreign Office in Tokyo as to the steps which should be taken. But while the members of the American State Department were following the case, no immediate apprehension was caused in our minds.

When the news of the clash in Manchuria first reached us there was the usual conflict of divergent stories, each side giving an entirely different version. I reported in my diary on Saturday morning, September 19th:

> Trouble has flared up again in Manchuria. The Japanese, apparently their military elements, have suddenly made a coup. They have seized Mukden and a number of strategic towns centered all along and through southern Manchuria. The situation is very confused and it is not clear whether the army is acting under a plan of the government or on its own.

But very quickly the important features became clear. The incident which was claimed by the Japanese to have caused their action, namely an alleged act of sabotage by the Chinese on the South Manchuria Railway, diminished to such small proportions[1] as strongly to suggest its actual non-existence. Meanwhile the Japanese army was found to have acted with such promptness and celerity as to make it evident that they were moving under a previously arranged strategic plan. Although the clash on the railway line did not occur until ten o'clock at night on September 18th, that same night the Japanese attacked and captured the Chinese barracks and the great arsenal in Mukden, in which the main war supplies of the entire Manchurian Chinese army were stored, and before daylight all their forces

[1] Cf. Westel W. Willoughby, *The Sino-Japanese Controversy and the League of Nations*, pp. 24 *et seq.*

in Manchuria and some of those in Korea had been brought into action throughout the whole area of Southern Manchuria.

By the afternoon of September 19th cities like Antung, Changchun, and Newchwang, several hundred miles away from one another, had been occupied by the Japanese forces. The Japanese at once assumed the place of the civil authorities in these cities, operating the public utilities, closing the telegraph offices, putting the radio stations out of commission, and permitting the telephones to be used only under Japanese supervision. Within forty-eight hours the whole of southern Manchuria, not only along the Japanese South Manchuria Railway, but also along some of the railroads built by the Chinese, had been thus effectively occupied. The evidence pointed to a deliberate action planned and authorized by the highest Japanese authorities in Manchuria and possibly with direction from the high military command in Tokyo. The orderliness, precision, coördination of time and comprehensiveness with which the vital strategic points in South Manchuria were seized indicated a perfection of staff work which could hardly have taken place without such authority. The Chinese made practically no resistance, announcing that an order not to resist had been given by the Young Marshal Chang Hsueh-liang. In this way Chinese forces amounting perhaps to nearly one hundred thousand men were dispersed, disarmed, and put out of action by the Japanese forces, which consisted mainly of the Japanese military guards of the South Manchuria Railway and probably aggregated not much more than fifteen thousand men.

The evidence was almost equally clear that the coup had not been engineered or acquiesced in by the civil authorities in Japan, but had probably taken place

without their previous knowledge. This was the concurrent opinion of well-informed observers on the spot,
including our representatives not only in Japan but in
China. While there were reports that Baron Shidehara
and the Foreign Office had been dreading some such
coup by the army, the presumption was strong that he
had not been a party to it and that it was contrary to his
entire policy. This was the conclusion which we in the
Department reached by Monday, September 21st.

The passage of time has confirmed my belief in this
explanation. The subsequent events, the violent political
controversies between the army and the Foreign Office
which became manifest even to foreigners during the
succeeding months, all pointed to its correctness, and
impartial historians have asserted the same view.[2]

II

REASONS FOR OUR INITIAL POLICY

I do not recall that there was any difference of opinion
whatever in our group at the State Department as to
the policy we should follow in the face of this diagnosis
of the situation in Manchuria. The evidence in our
hands pointed to the wisdom of giving Shidehara and
the Foreign Office an opportunity, free from anything
approaching a threat or even public criticism, to get
control of the situation. We were well aware of the
incomplete development of parliamentary government in Japan and that the Japanese Constitution,
instead of placing the army under the direction of
the Cabinet, gave it a direct and independent access
to the Emperor as the chief of state. We of course
knew of the imperious economic problem Japan

[2] Cf. Royal Institute of International Affairs, *Survey* for 1931, pp. 439, 440.

faced in the necessity of providing livelihood for a constantly increasing population and we were well aware that in grappling with this problem during the period of the Great War she had sought to use the tactics of conquest and colonization over China for its solution. But for nearly ten years under the guidance of Shidehara and his fellow liberals she had been "studiously and persistently sailing on the opposite tack to the militant course"[3] which she had previously followed. All through the decade from the Washington Conference to September, 1931, instead of seeking markets by force, she had been following the entirely opposite plan of "commercial expansion and political good neighborliness." She had been seeking to supply her growing population by the development of friendly trade with the outside world instead of by forcibly acquired outlets for emigration. She had followed this course patiently and in the face of considerable difficulty and provocation. She had withdrawn her troops from Siberia and from Shantung despite the severe opposition from her militarist party. She had acquiesced in the lapse of her alliance with Great Britain and had thus made possible the settlements which followed the Washington Conference. She had exercised great self-restraint in the presence of what seemed to her the needless and insulting methods in which our American Congress had treated the subject of Japanese immigration, and she had exercised a consistent policy of non-retaliation to a continuing series of Chinese provocations during the progress of the Chinese civil wars.

More than that, we had witnessed a very recent example of Japan's spirit of responsibility and fidelity to modern views of international relations in the course

[3] Royal Institute of International Affairs, *Survey* for 1931, p. 400.

which the Minseito Cabinet had followed in the ratification of the London Naval Treaty of 1930. In that matter they had quite the most difficult task of any of the nations involved. That treaty was highly unpopular with the naval authorities in Japan. But Premier Hamaguchi had carried it through to ratification in the face of tremendous opposition as a result of which he had lost his life. Mr. Wakatsuki, who had been the chairman of the Japanese delegation in London and had been active in securing the ratification of the treaty, was now Premier.

The Japanese government had thus for ten years given an exceptional record of good citizenship in the life of the international world. Shidehara was still in office. We knew he had been laboring hard for moderation against the pressure of the army leaders in Manchuria. We had reached the conclusion that those leaders had engineered this outbreak probably without his knowledge and certainly against his will. It seemed clear to us that no steps should be taken which would make his task more difficult because certainly our best chance of a successful solution of the situation lay in him.

History is full of lessons which point to the dangers of an opposite course. A century and a half ago the intervention of the European allies had only served to fan the flame of nationalism in revolutionary France and, by rousing the patriotism of her armies, had strikingly demonstrated the danger of outside interference in a domestic struggle such as was now going on in Japan. Furthermore, the history of our own English-speaking nations has shown that the constitutional corner stone of parliamentary government—the subordination of the military to the civil authorities—is developed only by domestic evolution. In the case of a people as keenly sensitive and patriotic as the Japanese, the danger of a false reaction from foreign interference was particularly great.

At the same time, while the importance of great caution in order not to inflame the passions of the Japanese people was thus in our minds, the other side of the picture of necessity was also clearly before us. If the military party should succeed in having its way, if Shidehara eventually should yield to them, the damage to the new structure of international society provided by the post-war treaties would be incalculable. There was no danger of our losing sight of this. Two years before there had been presented to us in the same locality a similar problem. In the summer and autumn of 1929, just as the nations of the world were on the point of celebrating the ratification of the Pact of Paris renouncing war, hostilities between the Russians and the Chinese had flamed up in northern Manchuria which threatened to throw discredit on that treaty at the very moment of its birth. Acting under the newly born treaty, the American State Department had then promptly taken the lead in mobilizing a very general expression of world opinion cautioning those two nations against a breach of that Pact. The memory of our efforts at that time at once rose in our minds now.

Thus, in the face of these two opposite dangers I find that as early as September 23rd I jotted in my diary the following entry:

> My problem is to let the Japanese know that we are watching them and at the same time do it in a way which will help Shidehara who is on the right side, and not play into the hands of any nationalist agitators.

III

OUR POLICY AS AFFECTED BY LEAGUE ACTION

At the time this crisis broke out in Manchuria the League of Nations was holding its regular September meeting in Geneva. On September 14th the Assembly of the League by a unanimous vote had elected China a member of the Council. Japan was already a member of that body. On the very day that the first news of the outbreak in Manchuria was going out over the wires to the rest of the world, Dr. Sao-ke Alfred Sze was formally taking his seat as the representative of China in the Council of the League of Nations.[4] At that very session the disturbances in Manchuria were called to the attention of the Council by Mr. Yoshizawa, the Japanese representative. Dr. Sze also commented on them. At the next session of the Council two days later, on the 21st, China formally appealed to the League through Dr. Sze, and under the terms of Article XI of the Covenant requested that the Council take immediate steps

> to prevent the further development of a situation endangering the peace of nations; to reestablish the *status quo ante*; and to determine the amounts and character of such reparations as may be found due to the Republic of China.[5]

By this action the League of Nations was at once put into full jurisdiction of the controversy.

Such action by the League of necessity had important

[4] It is well to remember, in the light of some of Japan's subsequent criticisms of the competency of China as an organized nation to sit in the League of Nations, that she had taken her post as a member of the League's governing body, the Council, on the special endorsement of Japan.

[5] The full text of Article XI of the League Covenant may be found in Appendix I.

effects upon our policy. We were not a member of the League. Yet we were greatly interested in the matter over which it had thus assumed jurisdiction. By virtue of our propinquity and of our historic interest in the opening up of both China and Japan to the modern world we had in some ways a greater direct interest than any other nation in the world. Furthermore, we were vitally concerned not only in the preservation of peace on this particular occasion, but also in the precedent which a breach of it might have on the post-war peace treaties above mentioned.

Such a situation at once presented a problem in international coöperation—always a difficult matter, but particularly so here where a system of coöperation between the United States and the League of Nations not only had never been worked out in any previous case, but where violent party feeling within the United States had been excited by the political struggle over the ratification of the League Covenant a decade before. Even the most normal and rational steps which might be taken by an American Secretary of State in such a situation were certain to be the subject of critical scrutiny and possible attack from some of his countrymen.

In the first place, there was the problem always present in such a situation of seeking to avoid the crossing of wires with the other parties. This is a problem the persistency and difficulty of which is familiar to every Foreign Minister. No matter how clear the common objective, no matter how genuine the zeal in its support on either side, there is always the danger, when nations are thus endeavoring to coöperate, of unexpected clashes of method or of action. That is true in cases of all joint human endeavor. But in international coöperation, where the situation is complicated by underlying national differences of viewpoint and of interest and where the whole matter is constantly subject to the scrutiny, publicity, and attacks of the never sleeping modern press, the situation is inconceivably more difficult. These difficulties can never be entirely eliminated; they can be minimized only by complete friendly frankness and never failing tact—the ability to see the problem from the other man's point of view.

Concerning then this particular problem before us, there were on its face two considerations which seemed to govern the method of coöperation on our part:

First: On the one side the League of Nations was a world organization comprising over sixty nations. On the other hand, the United States stood alone. Consequently if any controversy should arise with Japan as a result of the activities of her army in Manchuria, if that controversy took place between her and the League, it would present the picture of an issue between Japan and the whole world. It would thus give the maximum effect to world public opinion. On the other hand, if it arose with us, it would inevitably assume the picture of a private quarrel between two nations.[6]

Second: The organization of the League had created machinery which stood ready at hand for the investigation, the conciliation, and the solution of controversies. This mechanism had been under way for ten years and already a *modus operandi* in case of international controversies had been partially worked out. The members of the League by constantly recurring meetings had already developed a method of operation which constituted a long step forward in world history. On the other hand, although the United States was a party to two post-war treaties whose purposes were germane to

[6] We felt that such a position of antagonism between the United States and Japan would be peculiarly unfortunate in view of Japan's sensitiveness arising out of our insistence on the termination of the Anglo-Japanese treaty and the action of our Congress in regard to immigration.

the present situation, namely the Pact of Paris (called the Kellogg-Briand Pact) and the so-called Nine Power Treaty relating to the Far East, in neither of those treaties was there any such detailed system of machinery provided, nor had there been any similar experience in coöperation thereunder. Whatever steps were taken under our treaties would meet all of the difficulties and opposition that come from novelty.

Both of these considerations, coupled with the important fact that the League had already taken jurisdiction of the matter, pointed in the same general direction. They indicated that our most useful function would be to furnish independent support to the League rather than to play a rôle of leadership. In that respect they served to confirm the policy of cautious action which we determined on. Our policy should be to coöperate and support and so far as possible to avoid clashing with League policy.

We must create no doubt in the minds of our friends of our warm support of their general objectives. On the other hand, we must leave to them the work of examination and conciliation which they had assumed under Article XI and, in the light of our historic policy not only towards the League but in all other matters of international coöperation, we must make it clear from the beginning that our ultimate action must always be the result of our own independent judgment.

On Monday, September 21st, came the first communication from the League to us. It was a message from Sir Eric Drummond of the Secretariat evidently to sound out our attitude and views particularly as to whether we thought the Kellogg-Briand Pact was involved. In my reply I tried to make clear an attitude on our part of coöperation and frankness, giving him such information as we had received from Manchuria and telling him that we were following closely the development with a view to our treaty obligations under both the Nine Power Treaty and the Kellogg-Briand Pact, but were still somewhat embarrassed by lack of complete information. At the same time I called to his attention the evident issue between the Japanese military chiefs and their Foreign Office and my own impression that, while preparing to uphold treaty obligations, it would be wise to avoid action which might excite nationalistic feeling in Japan in support of the military and against Shidehara.

The very next day matters began to turn up which illustrated the inevitable difficulties which are sure to arise in such coöperation springing from the differing viewpoints, restrictions, and limitations of the two bodies concerned and of the respective localities in which they act. Late in the evening came a cable reporting that the League was contemplating sending to Manchuria an investigating commission appointed by itself; that Japan objected but that the investigation would probably be made anyhow, if necessary under Chinese authority as the local sovereign of Manchuria. They wished to know whether we would join with an American member serving on such a commission. The following morning, while I was considering the cable, it was reinforced by a message conveyed through our Minister to Switzerland over the telephone telling me of the proposal to send such a committee of investigation and also to send diplomatic notes to Japan and China making representations on the subject of the outbreak. In the same telephone message it was suggested that if we would permit an American representative to join in the discussions of these proposals at the table of the Council of the League or on its special committee appointed for the consideration of this matter, the effect would be dramatic and beneficial.

I had no doubt as to the dramatic effect, but I was very gravely concerned as to the effect which that drama would have upon the people of Japan. By the telephone as well as a long cable sent the same day, I tried to make clear my views. I at once accepted the suggestion that we should support by a similar diplomatic note the League's proposed representation through the diplomatic channels to China and Japan. But I deprecated the proposal of sending by the League at that time an investigating commission to Manchuria *over and against the objection of Japan.* I suggested that inasmuch as Oriental people were not so well acquainted as Occidentals with the method of judicial investigation and findings by third parties, but in my opinion were more inclined to settle their difficulties by direct negotiation between the parties involved, they should be permitted to try this method first. I told them that I felt there would be serious danger that, if the League sought to impose such an investigation upon Japan against her opposition, it would be popularly resented and would throw at once additional difficulties in the path of Shidehara's efforts at solution. I thought this danger would be accentuated if the United States, which was not a member of the League and had no right to sit on the Council, should participate in the sending of such a commission. I urged them, in case they felt that the need of such a committee was now imperative, to follow the method which had become common in international matters of having such a commission appointed by the two nations themselves, China and Japan, with a membership from neutral nations, this method being one which was well understood and in general use in various treaties of conciliation.[7] In summary I suggested that the most effective line of coöperation in the delicate situation prevailing in Manchuria would be for the American government, through the diplomatic channels, to support the League in urging a settlement by the two countries themselves through direct negotiations; secondly, if this should not prove effective and outside action became necessary, that it should be taken through the machinery of the League, to which both countries were parties and which had already been invoked by China. Finally, if this should not be effective, we should all consider such action as might be possible under the Nine Power Treaty and the Pact of Paris.

I have gone into this matter somewhat at length because it has been subsequently suggested by certain writers, that my refusal to assist in the appointment of this commission at that time may have prevented a successful solution of the entire Manchurian incident. My action was based upon my former experience with the Far East and I think my judgment has been confirmed by the subsequent events. I believe that the imposition of such an inquiry at that moment upon Japan would have accelerated the outbreak of nationalistic feeling which subsequently occurred; that it would have hastened the downfall of the Minseito Cabinet which at that time was doing its best to check the army; that whereas Shidehara was able to remain in office until December 10th and eventually to consent on behalf of Japan to the sending of the Lytton Commission of In-

---

[7] I also pointed out that the Manchurian situation differed widely from the Greek-Bulgarian boundary controversy in which such an investigating commission had been sent by the League. In that case the issue was over the determination of a geographical fact and the commission's duties were virtually to determine a geographical line; while here the investigation would involve an inquiry into a large number of deep and complicated political differences.

quiry, if we had overridden Japan at that early stage of the proceedings, we probably should have lost the invaluable results which came from the work of that commission.

At the same time I moved effectively to accomplish the real end which the League had in mind and to do it without the dangers which I had anticipated from their proposal. Through our embassy in Tokyo I informed Baron Shidehara that I desired to send two of our American representatives in the Far East to make an immediate investigation on the spot as to the occurrences in Manchuria, and I requested that they be given complete freedom in the prosecution of such an inquiry. As such investigators I selected Mr. Salisbury, a Secretary of the embassy in Tokyo, and Mr. Hanson, the American Consul General at Harbin, both of them men of long experience in the Far East, of tested capacity and thoroughly trusted by us. My request was immediately granted by Baron Shidehara, who promised that these envoys should be given full freedom of action and protected and facilitated in every way. On September 28th I telegraphed my confidential instructions to these two gentlemen. The scope of those instructions indicated the importance which I attributed to their mission.[8] Hanson and Salisbury promptly took

[8] They were to visit the various points where there had been fighting or where the Japanese troops had advanced beyond their treaty boundaries. They were to report their judgment as to the justification for these troop movements; their scope and extent and the reasons alleged for them. They were to gather evidence as to whether the proposed occupation was really temporary and whether the troops were to be withdrawn after the danger passed. They were to report on the form of civil administration, if any, set up by the Japanese in the Chinese cities and to report all interference by the Japanese military with the Chinese civil administration, particularly in respect to the native and international sections of Mukden and as to whether the civil administration had been in any respect restored in that city so that it could act with independence. They were also to report as to the attitude of the Chinese population in Manchuria towards the Japanese and whether it was such as to offer a genuine excuse for the non-withdrawal of

up their work and within a very short time I was beginning to receive from them on the ground a series of
reports upon the situation which was of the utmost
value in crystallizing my own judgment both as to
what had occurred and what was likely to be the outcome of events soon to be set in rapid motion.

IV

THE SITUATION AND ISSUES BETWEEN JAPAN AND CHINA
AS DEFINED BY THEM AT THE OUTSET OF THE CON-
TROVERSY BETWEEN SEPTEMBER 19TH AND 30TH

On September 22nd the President of the League of
Nations sent identic telegrams to China and Japan
pursuant to Article XI of the Covenant (1) appealing
to them to refrain from any further act of hostility
which would prejudice a peaceful settlement of the
problem; and (2) urging them to find means to withdraw their troops at once without endangering the
safety of their nationals and property, and informing
them that the Council was about to begin consulta-
tions with each of them with a view to such a withdrawal of troops.

On September 24th the American government in
support of this action by the League sent similar identic
notes to China and Japan expressing its hope that their
military forces would refrain from any further hostilities and that they would each take steps to satisfy the
requirements of international law and treaties in respect
to the situation.

On September 22nd before the dispatch of these notes
I had sent informally through the Japanese Ambassa-

---

the Japanese troops. In summary they were to report how far the Japanese
occupation in Manchuria had been extended and whether there was any
justification for the extension; also whether there was any intention manifested to restore the *status quo ante*.

dor an earnest memorandum to Baron Shidehara, expressing our serious concern in regard to the situation and pointing out the responsibility that necessarily rested upon Japan in view of the fact that by the action of her army the Japanese government had taken complete control of South Manchuria. I pointed out that the situation was necessarily of concern, morally, legally, and politically, to a number of neutral nations and that it was our hope that steps would be taken by both the Japanese and Chinese governments to refrain from further hostilities and to demonstrate that neither government had any intention to further its peculiar interests in Manchuria by the use of force.

In its replies to these notes the Japanese government asserted that its troops had acted only to the extent necessary to insure their own safety, the protection of the railway and the safety of Japanese nationals. They announced that they had already withdrawn the greater portion of their forces back into the railway zone, leaving only a few small bodies quartered in several places outside, and that their forces were being withdrawn to the fullest extent consonant with the safety of their nationals and the safety of their railroad. They also asserted their profound desire of reaching a peaceful settlement of the problem "as rapidly as possible by negotiations between the two countries."

In a longer public statement issued by the Japanese Cabinet on September 24th, after reciting various alleged Chinese provocations leading to the incident on September 19th, they repeated the statements in the notes as to the steps they had already taken towards withdrawal and for a solution of the situation; they asserted that Japan harbored no territorial designs in Manchuria and desired merely to protect her subjects engaged in various peaceful pursuits for the development of Manchuria by means of capital and labor, and pledged their readiness to coöperate with the Chinese government to solve the present incident and work out constructive plans to eradicate once for all any causes for future friction.

On the other hand, the Chinese government in its reply notes of September 22nd and 24th, respectively, disclaimed all responsibility for the outbreak; asserted that it had been entirely caused by Japanese aggression and that their own troops had not even offered resistance to the attacks of the Japanese; recited that the acts of aggression were continuing; pledged their readiness to abstain from any aggravation of the situation and assumed full responsibility for the protection of life and property as soon as the occupied areas should be evacuated by the Japanese troops.

Furthermore, in the discussions before the Council of the League on September 28th, Dr. Sze for China expressed the readiness of China for the dispatch of a neutral commission to Manchuria to determine the true facts. Mr. Yoshizawa, the representative of Japan, was unable to approve of this suggestion.

Thus at the very outset of this controversy the outline of the issues was clearly drawn. Japan asserted that the action of her army had been taken solely as a matter of self-defense and that, as soon as the safety of the Japanese residents could be assured, the army would be withdrawn into its original position—in fact she asserted that this movement was already taking place. On the other hand, China asserted that there had been no provocation for the movement; that it was sheer aggression and was continuing; and she pledged herself to assume at once full responsibility for the protection of life and property in the invaded areas as soon as they were evacuated by the Japanese troops. China was willing that the facts should be investigated by a League neutral commission on the spot; Japan was unwilling.

On the 30th of September the Council of the League took action on this situation by a resolution agreed to by all its members, including the representatives of both China and Japan.

(1) It noted Japan's disclaimer of territorial designs in Manchuria.

(2) It noted Japan's promises to continue the withdrawal of its troops "as rapidly as possible" into their lawful area of the railway zone "in proportion as the safety of the lives and property of Japanese nationals is effectively assured."

(3) It noted China's assumption of responsibility for the safety of the lives and property of Japanese nationals outside the railway zone as the withdrawal continued and the Chinese local authorities and police forces were reëstablished.

(4) It noted the assurances of both China and Japan "to prevent any extension of the scope of the incident or any aggravation of the situation."

(5) It requested both parties to do everything possible to hasten the restoration of normal relations and to that end to continue and speedily complete their foregoing commitments.

(6) It requested both parties to furnish full information at frequent intervals as to this development.

(7) It retained jurisdiction of the controversy and decided to meet again on October 14th to consider the situation as it would then stand.

The important thing about this resolution was the commitments assumed by the Japanese representative. That action and the consequent unanimity made the resolution legally binding upon all parties. We were to that extent much cheered and encouraged. It seemed as though the outbreak might be in a fair way to be terminated and the *status quo ante* eventually restored. It looked as though Baron Shidehara might succeed in maintaining his authority and former policy and that, while there might and undoubtedly would be difficult questions to solve before normal relations could be resumed, they might be nevertheless solved without further hostilities and in a way satisfactory to both nations. I was personally encouraged by Baron Shidehara's prompt readiness to give my investigators access to the locality, a permission which had been acquiesced in by the military authorities.

There was, however, still cause for anxiety. Baron Shidehara had been compelled to adopt in his notes a position on behalf of his government which strained our credulity; his excuses for Japanese action did not sufficiently tally with the facts even as they were thus far disclosed. Making all possible allowance for provocation by the Chinese, we knew of nothing which would justify as a necessary protection of life and property the actual steps taken by the Japanese army. It had acted with a promptness and vigor which indicated careful planning. It was now in possession of all of Southern Manchuria. It was hardly to be expected that it would be dislodged from that advantageous position until it had obtained its "pound of flesh" as a *quid pro quo*, and certain features already disclosed in the correspondence indicated that the Japanese government itself might ratify and assume such a position behind the army.

While we should welcome a negotiated settlement between the two parties concerned, the kind of negotiation which we had in mind was quite different from one in which one of the negotiators was backing up its arguments with an armed force holding the other by the throat. Such a negotiation could not be reconciled with the terms of the great treaties to which we were all parties. I think, however, it is accurate to say that few if any observers then expected that the Japanese forces and government would develop such a complete disregard of treaty obligations or world opinion as was exhibited within a few months.

On the other hand, our task of coördinating our efforts with those of the League had been well begun, although there already had been revealed some of its inherent difficulties. In order to register our appreciation of the League's success thus far and at the same time to crystallize our methods of coöperation, I sent on October 5th the following telegram to Sir Eric Drummond:

> I believe that our coöperation in the future handling of this difficult matter should proceed along the course which has been followed ever since the first outbreak of the trouble fortunately found the Assembly and Council of the League of Nations in session. The Council has deliberated long and earnestly on this matter and the Covenant of the League of Nations provides permanent and already tested machinery for handling such issues as between States members of the League. Both the Chinese and Japanese have presented and argued their cases before the Council and the world has been informed through published accounts with regard to the proceedings there The Council has formulated conclusions and outlined a course of action to be followed by the disputants; and as the said disputants have

made commitments to the Council, it is most
desirable that the League in no way relax its
vigilance and in no way fail to assert all the
pressure and authority within its competence
toward regulating the action of China and
Japan in the premises.

On its part the American government acting
independently through its diplomatic representatives will endeavor to reinforce what the
League does and will make clear that it has a
keen interest in the matter and is not oblivious to the obligations which the disputants
have assumed to their fellow signatories in the
Pact of Paris as well as in the Nine Power
Pact should a time arise when it would seem
advisable to bring forward those obligations.
By this course we avoid any danger of embarrassing the League in the course to which it is
now committed.[9]

This message was first sent informally to Drummond.
He subsequently requested permission to make it pub-
lic and to circulate it among the members of the
League.

V

THE CONTINUANCE OF AGGRESSION BY THE JAPANESE ARMY THROUGH THE AUTUMN OF 1931

1. Our respite was of brief duration. Almost at once
a succession of events began to occur which indicated
that the Japanese army chiefs in Manchuria had quite
different objectives from those professed to us by their
civil government at Tokyo and that they were bent on

[9] "Conditions in Manchuria," Senate Document 55, 72nd Congress, 1st Session, p. 14.

pursuing those objectives in entire disregard of any commitments or promises which might be made on their behalf by their Foreign Office.

After the capture of Mukden by the Japanese on September 19th the headquarters of the Chinese government and forces had been removed to Chinchow in the extreme southwestern corner of Manchuria, close to the borders of Chihli and northern China. Within a week after the League of Nations resolution of September 30th, General Honjo, the Japanese Commander-in-chief in Manchuria, publicly announced that this government of the Young Marshal, Chang Hsueh-liang, would no longer receive Japanese recognition. Other statements followed to the effect that Japanese forces would not cease their activities until the Young Marshal and his government were driven entirely out of Manchuria. Not only were these statements left without reprimand from the Tokyo government, but Japanese military airplanes began to enforce this policy in a most drastic manner. On October 8th a squadron of eleven Japanese planes dropped thirty or forty bombs upon the unarmed and unwarned city of Chinchow, killing and wounding a number of the inhabitants. On its face this was an indefensible act of aggression. Our protests to Tokyo brought expressions of regret which seemed quite inadequate.[10]

2. Shortly afterwards in the latter part of October the Japanese high command in Manchuria proceeded to send a military expedition to Tsitsihar, the capital of Heilungkiang, the northernmost province of Manchuria. This was several hundred miles north of any portion of the South Manchuria Railway and far outside the zone of any of the treaty rights which Japan

[10] See "Conditions in Manchuria," Senate Document 55, 72nd Congress, 1st Session, p. 16.

claimed in Manchuria. The expedition followed the route of a Chinese-owned railway which penetrated north to and crossed the Russian-owned Chinese Eastern Railway and thus constituted a potential strategic threat at the Russians in Vladivostok. This expedition defeated and destroyed the forces of the Chinese General Ma Chan-shan who commanded the military forces of Marshal Chang in Heilungkiang, and it thus destroyed all the organized forces of the Young Marshal in North Manchuria.

3. The capture of Tsitsihar left the Chinchow District in the southwest as the only fragment of Manchuria in which the Young Marshal's authority remained intact, and towards the latter part of November the Japanese forces in Manchuria began to move towards Chinchow. Although vigorous representations by the League and ourselves, which will be narrated below, succeeded in getting action from Tokyo which countermanded these original preparations and caused a withdrawal of the Japanese expeditionary force to Mukden on November 28th, this was only a temporary respite. After the fall of the Minseito Cabinet on December 11th, the movement towards Chinchow was resumed and that city was seized by the Japanese army on January 3, 1932. This completed the destruction of the organized forces of the Young Marshal and left the control of all Manchuria in the hands of the Japanese.

VI

THE GRADUAL EFFECT OF THESE MOVEMENTS
UPON THE DIPLOMATIC OBJECTIVES

This demonstration of the Japanese army's defiant disregard of the promises of its government unrolled before our eyes as a grim picture during the autumn months. Gradually during those months it also became evident that the army was gathering behind itself as it made these successive moves the support of a powerful nationalistic feeling among the people of Japan. At the same time the still more discouraging fact became almost equally clear that the Japanese civil government not only could not check the army's course, but that in some important respects it was willing to profit by the army's action. It insisted that Japan should be left alone to negotiate with China and it also insisted on widening the scope of such negotiations so that not merely should it include the solution of the present clash, but that advantage should be taken to clean up the entire area of long-standing controversies between the two nations. For many years China had disputed the extent of Japan's rights in Manchuria, asserting that some of those rights were based upon alleged agreements which either did not exist or which had been extorted by force. It now gradually became evident that the Japanese government was insisting that all these disputes should be settled and settled in Japan's favor while the army still remained in possession of the Chinese cities;—in other words that they should be settled by the power of the sword.

This was a position quite incompatible with Japan's obligations under the post-war peace treaties—not only her obligations under Article X of the League Covenant and Article I of the Nine Power Treaty, but also her promise under the Kellogg-Briand Pact, viz.: never to seek the solution of an international controversy save by pacific means. Thus the progress of the long-drawn-out and discouraging negotiations of that autumn served gradually to bring out and make more clear the ugly probability that, as applied to the Far East and to

Japan, this great post-war effort to place the world upon a higher level of international life was in jeopardy; the obligations of those treaties were being completely flouted and treated as though non-existent.

Such a possibility, of course, had faced us from the beginning. In one of my early reports to my colleagues in the Cabinet on October 9th, I find from my diary that I had voiced the apprehension that these modern treaties initiated by Western nations, and especially designed to fit the exigencies of the industrialized world of Europe and America, might not be taken very seriously in the Orient. But, as I then pointed out to my colleagues, those treaties existed; for better or worse they represented the earnest hopes of our part of the world, and if we surrendered and permitted them to be treated like scraps of paper, the hope of peaceable development in the world would receive a blow from which it would not soon recover.

In the face of such a situation certain basic facts had to be faced. The group of interrelated treaties entered into at the Washington Conference in 1922, under which America and Britain reduced the size of their respective navies in relation to that of Japan and agreed to leave their possessions in the Far East without further fortification, had been intended to make and had made it physically impossible for any single Western nation successfully to intervene by military force in such a matter as the Manchurian dispute even if it should desire so to do. Quite apart from such limitations, no fact was more clear to any observer than that at this period of the great depression none of the nations in Europe or America, even if able, had the slightest desire to go to war in such a controversy. These facts had evidently reduced the area of possible action before us to

(1) some form of collective economic sanctions against Japan, or in default of that

(2) by the exercise of diplomatic pressure and the power of world public opinion, to try to get as fair play as possible for the weaker power, China, in the eventual negotiated settlement, and

(3) by a vigorous judgment against Japan backed by the public opinion of the world, to save as much respect as possible for the great peace treaties which had been publicly flouted by Japan's action.

These in substance were the objectives which one after another were discussed by us at the State Department during the autumn weeks while the proceedings of the League were taking their discouraging course at Geneva and Paris.

VII

OUR PROCEEDINGS UNTIL THE CLOSE OF THE OCTOBER SESSION OF THE LEAGUE—MR. GILBERT SITS WITH THE COUNCIL

These events will be treated as briefly as possible. The League continued its efforts to solve the controversy by negotiation under the authority of Article XI of the Covenant. China had made her appeal under the authority of this article undoubtedly for a variety of reasons. In the first place this might fairly be called the favorite article under which the Council of the League had previously acted in many cases. Under it there was granted to the League a wide discretion as to the action it might take and there had been established a familiar procedure for dealing with controversies. Its chief limitation was that it required unanimity, including the consent of the disputants themselves. At the time when China appealed to it this limitation, though considered probable, had not yet been definitely determined and it was not until later in the October session of the Council that such a decision was made.

The League's efforts under Article XI were thus strictly limited to attempts to reach a solution of the dispute by conciliation and agreement of both disputants. Action under Article XI would not lead automatically to sanctions, either military or economic, against an aggressor nation. No effort thus far had been made by China to invoke any such action and, so far as I know, no suggestion of the invocation of such sanctions had thus far been made by anyone, at least to us. On the contrary, as early as September 26th it had been reported to us informally that Geneva was opposed to using sanctions. Furthermore, it must be remembered that China's appeal to the League was made within two days of the original clash; and at that time, while it was known that a very serious situation had been created, Japan was taking the position that she had acted solely for defensive purposes and that as soon as that defense should no longer be necessary her troops would be withdrawn. It undoubtedly was not believed at Geneva that Japan, in the face of the protests of the entire world, would be prepared to continue, much less extend, her military occupation of China's territory. So the flexible and well-tried provisions of Article XI were doubtless deemed most appropriate and sufficient for bringing to bear upon the situation the persuasive pressure of negotiation and conciliation backed up by the massed opinion of the world.

M. Briand of France assumed the chairmanship of the Council at its meeting on October 14th and thereafter conducted its proceedings with infinite patience and resourcefulness. Under the skillful advocacy of

Dr. Sze, China presented her case in such a way as to bring out with increasing clarity the continuing aggression of the Japanese army and to emphasize the force of China's appeal for protection to the pledged faith of the nations united under the Covenant. The United States continued its policy of endeavoring to support the persuasions of the Council by representations through diplomatic channels.

While the deadlock to which I have already alluded between the Chinese and Japanese in respect to negotiations continued, Japan insisting that the controversy should be settled by such negotiations between the two parties alone and China refusing, we remembered at the State Department that a similar impasse between China and Japan had been successfully solved during the Conference at Washington in 1922 by the device of having neutral observers sit with the negotiating parties. In that case Lord Balfour and Mr. Hughes or their representatives, by taking seats on the side lines during the negotiations, had helped to bring a very delicate controversy to a successful solution. It seemed to us that possibly the same plan might now be made effective to enable China to consent to negotiate with Japan and to do so without the fear of being placed at a disadvantage by Japan's superior military strength. Thinking, however, that the suggestion might have better chance of acceptance if it came from the Council at Geneva, we telegraphed the suggestion informally to the Secretariat, and it was thereafter made by the Council. Japan, however, refused to accept it.

When the Council of the League adjourned on September 30th, it had planned to meet again on October 14th. As that date approached it was not only clear that Japan was not making the promised progress towards the withdrawal of her troops from the occupied area, but the situation had grown much more serious than had been anticipated at the adjournment of the last meeting.

The attack on Chinchow and the unprovoked bombing of several railroad trains on the Chinese railroads by Japanese airplanes had created a very bad impression among our people and abroad. In both Washington and Geneva thought was being given to any possible way of bringing further moral pressure to bear upon the Japanese government and people which might impress them with the seriousness of the popular feeling against them throughout the world. In Washington we were considering whether it was not time to invoke an expression of opinion under the Kellogg-Briand Pact among its signatories as a means of showing this feeling. On October 9th I had discussed the matter in all its aspects before the Cabinet. On October 10th I had a long talk with the President, whose mind up to that time had been so preoccupied with the financial crisis at home that necessarily he had been able to give but little thought to Manchuria. On that morning, however, domestic matters were momentarily quiet and I found him keen and interested on the subject of my problems in the Far East. The League had long been anxious for us to make a demonstration of the solidarity of American and European opinion by inviting us to sit jointly with them in some discussion of this matter. As I have already stated, they had made the suggestion informally at the very beginning of the trouble. At this conference on October 10th President Hoover, having evidently been thinking over the matter since my Cabinet discussion the day before, plunged vigorously and sympathetically into my problem and expressed himself quite ready to authorize such a joint session centered on the subject of the Kellogg-Briand Pact.

This, of course, was a proposition which involved patent difficulties both at home and abroad. The risk of a hostile reaction at home had been so manifest and any adverse consequences would be so personal to the fortunes of the President that I had hesitated to urge it upon him until he thus voluntarily expressed himself ready for it. Furthermore, the risk of adverse reaction on the part of Japan was to be carefully considered. The United States had no right to partake officially in either the activities or the responsibilities of the League Council. It had no right to participate in the machinery of the League or even to share in the discussions which related solely to actions being taken under that treaty by its signatories. But all the nation-members of the Council and nearly all the nation-members of the League were also signatories of the Kellogg-Briand Pact, and there seemed to be no reason, if those nations wished to discuss with us through their representatives at Geneva action to be taken solely under that Pact, why we should not do it with them. The two jurisdictions, however, must be kept sharply distinct.

There was a further precaution to be observed. The Kellogg-Briand Pact contained two articles. The first one related exclusively to war and consisted of declarations renouncing war as an instrument of national policy. The second article was quite different and consisted of a covenant by the signatory nations never to attempt to solve their controversies except by pacific means. If we invoked the Pact we must make it clear that we took action only under the second article. No war had been declared by either party and it was most important, from the standpoint of preserving the rights of China, that a meeting of the nations on the subject of the Pact should not amount to a recognition that war existed. Otherwise it might play directly into the hands of further aggression by Japanese militarists. For example, had an avowed state of war become existent between the two nations, the recognized rules of war might be claimed to give Japan a free hand to blockade the maritime ports of China or conduct military operations anywhere throughout her territory.

Finally there was the consideration to which I have already referred and which had been constantly in our minds throughout our coöperation with the League. That was the importance of preserving League initiative as distinguished from initiative by the United States. The original suggestion of joint action had come from the nations at Geneva. It arose from their united impulse, not from our suggestions. For the sake of preventing misunderstanding in Japan it was important not to blur the truth of that situation. Not only should the invitation for the joint session come from the nations who were members of the League, but it also was important, if as a result of such conference it were decided to invoke the Kellogg-Briand Pact, that it should be the members of the Council who took the leadership in carrying out the various steps necessary to set in motion the signatories of that treaty. Otherwise I foresaw that America would be represented to the Japanese people as the instigator of the entire matter—of having wormed herself into League councils in order to stir up hostility against Japan.

When on October 14th the Council reconvened at Geneva the steps for such a joint meeting were carried through. On October 16th M. Briand, the President of the Council, addressed an invitation to me in the following terms:

I have the honor to inform you that the Council of the League of Nations has ap-

proved today the terms of the following proposal which I had the honor to make to it in
my capacity as President of the Council:

In the course of the discussion the opinion
has been expressed that the very important
question before the Council concerns the
fulfillment of obligations arising not only
from the Covenant of the League of Nations
but also from the Pact of Paris.

This opinion is certainly well founded
since, in accordance with Article 2 of that
Pact:

The high contracting parties agree that
the settlement or solution of all disputes
or conflicts of whatever nature or of whatever origin they may be, which may arise
among them, shall never be sought except
by pacific means.

Foremost among the signatories of the
Pact of Paris appear the United States of
America. The United States were one of the
proponents of the Pact, and I may be
allowed to recall that I had the honor to be
associated with the then Secretary of State
of the United States as joint author. In consequence, the United States may be regarded
as being especially interested in insuring a
settlement of the present dispute by pacific
means.

Moreover, the Government of the United
States, with which communications regarding the dispute before the Council have already been exchanged, has expressed its
whole-hearted sympathy with the attitude of

the League of Nations, and has affirmed its desire to reënforce the action of the League.

I feel confident that I shall be meeting the wishes of my colleagues in proposing that we should invite the Government of the United States to be associated with our efforts by sending a representative to sit at the Council table so as to be in a position to express an opinion as to how, either in view of the present situation or of its future development, effect can best be given to the provisions of the Pact. By this means also the opportunity will be afforded him of following our deliberations on the problem as a whole.

I am sure that any action that might be taken under the Pact could not but strengthen the efforts which are now being made by the Council in accordance with the obligations imposed upon it by the Covenant of the League of Nations to effect the peaceful settlement of the problem under discussion.

In consequence, I have the honor to address to the Government of the United States the invitation contained in the said proposal.

In response to this invitation on October 16th I authorized Mr. Prentiss Gilbert, the American Consul at Geneva, who for some years had acted as the unofficial observer of the United States at meetings of the League, to accept the invitation and to act as our representative in the discussion. My instructions were as follows:

You are authorized to participate in the discussions of the Council when they relate to the possible application of the Kellogg-Briand Pact to which treaty the United States is a party. You are expected to report the result of such discussions to the Department for its determination as to possible action. If you are present at the discussion of any other aspect of the Chinese-Japanese dispute, it must be only as an observer and auditor.

On the same date Mr. Gilbert appeared in the Council, handed to M. Briand his acceptance and made a statement which, while expressing in felicitous language our desire to coöperate within the limits of our authority under the Pact, made quite clear the necessary limitations which precluded action outside of that authority.[11]

The members of the Council and Mr. Gilbert proceeded at once with the discussion of the invocation of the Kellogg-Briand Pact and on the following day, October 17th, all the members of the Council except the representatives of China and Japan decided that their governments should call the attention of the Chinese and Japanese governments to the obligations which they had undertaken under Article II of the Pact. Following this decision the governments of France, Great Britain, Germany, Italy, Spain and Norway on the same day sent such notes to China and Japan, and the French government undertook to notify the other signatories of the Pact, including the United States, of the decision of these governments. On the receipt of this notification from the French government, we on October

[11] For M. Briand's and Mr. Gilbert's remarks see Willoughby, *The Sino-Japanese Controversy and the League of Nations*, p. 104.

20th sent to the governments of China and Japan identic notes calling attention to their obligations under the Kellogg-Briand Pact.

As soon as this invocation of the Kellogg-Briand Pact was concluded and nothing remained before the Council except the transaction of its League business, I directed Mr. Gilbert to retire on October 24th from his temporary seat at the table of the Council and to resume the normal position which he had always occupied in the Council room as one of the observers.

Our joint meeting with the Council thus followed the exact course to which we had intended it to be limited and observed the jurisdictional precautions with which we had surrounded it. Nevertheless, incidents occurred which illustrated the difficulties of such coöperation between the United States and the League, particularly when undertaken, as we were obliged to undertake it, as a novel proceeding.

When M. Briand broached in the Council the subject of the invitation to us, he was at once met by the constitutional objection of the Japanese representative that the United States as a non-member had no right to sit and participate in the discussions of the Council. He presented a written statement of these objections which on their face indicated complete misunderstanding as to the scope of our proposed participation. This was clearly explained in a reply of M. Briand the same day.[12] On October 15th the other members of the Council overruled Mr. Yoshizawa's objection, holding that the question was a matter of procedure and not of substance and thus did not require a unanimous vote. But this objection coupled with a rather surprising simultaneous public attack on the American government from

[12] See Willoughby, *op. cit.*, pp. 90-91.

the press spokesman in the Foreign Office in Tokyo emphasized the sensitiveness of the Japanese government and the danger which we had foreseen of any steps which would line us up *vis-à-vis* Japan.

Nevertheless, in spite of these minor *contretemps* I have felt that our main object in accepting the League's invitation was accomplished. That object was publicly to demonstrate and emphasize the support and cooperation given by the United States to the League in this matter and thus to encourage them in the knowledge that they would have the full moral backing of our government in achieving their general objective of securing a peaceful solution of this controversy. They had shown on their part decision and courage in handling the Japanese objection. For us to have drawn back in the face of that objection would have opened a cleavage between us and the League which could not have failed to discourage them and to have destroyed the momentum with which we approached the far more important issues of peace and war which were involved in the controversy before us.

The October session of the League terminated on October 24th with the passage of a resolution which obtained the votes of all of the members of the Council except Japan. Japan voted against it. The chief point of this resolution[13] was that the Council, basing its action upon the resolution of September 30th, proceeded to direct the Japanese government "to begin immediately and to proceed progressively with the withdrawal of its troops . . . so that the total withdrawal may be effected before the date fixed for the next meeting of the Council," viz.: November 16th. By its opposition to this resolution Japan prevented unanimity, and this

[13] For text of Resolution, see Willoughby, *op. cit.*, p. 113 *et seq.*

fact was impliedly admitted by M. Briand as depriving the resolution of legal validity, although in his closing announcement he asserted that it retained its "full moral force." In the preceding debate upon the resolution Japan objected that the proposed withdrawal would be premature and would expose her nationals to danger. She reasserted her readiness to negotiate privately with China and had mentioned that "she had determined upon a number of fundamental points" upon which normal relations between China and Japan should be based. On being pressed as to what these points were, her representative refused on that occasion to state them. But two days after the adjournment of the Council the Japanese government on October 26th at Tokyo made public the fundamental points, and it then appeared that they included the settlement of the entire question of the disputed treaty rights of Japan in Manchuria.[14]

While Japan's representatives officially disclaimed her intention to use military force to achieve her national objectives, the situation disclosed by these interchanges and by her attitude at the October session of the League made it very clear that in fact she was bent on doing just that very thing. Her army was not withdrawing. It was actually pushing forward its operations and the Japanese government was declining to

[14] These fundamental points were as follows:

1. Mutual repudiation of aggressive policy and conduct.
2. Respect for China's territorial integrity.
3. Complete suppression of all organized movements interfering with freedom of trade and stirring up international hatred.
4. Effective protection throughout Manchuria of all peaceful pursuits undertaken by Japanese subjects.
5. Respect for treaty rights of Japan in Manchuria. (In this fifth point Japan thus included some of the oldest and most fundamental controversies which existed between the two countries.)

interfere with these movements until all these fundamental questions of national policy between the two
nations should be settled.

M. Briand as President of the Council on October
29th and the American government by a note to the
Japanese government through our Ambassador at
Tokyo on November 5th, gave our views on the situation thus presented and endeavored to point out to
Japan the position in which such an attitude left her.[15]
On the other hand, the Chinese government on October
24th had announced its willingness to conclude with
Japan a treaty of arbitration for the very purpose of
settling in a peaceful and legal manner all these disputes as to treaty interpretation. Japan remained
obdurate. Her position at the end of October, as it has
been described by another historian, thus was that Japan

> having broken the peace by taking a military
> offensive and having accomplished by this un-
> lawful means a far-reaching Japanese occu-
> pation of territory that was lawfully under
> Chinese administration, impenitently took
> her stand upon two fundamental conditions:
> a refusal to withdraw her troops to the limits
> within which she was entitled to station them
> . . . until negotiations on the substance of her
> dispute with China had taken place; and an
> insistence that these negotiations should not
> only be antecedent to a withdrawal of the
> Japanese troops but should be conducted be-
> tween the two parties *à deux*[16] [i.e., without
> the intervention of neutral observers].

[15] See "Conditions in Manchuria," Senate Document 55, 72nd Congress, 1st
Session, pp. 25, 30.
[16] Royal Institute of International Affairs, *Survey* for 1931, p. 476.

VIII

OCCURRENCES FROM THE CLOSE OF THE OCTOBER SESSION
OF THE LEAGUE UNTIL IT RECONVENED ON NOVEMBER
16TH; THE MILITARY OPERATIONS IN NORTH MAN-
CHURIA; RISE OF NATIONALISTIC FEELING IN
JAPAN; CONSEQUENT EXCITEMENT IN THE
UNITED STATES

Almost as soon as the echoes of Japan's protestation
of peaceful intentions at the Geneva October meeting
had died away, news began to arrive of the movement
of the Japanese army into the far north of Manchuria.
This was a movement along the Chinese-owned railway
from Ssupingkai to Angangki on the line of the Russian-
owned Chinese Eastern Railway. It was an expedition
which not only took the troops hundreds of miles beyond their zone in South Manchuria, but was aimed directly at Tsitsihar, the capital of Heilungkiang, the
northernmost province of Manchuria. It was thus not
only a blow at the last remaining untouched province of
the Young Marshal but it also threatened Russia's
shortest line of connection with Vladivostok. By no
flight of imagination could these operations be connected with the protection of Japanese nationals and
property in South Manchuria. On November 4th to 6th
there occurred a three days' battle between this Japanese force and General Ma Chan-shan. By November
18th the forces of General Ma, who was one of the supporters of the Young Marshal, had been scattered and
destroyed, and the capital, Tsitsihar, had been occupied
by Japanese troops. During this period the Japanese
government had been sending to us and to the League
explanations as to this movement of its troops—that
they had merely gone north to protect the rebuilding of

the Nonni River Bridge which had been destroyed by Chinese brigands; that General Ma's troops were threatening their interest in the south even at that distance; that they would retire immediately after their protective mission had been finished. These explanations were on their face rebutted by the geographical situation and by the movements of their troops.

Contemporaneously we were getting dark news as to the popular excitement in Japan which was steadily rising as her troops moved forward. This came to us through many channels—our embassy at Tokyo, the Japanese embassy in Washington, our observers in contact with representative Japanese in various quarters of the world. Not only was the general feeling among the people aflame with patriotic hostility to China and the outside world, but fanatical secret societies existed which were overawing the chiefs of the army itself as well as threatening violence to the heads of the civil government. Our Embassy in Japan reported that the Wakatsuki-Shidehara Cabinet was tottering and could not last long in the face of the excited populace. Later messages from Japanese sources told us that plots had been uncovered to murder Mr. Wakatsuki, the Premier; Baron Shidehara, the Foreign Minister; Mr. Inouye, the Finance Minister. We also heard that even the heads of the army itself were personally threatened by a cabal of the younger officers who were attempting to influence the actions of their chiefs in a way which it was difficult for foreigners to understand.[17] On October 19th I wrote in my diary, after enumerating some of these messages:

[17] On February 9, 1932, Finance Minister Inouye was murdered by a group of these fanatics. On March 5th Baron Dan, the head of the great commercial concern of Mitsui & Company and one of the most influential men in all Japan, was similarly murdered. On May 15th the new Prime Minister, Inoukai, was similarly murdered.

In other words, the Japanese government which we have been dealing with is no longer in control.

At the same time the feeling in our own country was rising. Throughout the period of these negotiations I had been very fortunate in the treatment which had been accorded me in my difficult situation by the American press. Soon after the original outbreak of September 18th at Mukden I had held a conference at my home at Woodley with the chiefs of the various press associations and the heads of the Washington bureaus of the most important dailies, in which I had outlined to them the background of the Manchurian situation, the broad issues which were probably involved, and the difficulties with which we would undoubtedly be concerned. Thereafter on various occasions I had supplemented my regular press conferences at the Department with similar special meetings of these senior Washington journalists. Their response throughout this period to my appeal for patience and self-control on the part of our press had been admirable. They had as a whole kept the press from becoming inflamed and had endeavored to protect me from having my elbow joggled during the ticklish times through which we were passing.

But with the repeated acts of defiance of world public opinion on the part of the Japanese army and the failure of the Japanese government to make good its assurances, popular criticism throughout the country had been rising. Through the press the growth of this American feeling became very manifest to us at the Department. It was clear that the American people were following the proceedings both here and at Geneva with great interest. It was also clear that they were growing puzzled and angry at the silence of their own government in the face of the defiant attitude of the Japanese army towards the representations made by us and the League. This attitude was accentuated by the fact that the terms of most of our notes and diplomatic representations, having been made through the diplomatic channels, were unknown to them. They knew simply that a representation had been made and disregarded. They did not know in any fullness the assurances which had been given by the Japanese government to us and the way in which that government itself had been flouted by its army. Nor did they know our reason for exercising such patience.

I finally concluded that the time had come when the cause of peace was no longer best served by a situation in which the normal methods of diplomacy left the public opinion of America practically unguided and voiceless in dealing with this controversy. I felt that we had gone to the limit in our desire to protect the moderate government in Japan and to give it an opportunity to regain control of its own truculent elements; that we were approaching a time when, willy nilly, there would be a showdown between the law-abiding elements of the world and the law-defying elements represented by the Japanese army. I felt that it was the part of wisdom to prepare for this situation in order that there might be no misunderstanding with Baron Shidehara.

Accordingly, on November 19th, the day on which we received the final news that the Japanese had destroyed General Ma's army and had taken Tsitsihar, I invited in Mr. Debuchi, the Japanese Ambassador, and summed up my view of the situation to him fully and frankly, to be reported to his chief. I told him that the picture presented to me by the occurrences of the autumn was concisely as follows: that on September 18th the regular organized Chinese government in Manchuria consisted of the government of the Young Marshal, Chang Hsueh-liang; that this government had been recognized by the Central Government at Nanking and was the only regular government in Manchuria; that on that day and thereafter the Japanese army had attacked and destroyed the forces of Marshal Chang wherever they could find them and that, instead of withdrawing as promised by their own government, they only stopped attacking when there were no more Chinese forces left to attack; that in this latest instance they had penetrated to the extreme northern part of Manchuria many hundreds of miles beyond the Japanese railway zone in order to attack General Ma and to take Tsitsihar, and that I could not but regard this as a violation by the Japanese army of the provisions of the Kellogg-Briand Pact and of the Nine Power Treaty.

I then told the Ambassador that under these circumstances I must ask him to tell his government that I must reserve full liberty to publish all the papers and communications which had passed between our two governments on this subject; that I did not intend to publish them at once, necessarily, but that I must retain full liberty to do so. I told the Ambassador that, as he knew, for two months I had been keeping these papers from publication in the hope of a settlement so that it might not embarrass the Japanese government or the chance of such a settlement. I reminded him that I had gone so far in this hope as to urge our own press not to publish any matter which would inflame American sentiment against Japan, but that now in the interest of the position of my own government I must reserve full liberty of action to make public the whole matter.

I was very sorry for Mr. Debuchi, whom I believed to have been from the beginning earnestly and sincerely desirous of helping to seek an honorable solution of this matter. He admitted this was a dark day for him, but he frankly said he had no complaint to make as to the way we had treated him and that he would report the entire matter to his government.

IX

THE NOVEMBER MEETING OF THE LEAGUE

The Council had reconvened at Paris on November 16th in the face of the gloomy and humiliating situation which I have just described. In the light of the serious problem before us I determined to be represented in our coöperation with the League at this meeting by the most prominent and experienced public man of whose services we could avail ourselves at this moment—our London Ambassador, Charles G. Dawes, the former Vice President of the United States. His instructions were similar to those which had been given to Mr. Gilbert in October, except that it was left entirely to his discretion as to whether and when he should attend in person the actual meetings of the Council. In view of his prominence as a public man, I counted on his having easy opportunities for informal discussions with the representatives of other countries and at the same time I believed that his personality and reputation would do much to assure the people in this country of the importance of his work as well as the discretion with which he would carry it on. In both respects my anticipations were fulfilled.

He was able to keep in close touch with M. Briand and the other representatives of the important powers at the Council meeting. He was also in close touch with

Dr. Sze, who was representing China, and with Mr. Matsudaira, the Japanese Ambassador to Britain, who also was in attendance at Paris. As a result he was able to keep me posted by cable and telephone of both the official occurrences and the informal discussions which were going on during the crowded and exciting weeks while the Council was in session. At the same time his appointment as our liaison officer at Paris was received with cordiality by the American press.

November 19th, when the news came of the Japanese defeat of General Ma and the capture of Tsitsihar, was a day of excitement in Paris. Dr. Sze was reported as being anxious on behalf of China to invoke Article XV of the Covenant with a view to leading ultimately up to the imposition of sanctions. Members of the League were reported to have inquired from Mr. Dawes what our attitude would be in case they should proceed on that line. They were anxious to obtain commitments from us before they even discussed such action themselves. On our part we manifestly could give no such commitment. Our Congress was not in session and there was no statutory authority under which the Executive could impose economic sanctions. Furthermore, it was quite unlikely that any such authority would be granted by the Congress. In the public discussions in America a decade before as to joining the League much opposition had been manifested against the provisions for either military or economic sanctions expressed in the League Covenant. In the treaties to which it had afterwards become a party, viz. the Pact of Paris and the Nine Power Treaty, the American government had confined itself to a reliance upon the sanctions of public opinion alone. Under such circumstances manifestly we could not commit ourselves to the imposition of sanctions. On the other hand, if the League of Nations desired to proceed under Articles XV and XVI of the Covenant and themselves to impose such sanctions, we were anxious not to discourage them or to put any obstacles or dangers in their path. With the authority of the President, after a conference with him on that day —November 19th—I informed Mr. Dawes to that effect and authorized him in his discretion to make our whole position absolutely clear to M. Briand. The following morning he reported to me that he had done so and that M. Briand was perfectly satisfied with our attitude.

The situation had been complicated by the insistence of some of the members of the Council that Mr. Dawes should take this precise time to attend publicly a meeting of the Council and confer there with its members. Mr. Dawes was very much opposed to doing this at this particular time on account of the patent danger which would be involved of having his presence at such a meeting misinterpreted as a commitment by our government on the subject of sanctions which might there be discussed. In this I fully concurred with him. The nature and imminence of this risk can be realized by the fact that at this very moment one of the most important papers in New York City was falsely accusing us of intentional double dealing—that we were making representations in public before the League of Nations to one effect while in private we were reassuring the Japanese that we would not do anything to harm them. It would have been very unwise further to encourage such a misunderstanding. Through Mr. Dawes's caution we were able, I believe, to make our position absolutely clear to the members of the League.

Just after this the Japanese government took two steps which were in sharp contrast with its preceding attitude and which offered encouragement to us.

On November 20th it broached at Geneva the sending of a neutral commission of inquiry to Manchuria, and two or three days later it formally proposed such a commission and expanded the scope of the proposed inquiry to include all matters in controversy between the two nations. This proposal was a complete reversal of the attitude taken by that government since the beginning of the crisis. For the first time it offered an opportunity of an impartial judicial investigation of an international controversy which the Japanese had thus far studiously endeavored to preserve from discussion with outside nations. To be sure, they declined to couple the suggestion with an agreement to suspend hostilities pending the investigation, but even thus restricted it opened the door to the possibility of obtaining an authoritative report upon the rights and wrongs of a problem which was of paramount importance to the preservation of the peace of the world. It also constituted the first occasion of the application in the Far East of the methods of judicial examination and settlement of international controversies which the Western nations had been developing for many years.

The other step was also quite unexpected. On November 22nd we began to hear through the press rumors of a new movement by the Japanese army against Chinchow. On the 24th and again on the 27th I made vigorous representations through our embassy at Tokyo against this renewal of offensive action. Whether my success on this occasion was in part due to the warning of publicity which I had sent to Baron Shidehara on the 19th, I cannot be perfectly sure. From certain circumstances I am inclined to think that it was. But whatever the reason, Shidehara made on this occasion a very vigorous effort and for once was temporarily successful. The Japanese troops which had actually begun their advance from Mukden towards Chinchow were stopped on November 27th apparently by orders from Tokyo and returned to Mukden. General Honjo, the Commander-in-chief in Manchuria, apparently was for once overruled and checked by higher authority.[18]

These two steps, however, constituted the last effort on the part of the Foreign Office and the Minseito Cabinet to keep their country in alignment with world opinion. It became every day more clear that their tenure of office was brief and their hold upon official power rapidly failing. The army soon began to recover from its rebuff and to claim that it had been tricked into withdrawal in reliance upon corresponding promises of the Chinese to withdraw their army beyond the Great Wall which had not been kept. During these final days of the session at Geneva it was a race against time to carry the resolution for a neutral commission which had already been virtually agreed upon. By a narrow margin that race was won. On December 10th the resolution was successfully carried with the assent of the Japanese representative, and on the following day, December 11th, the Minseito government resigned at Tokyo and went out of office.

[18] "On the very day (Nov. 27) on which the Civil Government at Tokyo were giving this conditional yet explicit undertaking, the Japanese Commander-in-chief in Manchuria, General Honjo, was sending his aircraft to bomb Chinchow, entraining all his forces at Mukden and sending them southwestward along the Peking-Mukden Railway, and calling up all the Japanese reservists resident in Mukden to garrison the city after the first-line troops had left. The same evening, however, General Honjo countermanded his own orders—apparently in deference to imperative instructions from Tokyo—and the withdrawal of the Chinchow expeditionary force to Mukden duly began on the 28th.

"The turn of the screw which produced this unwonted effect appears to have been given neither by Monsieur Briand nor by Sir John Simon, but by Mr. Stimson, in a communication on the subject of Chinchow which was read by the American Ambassador at Tokyo to the Japanese Minister for Foreign Affairs on the 27th November itself, in reinforcement of representations which had been conveyed by the same procedure on the 24th." Royal Institute of International Affairs, *Survey* for 1931, p. 455.

The resolution as finally adopted also provided that China and Japan were "to avoid any further aggravation of the situation and to refrain from any initiative which may lead to further fighting and loss of life." But in assenting to this provision Mr. Yoshizawa, the Japanese representative, made reservations which much impaired its value. Immediately after the passage of the resolution I made a public statement describing the long course of the negotiation conducted by the League, the efforts of the United States to coöperate with and support these negotiations, and my gratification at the decision to appoint the neutral commission of investigation. I concluded my statement with the following paragraphs:

The ultimate solution of the Manchurian problem must be worked out by some process of agreement between China and Japan themselves. This country is concerned that the methods employed in this settlement shall, in harmony with the obligations of the treaties to which we are parties, be made in a way which shall not endanger the peace of the world and that the result shall not be the result of military pressure. These are the essential principles for which the United States and the nations represented on the Council have been striving and it is in itself a signal accomplishment that there has been arrayed behind these principles in a harmonious coöperation such a solid alignment of the nations of the world.

On the other hand the adoption of this resolution in no way constitutes an endorsement of any action hitherto taken in Manchuria. This government, as one of the signatories of the Kellogg-Briand Pact and the Nine Power Treaty, cannot disguise its concern over the events which have there transpired. The future efficacy of the resolution depends upon the good faith with which the pledge against renewed hostilities is carried out by both parties and the spirit in which its provisions directed towards an ultimate solution are availed of. The American government will continue to follow with solicitous interest all developments in this situation in the light of the obligations involved in the treaties to which this country is a party.[19]

With the passage of this resolution the Council of the League of Nations closed its session, and this adjournment virtually terminated the long period of negotiation under Article XI of the League Covenant which had been begun on September 21st. The Commission provided for by the resolution was promptly appointed. We assented to the inclusion in its membership of an American, and on the request of M. Briand I suggested and the League appointed Major-General Frank R. McCoy of the American army as that member. General McCoy had had long service in the Far East; had been a member of the Wood-Forbes Commission to investigate the Philippine situation in 1921, had also been the head of the distribution of American relief to Japan at the time of the great earthquake in 1923, and was well and favorably known to both China and Japan. The other four members of the commission

---

[19] For full provisions of the resolution of the Council, the declaration of the President of the Council and of the respective representatives of China and Japan, and the statement by the American Secretary of State, see Willoughby, *op. cit.*, p. 177 *et seq.*

were representatives of Great Britain, France, Italy and Germany, the chairman being the Earl of Lytton.

X

CONCLUSIONS FROM THE FIRST PERIOD

Thus our attempt to solve the Manchurian problem by discussion and conciliation had failed. We had been favored by there being in power at Tokyo a moderate government and I think we had made no mistake in placing our reliance upon the efforts of that government to solve the problem of controlling the army. It was our best chance under the circumstances, but it was not enough. A determined army, independent of Cabinet control, backed by the traditional Japanese feeling as to Manchuria, had vanquished the Cabinet and secured a united and inflamed nation behind it. By the perfection of its plans and the speed of its movements that army between Friday night and Monday morning (September 18th–21st) had presented an unready world with the *fait accompli* of a conquered South Manchuria and this had made its eventual success over the Cabinet sure.

Sir Edward Grey is said to have suggested that had he possessed the power to call a compulsory conference of the European nations during the fateful "twelve days of July, 1914" after the ultimatum to Serbia, the World War might have been prevented. This time the League of Nations possessed that power in September, 1931, and used it, but in the circumstances existing in Manchuria it was not enough. I doubt if in 1914 it would have been enough unless it could have been used before the first fatal order set in motion the interconnected mobilization of the various armies and thus transferred from the civil authorities to the military chiefs the direction of events. In 1931 the Japanese army had already acted before the rest of the world received any news of the crisis.

Some critics have blamed the nations for not at once setting in motion stronger machinery of compulsion against Japan; for not having at once invoked the pressure of economic sanctions. These critics disregard the limitations of man in international action. True, the power to invoke such measures existed within the League Covenant; but it had never been used. Mankind does not at once jump into the skillful use of new international machinery. The road of progress is much slower and is usually strewn with the wrecks of previous unsuccessful efforts. In this case the League turned first to the machinery with which it was most familiar and had had the best success in the past. And in that effort the League had for the first time the coöperation of the United States to an extent entirely lacking in previous efforts. For the reasons already pointed out, it could not have had during those early months the same American coöperation in the use of sanctions. Without the United States the League's use of sanctions would have been incomplete and comparatively ineffective—less effective than it could have been in the case of Italy versus Ethiopia. Roughly speaking, the United States possessed one-third of the world's trade with Japan; all the other nations combined, two-thirds. Although the League was assured of our moral sympathy and that we would interpose no obstacles to its economic sanctions, it took no step to invoke sanctions and even China, the party most concerned, did not insist upon them—did not even discuss them until near the end of November. In short, the League leadership was not ready to attempt sanctions in the autumn of 1931 in relation to Manchuria, and the government of the United States in its efforts at coöperation with the League under Article XI had gone to the limit of its legal authority and at least to the limit of its popular support. Thus the efforts at conciliation faded away, leaving only two definite constructive accomplishments. One was the new clear precedent of frank outspoken American coöperation with the League in a case affecting the general peace of the world. The other was the appointment with Japan's consent of an international commission of inquiry upon a vital Far Eastern problem. Each of these was in its way an accomplishment of signal importance.

PART THREE

CHINA APPEALS TO THE LEAGUE ASSEMBLY FOR JUDGMENT

CHINA APPEALS TO THE LEAGUE ASSEMBLY FOR JUDGMENT

I

THE CHANGED CONDITIONS AND PROBLEMS WITH WHICH WE WERE NOW CONFRONTED

WHEN on December 11, 1931, the Minseito government in Japan went out of office, an entirely new problem opened up before us. The Seiyukai party which then assumed control of the government represented a quite different attitude towards China and the Far East from that held by its predecessor. The statesmen whose names had been connected with the "friendly" policy towards China as well as a closer cooperation with the social and political views of the Western world had now passed off the stage. Shidehara, Inouye and Hamaguchi had all been outstanding men of the former type. They were succeeded by men whose connection with the views of the military leaders of Japan was closer and more sympathetic.

It was evident that what could not be done by their predecessors in checking the army would not be done by these last. This was quickly indicated by the immediate advance of the army, which moved forward and occupied Chinchow on the 2nd of January, 1932. At the State Department we realized that we were probably faced by a new era and that a period lay before us similar to the one which in 1915, during the Great War, had produced the Twenty-one Demands upon China, the occupation of Shantung and Siberia, and the long effort to persuade the Japanese forces to retire from those areas. We also were not unaware of the grandiose conceptions of Japan's mission towards her Asiatic neighbor, China, which at various periods had been voiced by some Japanese statesmen and which since then have been not only voiced but begun to be put into operation in the Japanese advances into North China and Mongolia.

Our policy during the past three months had been predicated on the hope of action from within Japan. That hope had now vanished. The most extreme manifestations of nationalistic feeling were being made by her people. What can only be called a reign of terror was going on, directed at her moderates—at the men who had been attempting to develop her progress towards constitutional government. Gentlemen high in public and social circles of the nation who were known and honored throughout the Western world were being driven into hiding for fear of their lives by the frenzied agitators for militarism and imperialism. For example, Dr. Inazo Nitobe, a man well known in Europe and America for his literary culture and distinguished public services, was reported to have been dragged from his sick bed in a hospital to appear before the Reservists Association of the Army and apologize for having said in a lecture that militarism might be as dangerous as communism. Every fresh advance of the army in Manchuria had been a signal for fresh outbursts of this spirit.

On its face it was evident that all hope for a solution of the Manchurian problem by conciliation and for a fair settlement by even-handed negotiation with China was ended for the present. It was quite clear that a nation in Japan's present frame of mind must be left to dash her head against the hard but slow-moving economic and social realities of the world. If the modern political and social faiths of the Western world, particularly the English-speaking world, were well founded; if the lessons taught by the downfall of colonial Spain and the colonial theories of George III were sound, sooner or later Japan also would learn that she could not permanently dominate and exploit by ancient methods a much larger nation than herself composed of people the intellectual and spiritual equals of her own. But this process might take ages and in the meanwhile much harm to the rest of the world would be done by the far-reaching disturbances which it would inevitably excite. There were, therefore, some very real and important problems left for us to solve in warding off and minimizing such evils.

The possible harm to the interests of the United States which I foresaw as inherent in this situation can be roughly divided into three divisions:

First: The direct material damage to our trade which would inevitably be caused; also the less certain but nevertheless quite possible jeopardy which in the future course of such a struggle between China and Japan might threaten our own people and their territorial possessions.

Second: The immense blow to the cause of peace and war prevention throughout the world which would inevitably be caused if without protest or condemnation Japan were permitted to violate and disregard the group of post-war treaties which she had ratified and upon which so many hopes of our race and of our part of the world had been predicated.

Third: The incalculable harm which would be done immediately to American prestige in China and ultimately to the material interests of America and her people in that region, if after having for many years assisted by public and private effort in the education and development of China towards the ideals of modern Christian civilization, and having taken the lead in the movement which secured the covenant of all the great powers, including ourselves, "to respect her sovereignty, her independence and her territorial and administrative integrity," we should now cynically abandon her to her fate when this same covenant was violated.

A word or two may be said as to some of these considerations. We have recently been so absorbed in our own sufferings and retrogression in the great depression that we forget the possibilities which should normally inhere in our commercial relations with China and the rapid strides which in normal times, particularly during the first decade after the Great War, have been made in the development of our commerce with that country. During that decade it increased at a much more rapid rate than our commerce with Europe. China is a country so vast and at present so undeveloped in the normal needs of a population of her type and intelligence that the possibilities of a commerce with her, which will supply her needs as she develops along the pathway of modern civilization, are literally enormous. Next to Japan we are the country to which a participation in that commerce most naturally belongs by virtue of our geographical location.

The third category includes in some respects the most important matters of all when measured by their possibilities of future good or evil to the world. Yet in current discussions on this subject it is most frequently ignored and forgotten. The future of the Far East will be very largely dominated by the future of the four hundred fifty million people of Chinese blood. For several centuries Eastern Asia has owed its character mainly to the peaceful traditions of this great agricultural nation. If the character of China should be revolutionized and through exploitation become militaristic and aggressive, not only Asia but the rest of the world must tremble. The United States has made a good start in the development of China's friendship. It would have been the most shortsighted folly to turn our backs upon her at the time of her most dire need.

II

THE INITIAL STEPS TAKEN

The first necessary step was one of popular education. The long discouraging negotiations of the autumn had necessarily been conducted largely behind the veil of diplomatic procedure. If they had been successful in accomplishing a fair settlement between the two countries in controversy, that would have been sufficient. No further enlightenment as to the facts of the controversy would have been necessary for the people of our country. They would have been satisfied with the result and would have let it go at that. But now when we were confronted with the indefinite continuance of a dangerous strife which might at any time flare up and involve our own material interests or even safety, it was important that the American people should know what it was all about to a much fuller and more accurate extent than they actually did.

In the second place, some way must be found to terminate the long-drawn-out process of note-writing which had produced such comparatively insignificant results and to wind it up with a snap—with a statement which should serve at the same time as a period to the interchange of unsatisfactory argument and as a reminder to Japan that the United States had important rights involved in the controversy upon which she proposed to stand without further discussion.

Finally, conciliation having failed, it was most important to find some way of formally expressing the moral disapproval of the world against the breach of the peace in Manchuria and, if possible, to put behind that expression a sanction which would bring pressure upon the party responsible to make amends. We had reason to believe that economic sanctions would not be invoked. The League from the beginning had been hesitant and reluctant to turn to the machinery for such sanctions which it had ready. We had no such machinery ready, and very evident difficulties lay in the path of its creation. If possible, some substitute upon which all nations could agree should be found which would at least carry the force and implication of a moral condemnation.

The first of these steps was in process of being taken. On November 19th I had given notice to Baron Shidehara that I must reserve the right, if necessary, to publish our correspondence. On December 17th the Senate, quite without my previous knowledge, had passed a resolution requesting the transmission to the Senate of the notes, correspondence and communications between our government and all other nations, relating to the situation in Manchuria. These documents were now being compiled and prepared. There was no reason for withholding them longer from publication. On January 26th, as soon as they were compiled, they were sent to the Senate.[1] Fortune played into our hands in that the time when they were published by the Senate coincided with the attack by the Japanese upon Shanghai. This was causing nation-wide excitement. Therefore the correspondence was given most earnest attention by both the Congress and the people and it helped powerfully towards clarifying the issues involved.

As soon as the actual taking of Chinchow by the Japanese army signalized the final flouting of all our efforts during the autumn's negotiations, I set to work upon the second step—the winding up of discussion by a final notice of our rights. The idea of using a notice of non-recognition as a warning to an aggressive power of course was not new. In 1915 Secretary Bryan had sent such a notification to China and Japan at the time when Japan had served the Twenty-one Demands upon China and was exercising pressure upon China to make agreements with her which might violate the rights of the United States under the Open Door policy or otherwise. The thought of using such a method to emphasize our position in the present controversy had been in our minds for many weeks. I find from my diary that as early as November 9th I discussed it with my assistants as an ultimate possible weapon to be used, and thereafter it was constantly cropping up in our discussions. Mr. Bryan had used it as an individual notification from the United States based upon rights of our government under treaties relating to China alone. But even on November 9th we were beginning to discuss the greater potentialities of the doctrine should the other nations of the world join us in establishing it. The force of a non-recognition of the fruits of aggression when concurred in by the entire world would manifestly have a more

[1] See "Conditions in Manchuria," Senate Document 55; 72nd Congress, 1st Session.

powerful deterring influence upon the aggressor than when used by a single nation.

Since Mr. Bryan's day the relations of the powers with China had been crystallized by the Nine Power Treaty of 1922, which placed the commercial rights of the signatory nations upon the far-sighted principle of respect for China's territorial and administrative integrity.[2] Furthermore, since Mr. Bryan's day this policy of self-denial of aggression by a stronger against a weaker power involved in the Nine Power Treaty had been powerfully reënforced by the execution of the Kellogg-Briand Pact pledging its signatories, including Japan, never to seek the solution of controversies except by pacific means. If our warning should be so extended as to include non-recognition of the fruits of a violation not only of treaties specifically relating to China, but also of the Kellogg-Briand Pact covering the whole world, it would not only rest upon a more elevated and broader principle, but it would appeal with greater force to a much larger number of nations in the world.

Many of these nations, while not expressly interested in China to the extent that we were, had been earnestly coöperating during the past month in the efforts of the League of Nations to restore peace in Manchuria. So gradually and naturally our efforts to achieve the second objective above mentioned, namely of terminating the discussion of this controversy with a positive statement of our rights, became blended with the hope that this same effort might also serve as a rallying point for the other nations who had been our associates in the autumn's negotiations. In this way it might possibly

[2] The Nine Power Treaty itself in Article II contains a direct covenant among its signatories against any such "arrangement" as Japan was now engaged in establishing in Manchuria. It thus directly supported the "non-recognition" policy. See Appendix II.

serve as the substitute for sanctions for which we all had been groping.

Thus in the Department we came to our note of January 7, 1932, by a natural and almost inevitable sequence, and the only differences of opinion that I remember were as to its scope and the definiteness and finality of its method of expression. But I felt that it was a serious decision and one on which the President should be consulted. On the evening of January 4th I therefore laid the matter before him at the White House. He was awaiting me in his study in the room which had been Lincoln's Cabinet office. It was at a time of great economic stress. The procession of countries which had followed Great Britain off the gold standard was putting serious pressure upon our own resources. World currencies were fluctuating and depreciating. Trade barriers were being everywhere erected to protect foreign exchanges. Our trade was constantly decreasing and our prices falling. The drain on our gold and the withdrawal of foreign deposits were putting a strain on our domestic banks, thereby stifling our industry. Unemployment was rapidly rising.

Furthermore, the new Congress under changed party leadership was not coöperating with the recommendations for the purpose of meeting this crisis which the President had made to it when it met in December. On the very day of my visit he had sent them a further urgent message hoping to expedite their action and to awaken public support for the long series of constructive remedies which he had previously urged upon them. The burden thus weighing upon him showed itself clearly in his face. It seemed almost fantastic to expect him to be able to turn from this domestic pressure, under which he was the pivot upon which turned the work of reorganizing our entire domestic economy, in order to consider new complicated problems arising out of a crisis in the Orient.

In order to simplify and facilitate explanations I had prepared two drafts of my proposed note, one in the narrow form following closely the precedent of the 1915 note and covering merely our commercial rights; and the other in the form which I myself preferred, taking in the general obligations under the Kellogg Pact. He read them through. I briefly explained the difference—the conservatism of the one; the possibilities and at the same time the novelty and risks of the second. He hesitated not a moment. "I agree with you," he said. "Let us put it on the broad basis." And in the discussion which followed he showed that he had at once grasped the possibilities of international reorganization which were involved in the proposal. The note thus approved reads as follows:

January 7, 1932.

With the recent military operations about Chinchow, the last remaining administrative authority of the Government of the Chinese Republic in South Manchuria, as it existed prior to September 18, 1931, has been destroyed. The American Government continues confident that the work of the neutral commission recently authorized by the Council of the League of Nations will facilitate an ultimate solution of the difficulties now existing between China and Japan. But in view of the present situation and of its own rights and obligations therein, the American Government deems it to be its duty to notify both the Government of the Chinese Republic and the Imperial Japanese Government that it can not admit the legality of any situation *de facto* nor does it intend to recognize any treaty or agreement entered into between those governments, or agents thereof, which may impair the treaty rights of the United States or its citizens in China, including those which relate to the sovereignty, the independence, or the territorial and administrative integrity of the Republic of China, or to the international policy relative to China, commonly known as the open-door policy; and that it does not intend to recognize any situation, treaty, or agreement which may be brought about by means contrary to the covenants and obligations of the Pact of Paris of August 27, 1928, to which treaty both China and Japan, as well as the United States, are parties.

III

THE NOTE OF JANUARY 7TH

The purpose and character of such a note obviously precluded a preliminary general conference in respect to it with other nations. Its primary purpose was to record the final decision of an influential government which had made earnest and patient efforts for a peaceful solution of this controversy; which had exercised great forbearance in the face of a long series of assurances, given and immediately disregarded and which had now been driven to a serious decision which was intended to be final. Any attempt to discuss such a note with a view to joint action by the entire group of signatories of the Nine Power Treaty or of the Pact of Paris would inevitably have produced hesitation, delays and leaks to the press. These would have impaired, if they had not destroyed, the psychological effect of the note. From its nature and the circumstances surrounding its inception the note was thus necessarily the setting up of "a standard to which the wise and honest may repair," leaving "the event in the hand of God."

But that did not mean that we did not hope that our action would be received at least with sympathy and perhaps with immediate support by those with whom as associates we had been laboring in a common cause during the preceding three months. In order to promote this possibility I communicated what we were going to do confidentially in advance to the two nations which throughout the autumn had been the leaders in the conduct of the negotiations by the League. On the morning of January 5th I saw the British Ambassador. I told him that now that the Japanese had occupied Chinchow I was about to send a note to both the Japanese and the Chinese governments notifying them that we did not intend to recognize any treaties, understandings or situations which might be entered into by China and Japan impairing the treaty rights of the United States or their citizens in China or impairing the sovereignty, independence or territorial or administrative integrity of China, or affecting the Open Door policy, or which might be arrived at by steps contrary to the Pact of Paris. I read to the Ambassador a draft of the note. I reminded him that we had done somewhat the same thing in 1915 at the time of the Twenty-one Demands, but I pointed out to him that our action now would be assisted and made more effective if other countries like Great Britain and France who were in a similar position to us took similar steps. I asked him to communicate our intention to his government and said that I intended to bring the same matter to the attention of the French. On the same morning immediately afterwards I saw the Ambassador of France, read to him the draft of the note and communicated our purposes and intentions to him substantially in the same way as I had to his British colleague. I told them both that I intended to act promptly within a day or two.

Two days later on the morning of January 7th I delivered the identic notes to Mr. Debuchi, the Japanese Ambassador, and to Dr. Yen, the chargé d'affaires of China. Immediately afterwards on the same morning I handed copies of these notes to the representatives of the six other signatories of the Nine Power Treaty. On the following day, January 8th, I made the notes public, having previously taken the precaution at a conference with the senior members of the press at Woodley to give them the broad background of the historic policy for which we were working in China and urging upon them a treatment of the entire step which would not be inflammatory or truculent and yet would give to the act its proper perspective in connection with our general policy in the Far East.

We naturally looked to the government of Great Britain for a sympathetic understanding of the position which we had taken as well as for possible coöperation in the subsequent steps that might make more effective our policy. Of all the European powers Great Britain had the largest commercial interests in China. Lord Salisbury's earnest coöperation with John Hay had originally established the Open Door policy. Lord Balfour's earnest coöperation at the Washington Conference had crystallized that policy into the Nine Power Treaty and had been most helpful in the general settlement in respect to the Far East which was achieved at the same time. Finally for the past two years our administration had been having the most complete and cordial understanding with the British government which had marked Anglo-American relations for many years. We had coöperated in many matters, including a successful international naval conference at London in 1930 and a successful international financial conference at London in 1931. This coöperation was largely based upon the effective influence of the Kellogg-Briand Pact in promoting the recent emergence of the United States from the accentuated isolationism which had marked its attitude towards the League of Nations since the Great War. At the Rapidan Conference in October, 1929, Prime Minister MacDonald had joined with President Hoover in the announcement that

> both our governments resolve to accept the peace pact [the Kellogg-Briand Pact] not only as a declaration of our good intentions but as a positive obligation to direct our national policy in accordance with its pledge.

Our note of January 7th represented the most signal effort by our own government to carry out that pledge. We knew that in Britain there had been a recent change in government and that a Coalition Cabinet had succeeded the Labor Cabinet with which for over two years we had had our dealings. But the new government had participated in the coöperative efforts which had been made in the attempted solution of this Manchurian problem during the past three months. We had no reason to anticipate that it would not view our action sympathetically even if it felt unable for any reason to follow us.

In the light of these anticipations we were disappointed by what actually occurred. On January 11th the British government published in the press a communiqué in reference to our note of January 7th.[3] The contents of this communiqué were such as to be taken by most readers, including—what was most important —the Japanese government, as a rebuff to the United States. It stated in substance that, in view of former statements by Japanese representatives Japan would adhere to the Open Door policy and would welcome participation and coöperation in Manchurian enterprise, the British government did not consider it necessary to address any formal note to Japan on the lines of our note but had requested the Japanese Ambassador in London to obtain confirmation of these earlier assurances of his government. Its omissions were the most important feature of the communiqué. It was entirely silent as to the preservation of the sovereignty, independence and integrity of China, the Kellogg-Briand Pact, and the assertion of the principle of the non-recognition of the fruits of unlawful aggression. It thus ignored entirely the questions of world peace and China's integrity which we had deemed the most important features not only of our

[3] The full text of the communiqué was as follows:

"His Majesty's Government stand by the policy of the open door for international trade in Manchuria, which was guaranteed by the Nine Power Treaty at Washington.

"Since the recent events in Manchuria, the Japanese representatives at the Council of the League of Nations at Geneva stated on the 13th October that Japan was the champion in Manchuria of the principle of equal opportunity and the open door for the economic activities of all nations. Further, on the 28th December, the Japanese Prime Minister stated that Japan would adhere to the Open Door policy, and would welcome participation and coöperation in Manchurian enterprise.

"In view of these statements, his Majesty's Government have not considered it necessary to address any formal note to the Japanese Government on the lines of the American Government's note, but the Japanese Ambassador in London has been requested to obtain confirmation of these assurances from his Government."

The British government on January 11th also delivered at the State Department a courteous memorandum containing substantially the same information as that made public in the foregoing communiqué. It did not reach me until January 12th.

note, but of the previous three months' negotiations in which we had been supporting the efforts of the League of Nations and the British government. The communiqué dealt solely with the single problem of continuing trade relations with Manchuria.

In a leading editorial published on the same day and on the same page with the communiqué (January 11th) the London *Times* confidently undertook to supply affirmative interpretations of these omissions of the communiqué. Its editorial began as follows:

> The British Government have acted wisely in declining to address a communication to the Chinese and Japanese Governments on the lines of Mr. Stimson's Note.

It then described my note and the Nine Power Treaty referred to therein and proceeded:

> In invoking its clauses (those of the Nine Power Treaty) the American Government may have been moved by the fear that the Japanese authorities would set up a virtually independent administration in Manchuria which would favour Japanese interests to the detriment of the commerce of other nations. It is clear that the Foreign Office does not share these apprehensions, and that, although the Nine Power Treaty provides for consultation between the interested powers, it was not in fact consulted before the Note was communicated to Nanking and Tokyo.
>
> In the circumstances it was fully justified in limiting its action to a request for a confirmation of the assurances given by Mr. Yoshizawa to the League Council in October and by the

new Japanese Prime Minister a fortnight ago,
to the effect that Japan would adhere to the
principle of the "Open Door" which her Government claims to be defending in Manchuria.

.   .   .   .

Nor does it seem to be the immediate business of the Foreign Office to defend the "administrative integrity" of China until that
integrity is something more than an ideal. It
did not exist in 1922 and it does not exist today. On no occasion since the Nine Power
Treaty was signed has the Central Government of China exercised any real administrative authority over large and varying areas of
its huge territory. Today its writ does not run
in Yunnan and in other important provinces,
and, while its sovereignty over Manchuria is
not disputed, there is no evidence that it has
exercised any real administration there since
Nanking became the Chinese capital.

The depth of the cleft between the views and policies
of our two governments indicated by this assumed interpretation can best be appreciated when we remember that in 1922, when Lord Balfour and Mr. Hughes
at Washington were executing the Nine Power Treaty,
the chaotic conditions created by civil war in China
were far greater than in September, 1931, when Japan
attacked and destroyed the government in Manchuria.[4] Nevertheless it had been the avowed intention of
those statesmen by that treaty to assure China of ample
time and freedom from foreign aggression to make successful her gigantic task of developing the free institutions of a self-governing state. The treaty was based

---

[4] See Report of Lytton Commission, Chap. I.

upon the assumption that in the long run the interests of the foreign nations trading with China would be better served by such a policy of self-denial as the treaty provided than by any selfish exploitation of China. Thus the assertions of the *Times* as to China's lack of "administrative integrity" were not only quite irrelevant to the purposes and validity of the Nine Power Treaty; they not only ignored the fact that Japan herself was responsible for the recent adverse change in Manchuria, but they were assertions on their face most welcome to a nation which, like Japan, was then engaged in tearing down the growth which the treaty was intended to build up. The imperialistic group of Japanese statesmen who for years had cherished the hope of a military and economic hegemony over China but whose hopes had been suppressed by the enlightened policy at Washington in 1922, joined in by the Japanese government of that day, could have asked for no more effective assurance in their favor.

From the beginning of the Manchurian crisis, in considering all possible influences and sanctions which conceivably could bring Japan back to the responsible attitude towards the outside world which in former periods her government had manifested, the sanction which I had always felt would be the most potent of all would be a belief on her part that in the fundamental principles governing this problem the United States of America and the British Commonwealth of Nations would see eye to eye and stand side by side. That was a feeling which I shared not only with the members of our administration, but with most responsible Americans with whom I had discussed this matter. Moreover, it was a belief which Japan herself might well have acquired by observation of the Anglo-American coöperation throughout the negotiation of the Nine Power Treaty itself at Washington in 1922 as well as throughout the long and difficult negotiations of the London Naval Conference of 1930. The chief evil result of these statements of the London *Times* which I have just described was that they tended to destroy at once any such belief on the part of Japan. The memory of this cleft necessarily colored and rendered difficult whatever was attempted throughout the subsequent months.

The protagonists of Japan were prompt to take advantage of this assurance of divided counsel which was thus offered them. In the long series of their attempted defenses for their Manchurian adventure during the autumn, they had not dared to argue that China's alleged lack of standing as an organized state operated to relieve them from the obligations of their covenants towards her in the Nine Power Treaty and elsewhere. Indeed, they could hardly do so in view of the fact that on September 18, 1931, China had become a member of the Council of the League of Nations upon the motion and endorsement of Japan herself. But now with this assurance offered them they were quickly emboldened to take this position.

On January 16th the Japanese government replied to our note of January 7th. Not only did the tone of the note on its face give evidence of the receipt of reënforcement to the Japanese cause[5] but in the following

[5] "The document (the Japanese reply to the American note) was conceived in a vein of elegant irony which came within an ace of insolence." Royal Institute of International Affairs, *Survey* for 1932, p. 545.

"The reply of the Japanese Government was of a peculiar character, for its second paragraph must have been intended to irritate rather than to answer the United States since it ascribed to the United States an assurance which by no straining of language could be read into its note." Willoughby, *The Sino-Japanese Controversy and the League of Nations*, p. 207.

paragraph it made almost literal use of the London *Times's* argument. It said:

It may be added that the treaties which relate to China must necessarily be applied with
due regard to the state of affairs from time to
time prevailing in that country, and that the
present unsettled and distracted state of China
is not what was in the contemplation of the
high contracting parties at the time of the
treaty of Washington. It was certainly not satisfactory then; but it did not display that dis-
union and those antagonisms which it does today. This cannot affect the binding character
of the stipulations of treaties; but it may in
material respects modify their application,
since they must necessarily be applied with
reference to the state of facts as they exist.

But while it gladly accepted the argument offered
by the London *Times* as to the lack of organized government in China, the Japanese government in this
note declined to lend any support to the happy assurance which the *Times* had asserted was held by the
Foreign Office against the fear of a future "Manchukuo," for in the note to us it at once proceeded to
lay the basis of the argument upon which "Manchukuo"
was immediately afterward constructed. It said:

My government desires further to point out
that any replacement which has occurred in
the personnel of the administration of Manchuria has been the necessary act of the local
population. Even in cases of hostile occupation—which this was not—it is customary for
the local officials to remain in the exercise of

their functions. In the present case they for the most part fled or resigned; it was their own behavior which was calculated to destroy the working of the apparatus of government. The Japanese government cannot think that the Chinese people, unlike all others, are destitute of the power of self-determination and of organizing themselves in order to secure civilized conditions when deserted by the existing officials.

The argument to the effect that China was not an organized state and that this fact relieved Japan from the obligation to carry out the covenants of the Nine Power Treaty and the League of Nations Covenant was thereafter regularly put forward by the Japanese government in its diplomatic utterances.[6] It may be fairly said to have become the argument upon which Japan thereafter relied with the greatest assurance. It was ultimately rejected as untrue and unsound by the unanimous report of the Lytton Commission in September.[7]

I learned informally from the French government that owing to the attitude of the British it would not make the *démarche* towards Japan which it had been previously considering, and several other powers, signatories of the Nine Power Treaty, including the Netherlands and Belgium, later informed me that they did not consider it necessary to send a note on the situa-

[6] Thus it was used on February 19th by the Japanese representative in the argument before the Council of the League of Nations in defense to an application of Article X of the Covenant. It was again used in the reply on February 23rd of the Japanese government to the appeal of the Council of the League of February 16th on the same subject, and it was used in the formal statement of the position of the Japanese government accompanying the foregoing reply of February 23rd.

[7] See Report of Lytton Commission, Chap. I.

tion to Japan or China. In the light of the division of opinion made clear by the British attitude, such a position on the part of smaller governments having territorial interests in the Far East was easily understood.

Vigorous criticism of the action of his government and a detailed analysis of the various causes which may have contributed thereto has been made by the Director of Studies of the Royal Institute of International Affairs in his *Survey of International Affairs for 1932.*[8] It would not be appropriate for me to attempt any such analysis and I think it is fair to say that, while deeply regretting the division of policy, we were not uncharitably disposed in our acceptance of it at the time. We were well aware of the great national strain which had enveloped Great Britain ever since the change in her government in September and which rendered it an especially difficult time in which to follow a difficult policy. We also fully appreciated the natural ties of sentiment and gratitude which had resulted from the former Anglo-Japanese Alliance. Moreover, as a former administrator in the Far East, I was well acquainted with the attitude of mind towards China which had been reflected in the editorial of the London *Times.* It was the typical attitude of the "Old Timer,"[8a] a man who has spent his life in residence and in business in the Far East and who has imbibed an attitude towards the native populations of that region which is quite common among such men. The "Old Timer" is also a familiar figure in the Philippines and during my stay there I had on more than one occasion checked up my own observations of his peculiarities with the

[8] See Royal Institute of International Affairs, *Survey* for 1932, pp. 523, *et seq.,* 540 *et seq.*
[8a] Sometimes also spoken of as the "Old China Hand."

similar observations of my British colleague at Hong-kong.

The Chinese are not an easy people to deal with in the mass, and these characteristics have been much accentuated by their efforts since the revolution to throw off the earlier shackles of extraterritoriality, consular courts, concessions and foreign settlements. The "Old Timer's" memory is full of small grievances and he is happy to welcome almost any opportunity to get even with the Chinese or any other Oriental people with whom he has been living through similar periods. His attitude often colors the vision of those engaged in Far Eastern commerce. So here it seemed to me merely that the British government had temporarily found it easy to follow the lead of those whose viewpoints were affected by commercial relations. Downing Street had temporarily yielded to the views of the "City."

IV

MILITARY OPERATIONS AT SHANGHAI

Seldom has the appearance of an international situation been so suddenly changed as was that in the Far East by the attack initiated by the Japanese navy on the Chinese at Shanghai late in January, 1932.

In the middle of January to all appearances Japan's aggression in Manchuria had achieved complete military and diplomatic success. Her army had occupied all the strategic points of Manchuria, had overturned and driven out the government of the Young Marshal, and had destroyed and scattered Chinese armies numerically very much larger than its own forces. At the same time her government had successfully resisted

attempts of the other nations of the world to intervene
with any effectiveness; had delayed and thwarted the
efforts of the Council of the League under Article XI,
and finally had seen a wedge of differing policies
driven between Great Britain and the United States,
the two principal nations interested in these international efforts. China was completely discouraged; the
other nations baffled and pessimistic. The collective
peace machinery had received a blow which made it
look entirely ineffective.

By the 1st of May this picture had radically changed.
Japan had attempted to extend her aggressive action to
the Yangtze River and to break up the efforts of the
Chinese at Shanghai to maintain an economic boycott
against her business. There she had received the most
striking military setback of her modern history. More
than five thousand marines, subsequently aided by two
divisions and a mixed brigade of infantry with a full
complement of artillery, tanks and bombing airplanes
had been checked, thrown back and held impotent for
over a month by a force of Chinese soldiers armed only
with rifles and machine guns.[9] Ultimately the Chinese,
when flanked out of their positions by a wide turning
movement which Japan for weeks had failed to make,
had retreated unbroken and in good order. In the face
of the indignation of a world shocked at the cruelty
with which she had bombed the helpless Shanghai sub-
urb of Chapei, Japan was withdrawing her forces from
Shanghai with her original purpose unaccomplished.
China, thrilled at the heroism of her infantry, was filled
with new courage; and Great Britain, roused by this
Japanese blow at the solar plexus of British interests

[9] A third division, the 14th, was also sent as reënforcements but did not
arrive until March 7th, after the fighting had ceased. The Chinese possessed
some pieces of artillery but these were so few and so ineffective as to play
virtually no part in the subsequent operations.

on the Yangtze, was throwing into the coöperative efforts of the nations to curb Japan a spirit which had been absent before. The entire group of the nations organized in the League had taken over the conduct of the Manchurian affair from the Council into the hands of the Assembly, and these nations thus organized had pledged themselves unanimously to the doctrine of not recognizing as valid the administrative changes which had taken place in Manchuria.

In order to make clear the general thread of the policy of our government during this period, it is necessary to explain somewhat in detail these military operations and some of the complex problems involved.

A

The Chinese Boycott

The Shanghai incident took its origin in the effectiveness of the boycott which ever since the preceding summer the Chinese had established on Japanese goods throughout China. This boycott was China's answer to Japan's aggression in Manchuria.[10] For many years an economic boycott has constituted China's weapon of pacific defense against external aggression. It has been a very effective weapon. A number of nations have suffered from it, including ourselves, and the dread of it has undoubtedly served as a very considerable protection to a nation like China which was unwilling or unable to use force. In fact its efficacy has been such as to make it worth while to consider carefully the even greater potentialities which would inhere in a system of collective economic sanctions such as is proposed

[10] A boycott had actually originated in June, 1931, as a result of trouble between the Chinese and Koreans, but it had been greatly strengthened and extended when the Japanese made their attack on Mukden on September 18th.

by Article XVI of the League Covenant. When we consider what has been done by China, alone and unaided, towards some of her aggressors and the deterring effect which it undoubtedly has had upon future aggression, we may well get a useful sidelight on the possible potency of such a system if it were sincerely applied collectively by a large group of nations instead of by one alone.[11]

In this case Japan had suffered very seriously, China being, next to the United States, the largest buyer of Japanese goods. The Japanese naval move at Shanghai undoubtedly was designed to break up the boycott, inasmuch as Shanghai was the chief industrial city of China and the center of her trade with Japan.

Thus the implications of this Shanghai controversy were broad and important. On the one hand, the Chinese in their effort to make the boycott effective without doubt had been guilty to a certain extent of violence in their attacks upon Japanese commerce and Japanese traders. Under international practice, if the Chinese government failed to protect from violence the citizens of Japan who were within her borders, Japan herself might intervene to give the requisite protection. On the other hand, if such an intervention was merely being used as a cloak to destroy the boycott by force, it represented a further unauthorized aggression by Japan against China and the destruction of the only peaceful weapon of defense which China had in her hands to redress the injury which had already been done to her in Manchuria. The rights and wrongs of the situation were thus complex and of far-reaching significance.

[11] In the year 1926 I visited Hongkong when it was suffering from the effect of the Chinese boycott imposed on British trade on account of the alleged "student massacre" at Shanghai the preceding year. The visible effect was very striking. Commercially Hongkong seemed almost like a dead city.

B

The International Settlement at Shanghai

Shanghai, where this controversy took place, was not only the chief commercial city of China, but it was a great cosmopolitan port where important commerce of many nations was centered. It was filled with their merchants and business men from all over the world as well as with their factories, their warehouses, their shops and their residences. It was the port of that great area in Central China which centers around the valley of the Yangtze River. Although the Japanese were the most numerous of foreigners living and doing business in Shanghai, that port and the Yangtze Valley were the center of Great Britain's chief commerce with China. The United States and France also had very large commercial interests there. Shanghai held a population of over three million and in the volume of its trade was one of the five or six largest commercial ports of the world.

The waterfront of Shanghai extends along the Whangpoo River, which runs into the estuary at the mouth of the Yangtze. The city lies near the base of a broad peninsula, which is bounded on the southeast by the Whangpoo River and on the northeast by the Yangtze. In composition and government the city is a curious mixture. Its center and principal portion consists of the area of the two foreign settlements known as the International Settlement and the French Concession. These settlements front on the north side of the Whangpoo River. Their population consists partly of foreigners and partly of the large numbers of Chinese who also have entered the settlements for the purpose of business, residence or protection. Around these two international settlements lies a great urban area chiefly occupied and entirely governed by the Chinese. A portion of this Chinese area projects as a salient into the International Settlement from the north and is known as Chapei. Another portion of this Chinese area projects into the French Concession from the south and is known as the Native or Old City.

Within the area of the foreign settlements foreigners are permitted to lease land for business and living purposes and to establish municipal governments with certain restricted local powers of police and taxation. The foreigners living there are entitled to the extraterritorial rights and privileges which have been granted to foreign powers by treaty throughout China. In other respects they and all other residents are subject to Chinese jurisdiction both in and out of the settlements. In the International Settlement these special local powers of police and taxation are exercised by a municipal council composed in part of foreign residents and elected by the taxpayers. In the French Concession the dominant local authority is the French Consul General, aided by an advisory Municipal Council. The International Settlement is policed by an efficient international police force composed partly of foreigners and partly of specially selected Chinese. In addition to these police there are usually stationed in the Settlement forces of sailors or marines belonging to the principal powers interested in the commerce of Shanghai. At the outbreak of the trouble on January 28, 1932, these foreign troops, other than Japanese, consisted of about 2,300 British, 1,250 Americans and 1,050 French, with some few Italians. There were in the harbor at that time twenty-three Japanese, five British, two French and one American war vessels.

To the visitor coming by the river, Shanghai thus presents the picture of a great modern city filled with broad busy streets, handsome buildings of commerce, manufacture and business, and comfortable residences and parks. The shape of this modern city, as will be seen from the accompanying map, is most irregular, and as soon as the visitor crosses certain invisible boundaries he finds himself at once among the frail structures and dense population of a typical Chinese city. These features accentuate the difficult problem of protecting foreigners in such emergencies as have arisen occasionally during the past ten or fifteen years.

During the turbulent period of civil war since the fall of the empire, it has been the effort of the authorities of the international settlements of Shanghai to establish the tradition that these settlements shall be treated as a neutral area into which the violence of this civil strife shall not be permitted to enter. There has been created an International Settlement Defense Committee consisting of the commanders of the foreign troops, the chairman of the Municipal Council, the Commander of the Police, and the Commandant of the Shanghai Volunteer Corps.[12] In case of such emergencies as arose in 1924, 1925 and 1927 during the civil war period, there has grown up the custom of establishing around the boundaries of the two international settlements a protective cordon composed of the foreign troops which thus constituted a guard against the intrusion of belligerent factions of the Chinese from without. This protective line did not always follow exactly the boundaries of the settlements. In some cases, in order to establish a defensible line, it was found

---

[12] This is an armed volunteer corps established from the residents of the foreign settlements.

necessary to extend the cordon of troops outside into the native areas, but its military purpose was to protect the foreign settlements. Whenever such an emergency was declared by the Municipal Council to exist it was the duty of the Defense Committee to allot the sectors in the line of defense among the different foreign forces and for each commander to establish his troops in the portion of that line allotted to his nation.

In these previous emergencies the controversies which excited the violence were between various factions of the Chinese themselves as, for example, between the forces of North China and the forces of Southern China in 1927. In all these cases the foreigners within the Settlement could act as a unit in a common spirit of neutrality.

But the controversy which now arose in January, 1932, was quite different. It was between one of the foreign nations and the nation of China, and the issue involved was not the clear and undisputed problem of protecting the city and its occupants from violence. Japan might and did claim that such was the case; but China, with a great deal of reason, did not admit that the issue was so narrow. She claimed and the actions of the Japanese gave good reason to believe that Japan's purpose was much broader; that it was not to protect Japanese citizens from violence, but that it was a continuance of Japan's national aggression against China which had been going on in Manchuria and was intended to cripple China's defense by a new attack upon her at Shanghai. Necessarily such a situation gave rise to much more difficult questions for the authorities of the Settlement and for the different foreign nations interested therein than had ever arisen in the earlier emergencies.

C

The Origin of the Hostilities

Although a most intensive and effective boycott of Japanese trade by the Chinese had been going on for over four months, and although the occurrences in Manchuria had resulted in tremendous feeling against the Japanese on the part of the Chinese population, it is fair to say that surprisingly little personal violence had resulted. Property had been destroyed probably by illegal methods and the Chinese courts had been lax in giving redress to Japanese claimants, but I believe there was no reported loss of life until January 18th, when a clash occurred in front of a Chinese factory in Chapei, in which two Japanese were seriously wounded, one of them subsequently dying from his wounds. Two days later some fifty members of one of the Japanese societies proceeded to the factory, set it on fire and clashed with the municipal police. In this clash three Chinese policemen and three Japanese were injured, one on either side subsequently dying.[13]

On January 20th the Japanese Consul General presented to the Chinese Mayor of Greater Shanghai (that is, the chief Chinese authority of the entire urban area) the following demands:

1. Formal apology by the Mayor.
2. Immediate arrest of those responsible for the attack on January 18th.
3. Payment of damages and hospital bills.
4. Adequate control of the anti-Japanese movement.

[13] Compare, for instance, this modest casualty list with the anti-Chinese riots in Korea in the preceding July which the Japanese authorities failed to control and where more than one hundred Chinese were killed, over five hundred injured, and a great amount of Chinese property was destroyed.

5. Immediate dissolution of all anti-Japanese organizations engaged in fostering hostile feelings and anti-Japanese agitation.

It will be noticed that these last two demands virtually amounted to a demand for a dissolution of the boycott organization. The next morning the Mayor replied that he was ready to consider the first three demands but would have difficulty in complying with the last two. Thereupon that same day, January 21st, the Japanese Admiral in command of the forces at Shanghai, Koichi Shiozawa, gave a public notice in the press that

> should the Mayor of Greater Shanghai fail to give a satisfactory reply to the Japanese and fulfill their demands without delay, the Admiral was determined to take the necessary steps in order to protect Japanese Imperial rights and interests.

Moreover, heavy Japanese reënforcements were at once ordered to Shanghai. These arrived partly on the 24th and partly at dawn on the 28th. They consisted of two cruisers, an aircraft carrier and sixteen destroyers, and brought the number of marines under Admiral Shiozawa's disposal for landing purposes up to about three thousand men.

A force of about thirty thousand Chinese troops, known as the Nineteenth Route Army, had been for some time regularly quartered in and near the Chapei district of Shanghai. Its mission was the national defense of the Nanking and Shanghai districts of China. This unit was composed of Cantonese troops and was one of the most experienced fighting forces of the Chinese army. Its presence in Shanghai was in no way connected with the boycott controversy in which its members apparently had taken no part. Moreover, after Admiral Shiozawa's warning, the Mayor of Shanghai announced that he would make every possible concession to avoid clashes and began trying to induce the leaders of the local Chinese to put an end to the anti-Japanese boycott association. He made a public statement to this effect on January 27th and, as a result of his efforts, various offices of that association were seized by the police during the night of January 27th–28th. On the side of the Chinese authorities therefore there was apparently no further provocation, but on the contrary efforts were being made to accede to the full Japanese demands.

But on January 24th the Japanese Consul uttered a further warning and again on January 27th he notified the Mayor that he would expect a "satisfactory reply to the demands by 6 P.M. next day, failing which the Japanese would take the necessary steps in order to enforce them." On January 28th at seven-thirty in the morning Admiral Shiozawa notified the commanders of the other national defense forces in Shanghai that he proposed to take action on the following morning (the 29th) if no satisfactory reply had been received.

As a natural result of these repeated threats, the apprehension of the Chinese and the other nationals in Shanghai became intense. If the Chinese failed to make satisfactory answer to these drastic demands, the community was faced with Japanese action of a nature not specified, but which, if measured by what had happened in Manchuria, might be expected to be of the most serious character. On the other hand, if the Chinese authorities yielded, there might be angry reactions from the Chinese population.

Under these circumstances the Municipal Council of

the International Settlement met at 2 P.M. on January 28th and declared the existence of an emergency, and at about 4 P.M. all of the international forces, except the Japanese, began to take up their allotted positions in their respective defense sectors. The sector allotted to the Japanese was in the northeastern portion of the Settlement. More than that, the defense line of the Japanese sector had been extended outside of the Settlement northward in a sharp salient so as to include the so-called Hongkew district where a large number of Japanese nationals resided. This Hongkew salient lay east of the Shanghai-Nanking Railway, which ran north from the North Station. The main portion of Chapei lay west of the railway, in some portions overlapping the railway. Somewhere in Chapei it was known that the Nineteenth Route Army was quartered. This, moreover, was the first time that such an extension of the Japanese sector outside the Settlement to Hongkew had ever been made; and no notice of the extension had been given to the Chinese authorities of the city by the Defense Committee—perhaps owing to the confusion and excitement of the moment. Therefore if the Japanese moved into that portion of their sector without ample warning on their part, it was morally certain that they would come into immediate proximity and perhaps into contact with the Nineteenth Route Army.

Early that same afternoon the Mayor of Shanghai finally transmitted to the Japanese Consul a reply accepting entirely the Japanese demands, and at 4 P.M. the Consul informed the other national consuls of the receipt of this reply, stating that it was entirely satisfactory.

After nightfall of the same day and at least five or six hours after all of the other national forces had taken their stations, the Japanese marines assembled at their naval headquarters in the International Settlement. At 11 P.M. Admiral Shiozawa sent proclamations to the Mayor notifying him that he had decided to send out troops to protect the Japanese nationals in Chapei and asking the Chinese authorities speedily to withdraw the Chinese troops now stationed in Chapei to the west of the railway and to remove all hostile defenses in that area. The Mayor received the message at 11:15. The Japanese forces began their movement at 11:45. It of course would have been quite impossible in the short time at their disposal after the notification from the Admiral for the Chinese authorities to have arranged for the actual withdrawal of the Chinese troops in the area mentioned.

The Japanese force consisting that night of approximately two thousand marines and sailors, together with armored cars, trucks and light artillery, advanced along the North Szechuan Road running north out of the Settlement parallel to and east of the railway. At the entrances to streets running westward they dropped parties of troops. At midnight on a given signal these separate detachments advanced westward towards the railway and the main section of Chapei and very shortly came into conflict first with Chinese police and later with the soldiers of the Nineteenth Route Army who were quartered in that section.

In defending themselves for the responsibility of this initial clash, the Japanese rest their case upon the claim that they were doing no more than they were authorized to do by the International Defense Committee and the Municipal Council of the Settlement, and that their troops, while moving out to their allotted sector, were first fired on by Chinese troops and civilian snipers. But even if one should admit these assertions, which are not at all undisputed, such a technical defense does not go to the bottom of the matter and reach the basis of ultimate responsibility. Any fair criticism must take account of a far broader situation for which the Japanese themselves were responsible. In the first place the September aggression in Manchuria in which their troops, on a similar pretext of protecting Japanese nationals, in forty-eight hours had overrun all of Southern Manchuria and scattered and destroyed all the organized Chinese forces of that region, was in everybody's mind. Now in Shanghai on the similar pretext of a comparatively trivial incident, they had at once mobilized a disproportionately large naval force in the harbor of Shanghai and were rapidly augmenting that force with new reënforcements. Thirdly, the warnings of the Admiral had given no accurate measure of what he intended to do except that he proposed to compel the Chinese to abandon their national boycott by an act of force. Finally, instead of marching his forces out to their sector in daylight as the other national commanders had done, he had assembled them under cover of night and made his movement with a notice so insufficient as to amount to no notice at all and had covered his operation with a veil of secrecy which was bound to excite alarm.[14]

[14] Press reports emphasized this secrecy. An Associated Press correspondent, learning late in the evening of the 28th that the Japanese were about to begin armed action, motored through the northern districts of the city and the areas outside the Settlement limits. Part of his account reads as follows:

> In the darkened streets almost deserted by civilians, Japanese bluejackets and marines were lined up rank upon rank, awaiting the order to begin the invasion. . . . The secrecy which was maintained over the Japanese plans was indicated by the fact that I saw Chinese police in the native city patrolling the streets as usual to the corners of their beats up to the very edge of the Japanese residential section. As the Japanese bluejackets deployed down these streets, the Chinese policemen stared open-mouthed and paralyzed in surprise. They stood transfixed while their rifles were taken away from them and some of them were marched to Japanese

Even in the minds of the foreigners resident in Shanghai this series of Japanese actions had excited the most lively apprehension as to what the Japanese intended to do. In the minds of the Chinese against whom it was directed such apprehensions were necessarily infinitely accentuated. Their Mayor had yielded to demands which seemed beyond any justification and was doing his best to prevent further outbreaks. In spite of this they saw the Japanese commander proceeding with his threat and carrying out movements which had no reasonable relation to any justifiable protective purpose.

Against such a background and bearing in mind such an atmosphere on the part of the Chinese, the fair-minded historian must reach the conclusion that when Admiral Shiozawa began his movement, he, to put it mildly, was not at all reluctant at the prospect of having an armed clash with the Chinese forces in the district into which he was moving. In fact he was courting such a clash and he must have known it.[15]

D

Summary of Military Operations
January 28th to March 3rd

If, as is not unlikely, the Japanese Admiral expected that no serious resistance would be made by the Chinese

---

headquarters. Just previously I had visited some of the streets of the Chapei section which was burned today. I found everything completely quiet and peaceful there. Even the railway station was deserted. Within half an hour these same streets were echoing with the rattle of machine guns and rifles and the great battle of Chapei had begun.

A Reuter correspondent touring the same area at about the same time substantially corroborates the above statement.

[15] Press reports stated that the Cabinet at Tokyo on January 26th had authorized the naval forces at Shanghai to "take positive action" in the event of no satisfactory reply being returned to the Consul's demands. See London *Times*, January 27, 28, 1932.

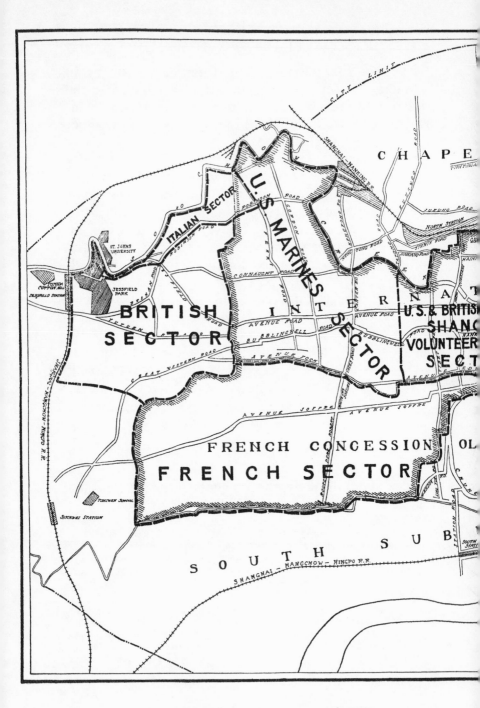

THE INTERNATIONAL SETTLEMENT AT SHANGHAI

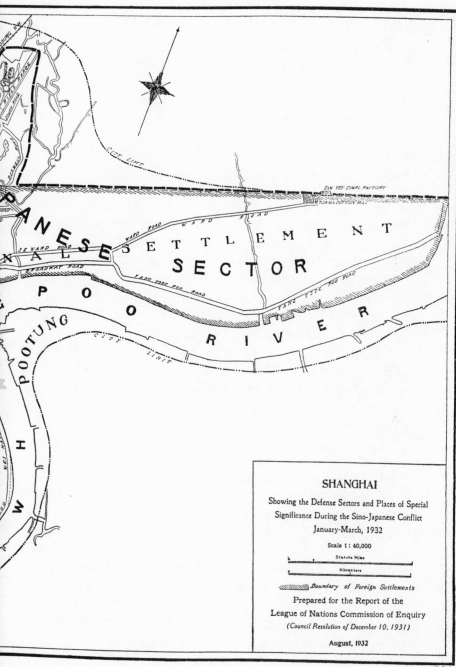

SHANGHAI

Showing the Defense Sectors and Places of Special
Significance During the Sino-Japanese Conflict
January-March, 1932

Scale 1 : 40,000

Statute Miles

Kilometers

Boundary of Foreign Settlements

Prepared for the Report of the
League of Nations Commission of Enquiry
(Council Resolution of December 10, 1931)

August, 1932

to his operations, he was soon rudely undeceived. His troops first came into conflict with Chinese gendarmes of the native city, but in about forty minutes thereafter they came up against some three thousand soldiers of the Seventy-eighth Division of the Nineteenth Route Army. These last brought the Japanese to a sharp stop and the position held by these Chinese soldiers that night remained substantially untaken for over a month of hard fighting. Parties of the Japanese who in their surprise advance had crossed the railroad and taken possession of the North Station, before the night was over were driven back by Chinese counter-attacks. The Admiral was soon sending for all the reënforcements he had, bringing his landing force up to at least three thousand men. Then at four-thirty in the morning he issued an order which must have been the act of either a perfectly ruthless or a badly excited man. He sent to the airplane carrier for his bombing planes and proceeded to bomb the unwarned and helpless civilian native quarter of Chapei. It was an act of inexcusable cruelty and has stained the Japanese record at Shanghai for all time. Not only were bombs dropped upon the positions held by the Chinese troops, but incendiary bombs were used which soon had the entire quarter in flames. According to Reuter's correspondent, by five-thirty that morning "Chapei had the appearance of one blazing bonfire" which seemed to be creeping towards the International Settlement. Flames were "leaping seventy-five to a hundred feet in the air and the roar of the conflagration was audible at a great distance." Thousands of helpless civilians met their death without warning and two hundred fifty thousand helpless refugees poured from the ruins of Chapei into the International Settlement. But it was as useless as it was cruel and utterly failed to shake the steady defense of the Chinese troops.

Unable to make headway against their military opponents in Chapei, the Japanese naval authorities vented their energies on the district within the Settlement which they were supposed to protect. They barricaded the streets; they disarmed the police and paralyzed all the regular municipal activities of the Settlement authorities, including the fire brigade. Numerous excesses against the Chinese population were committed, including many summary executions, and a veritable reign of terror resulted, during which almost the entire non-Japanese population of that part of the Settlement fled. Apparently believing their regular forces insufficient for the defense of that area, the Japanese command mobilized their so-called "reservists," and these imperfectly disciplined and armed civilian Japanese added to the excitement and terror.

The American sector of defense adjoined the Japanese sector on the west, and Japanese detachments, apparently losing all self-control in their excitement, rushed into the American sector, committing acts of violence therein against the Chinese and creating a very delicate and difficult situation for our troops to control. That a clash between the Japanese and American forces did not result during several turbulent days was almost solely due to the discretion of the American commanders and the admirable self-control of their men.

Vigorous protests by the Mayor of Shanghai backed by the American and British Consul Generals resulted by 8 P.M. on January 29th in a truce in the firing and the bombing. This truce at best was imperfect and temporary. The Japanese had lost prestige by their initial repulse on the night of January 28th. The bombardment of Chapei had also made a most painful impression against them throughout the world, evidence of which was coming to Tokyo through all their diplomatic channels. It soon became evident that they felt that they could not stop without accomplishing some sort of a military victory to "save their face." On February 4th they rejected the suggestions which they had invited on February 1st from the four great powers for a joint withdrawal of both Chinese and Japanese forces behind a neutral line which should be guaranteed and patrolled by the neutral powers.[16] A stream of their reënforcements, both naval and land troops, were beginning to arrive, and on February 3rd their attacks began again. The manner and results of these attacks, however, and the reënforcements and successive commanders who arrived, showed not only how greatly the Japanese command were surprised at the magnitude of their task and the fighting character of their opponents, but also revealed the basic defects in the tactics they were employing.

The reader can perhaps best understand the tactical situation by a rough comparison with that which existed on June 17, 1775, at Bunker Hill. There the American militia had established themselves in a precarious position on the tip of a peninsula projecting towards Boston. The British commander in Boston, whose fleet could entirely command the water approaches to the American position, by landing a few troops on the base of the peninsula at Charlestown Neck, speedily and with insignificant loss could have bagged the entire American force. Underestimating their defensive fighting power, however, he chose to land his disciplined troops on the tip of the peninsula and by a frontal attack tried to drive the Americans out through the neck of the

[16] These various diplomatic steps are discussed below, pp. 145-152.

bottle which so easily he could have stopped up. The result was great losses of men and prestige on his part followed by a very hard-earned success; while on the part of the Americans there was a great increase of

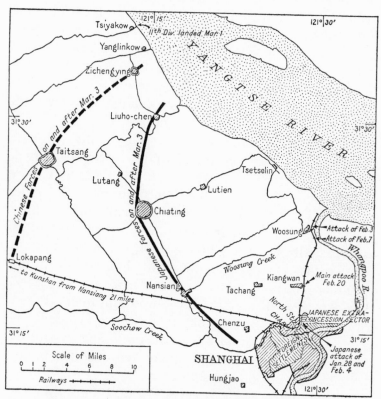

THE SHANGHAI BATTLE AREA

enthusiasm as well as of confidence in the fighting power of their militia.

At Shanghai the Chinese forces were distributed along a much broader peninsula from Woosung at its tip to Chapei near its base, but strategically they were all in a precarious position, for the Japanese at all times could have made a landing on the Yangtze River whence by an easy enveloping movement they could cut the single railroad running from Shanghai to Nanking and compel the Chinese forces to retire with comparatively little loss on either side. This they were eventually forced to do. But like Lord Howe in 1775, underestimating the fighting power of their opponents, for a month they wasted their constantly accumulating strength in a succession of frontal attacks at Chapei, at Woosung and finally at Kiangwan in the center between the two. Eventually they landed the Eleventh Division near Liuho on the Yangtze River and made the enveloping movement, at which the Chinese promptly retreated and the military operations ceased. Had the Japanese been willing to do this earlier, they would almost certainly have accomplished the same result and they would have saved nearly fifteen hundred casualties on their own side and over five thousand casualties in the Chinese army, to say nothing of the ruins of Chapei and the eight thousand dead and wounded civilians which was the price of the course they actually followed.[17] More important than all these factors to the Japanese, they would have avoided giving to China the impulse towards unity and patriotism which was created by the unexpected example of the devoted heroism of her soldiers.

For our purposes it is necessary only to outline the successive steps actually taken. On February 2nd Admiral Nomura arrived from Japan and assumed

[17] The Chinese Government announced at the end of May their military losses as 4,274 killed and 1,770 wounded. The Japanese Government announced their casualties on May 11th as 634 killed and 791 wounded. The Shanghai Bureau of Social Affairs in the middle of March estimated that 6,080 Chinese civilians had been killed and more than 2,000 wounded, while there were 10,040 missing.

command over the Japanese naval forces. On February 3rd the Japanese first attempted to take the forts at Woosung by a landing attack covered by the guns of their fleet. They were repulsed with considerable loss. On February 4th, their total naval landing forces having been brought up to about five thousand men, assisted by artillery and bombing planes, they renewed the attack on Chapei. Little or no advance was made by their troops but considerable damage was done to Chapei by planes and artillery. No further general attacks were made by the navy, though their artillery and planes continued to direct fire on Chapei with increasing damage to property. The Nineteenth Route Army, unsupported by artillery, held its ground in spite of casualties.

On February 7th the Japanese Twenty-fourth Mixed Brigade of land forces arrived and landed south of Woosung Creek. The Chinese had constructed defenses on the north side of the creek between the creek and the forts. That night and during the 8th the Japanese attempted to cross the creek and take the Woosung forts, but without success. On the 14th of February they crossed the creek further inland and renewed the attack on the forts, but a Chinese counter-attack forced them back with severe losses.

By February 18th the Japanese had assembled a land force of about 16,000 men, including not only the Twenty-fourth Mixed Brigade, but the Ninth Division. These were supported with howitzers, guns, tanks and planes. A landing-field had been constructed on shore to facilitate the use of the air service. Plans were made for a carefully concerted movement of attack. It was proposed to hold the Chinese at the Woosung forts with a small containing force on the right of the line;

to hold the Chinese at Chapei with the naval forces on the left of the line, and to break westward through the center at Kiangwan with the Ninth Division as a striking force. After thus breaking through in the center, this force was to turn southward towards Chenzu, thus forcing the stubborn defenders of Chapei out of their positions by a flanking movement on their left. In the meantime the Chinese had been reënforcing their lines at Woosung and Kiangwan by the Eighty-seventh and Eighty-eighth Divisions of the Fifth Route Army, which had been brought up from the interior of China to support the Nineteenth Route Army. These last Chinese troops during the civil wars of the past year had been fighting against the Nineteenth Route Army, but this threat from a common foreign foe healed the old antagonisms and the two armies now fought shoulder to shoulder with equal ardor.

General Uyeda arrived from Japan and took command, and the Japanese War Office at Tokyo announced that he had been authorized to hand to the Chinese commander an ultimatum requiring him to withdraw his troops from Shanghai within twenty-four hours. Whereas the proposal of the neutral powers on February 2nd had been that there should be a *simultaneous* withdrawal of both combatant forces backward from the points of conflict, this ultimatum required the Chinese to withdraw alone and for a distance of twenty kilometers. It also required that China should dismantle her forts and other military equipment within the entire area of the terrain and that she should not refortify them. Such a sweeping invasion of Chinese sovereignty could hardly be defended on any theory of protecting Japanese nationals. The ultimatum was evidently not intended to be accepted by the Chinese commander, and it was not.

The Japanese moved into position on the night of February 19th and began their attack early the following morning. At first the carefully organized offensive seemed to proceed smoothly and at 10 A.M. General Uyeda stated that he expected to be in Kiangwan by 4 P.M. that day. Then they ran up against the stubborn Chinese defense and for seven days the entire Ninth Division was bogged down against the Chinese defenses at Kiangwan. The terse words of military reports inadequately picture the courage of that prolonged unequal fighting. On the one side was the perfected Japanese fighting machine with coördinated movement raining down its bombs and shell fire upon an enemy which had no such means of reply. The American military observer with the Japanese army reported:

On this front during all the fighting not a single round of artillery was fired by the Chinese. They took the punishment of all that the Japanese could send over and still hung on at Kiangwan and Miao Hang Chen.

And whenever the Japanese infantry attempted to advance, they crawled out of their shell holes and drove it back with their rifles and machine-guns.

Again reënforcements were called for and on February 28th the Eleventh Division arrived from Japan. A new commander-in-chief in the person of General Shirakawa arrived on the 29th and took supreme command. A portion of the Eleventh Division was landed at Woosung to reënforce the stalled Ninth Division, but the main bulk of the Eleventh Division was sent up the Yangtze and at dawn on the morning of March 1st was landed near Liuho. The long-postponed enveloping movement was at last resorted to. The following night, March 1st–2nd, the entire Chinese army retreated from their positions in good order and by the 3rd had taken up a new position approximately twenty kilometers to the rear of their old one. This position ran from north to south approximately through the villages of Zichengying-Taitsang-Lokapang. The Japanese followed with caution, merely harassing the retreating Chinese with airplanes and making no attempt to close with them. On the same day, March 3rd, they took up the line running roughly from north to south through the villages of Liuho, Chiating and Nansiang. On that day, General Shirakawa promptly gave the order to cease firing and announced that with the retirement of Chinese troops from the area, hostilities were at an end and that the Japanese forces would advance no further and that unless attacked by the Chinese there would be no more fighting.

Military reports are not agreed on whether the retreat was solely caused by the threat of envelopment from Liuho. During the last two days the Japanese with their reënforcements had been making more progress at Kiangwan; and the completeness and success with which the Chinese retreat was conducted indicated that probably the Chinese commander had been preparing for it for several days. The news of the landing at Liuho may have only served to confirm a decision already arrived at. But from the standpoint of moral effect it was immaterial what was the determining factor. Upon foes and friends alike the long courageous defense had produced effects which were as fundamental as they were unexpected. Japan was only too ready to withdraw from a situation which was giving her nothing but embarrassment; and China, according to all advices, was for the first time in the history of the Republic thrilling with a national feeling of courage and unity.

V

PROBLEMS AND POLICIES RELATING TO SHANGHAI ATTACK

A

Preliminary Views

The impact of the Japanese move on Shanghai fell as unexpectedly upon us as upon the rest of the world. By sending our non-recognition note of January 7th to Japan we had intended to close an episode and terminate discussion.[18] We had anticipated a period of diplomatic silence. But instead we were now faced by new problems arising out of a situation of far-reaching importance. These problems were thrown in my face when I returned on January 24th from a forty-eight hour absence in New York. It was four days before Shiozawa's actual attack on Chapei, but the announcement on the morning of my return of Japan's great movement of warships gave us ample notice of the seriousness of the situation. I at once recognized that her real purpose was to break up the Chinese boycott and that the ostensible object of protecting her nationals in Shanghai was but a cloak.[19] Out of this were foreseen at once three results. In the first place the United States in common with the other foreign powers would have an

[18] We did not even reply to the provocative Japanese response of January 16th. The long correspondence of the autumn with Japan, which the Senate had called for, was on the point of being made public and we decided that those documents, with the vivid light which they cast on Japan's conduct in Manchuria, would constitute our most dignified rejoinder.

[19] My diary and personal records give an account of our discussions, conclusions, and actions taken on that day, January 24th, which, looked back on in the perspective of a four years' interval, shows an accuracy of prophecy which does credit to the departmental organization with which I was surrounded. It also brings out clearly the development of the farsighted policy which throughout we were consistently trying to maintain.

immediate and most difficult problem in protecting the Foreign Settlement and our commercial interests which centered there. The dangers to us which would arise from the use of the Settlement by the Japanese as a base for an attempt to suppress the Chinese national boycott were manifest on their face. It would inevitably involve armed hostilities in which the Settlement and all that it contained might become identified in the minds of the Chinese with Japanese aggression and thus a target for undiscriminating Chinese resentment and attack. If Japanese troops coming out of the Settlement should attack Chinese troops in the neighborhood, the danger of Chinese reprisals against all foreigners in the Settlement was manifest. Moreover, such an anti-foreign feeling would be likely to spread all through China. The Chinese government might even be driven to declare war on Japan.[20] Japan probably desired this and if it occurred she might blockade not only Shanghai and the river ports but all the other ports of China, which would result in great losses to the commerce of the rest of the world.

My second conclusion was that this coming threat to the British commerce centered in the valley of the Yangtze would probably at last startle the merchants of Great Britain into a realization of what Japanese aggression towards China ultimately meant to them and that we should find British coöperation with us more ready and willing now than we had found it on January

[20] Chiang Kai-shek, who throughout the Manchurian aggression had consistently sought to avoid a declaration of war with Japan and to trust to the public opinion of the world and the moral influence of the other powers to protect his country, had for a long time been under vigorous attack from Eugene Chen and other leaders who were clamoring for a resort to arms and a declaration of war.

7th. The foundation might thus be laid now for a unity of policy between us.

But in the third place I foresaw that Japan's purpose, in the long-distance view, might involve consequences to the whole world of the gravest character. If China should be deprived of her age-long peaceful weapon against an enemy—the boycott—she would ultimately be faced with one or the other of two alternatives: either to arm herself and become a military instead of a peaceful nation, or be thrown into total subservience to her more military neighbor, Japan. Either of these results would be fraught with ominous danger to the peace of the world and to the freedom of peaceful commerce for which we and Great Britain had been striving for many decades in the Far East. We knew that China was feeling deserted and helpless. Many of her statesmen already were insisting that in relying upon the League Covenant and the other peace treaties, she had depended upon a broken reed and been deserted by the powers upon whose influence she had counted. We felt that in such a crisis it was more important than ever before to maintain the sanctity of those treaties and to make it clear to China that her interests under them were not entirely forgotten.

We at Washington did not foresee—any more than anyone else in the world—the astonishing thing that actually did occur to revive Chinese courage. We did not foresee that a corps of Chinese soldiers apparently acting contrary to the prudent orders of their government would put up a defense against Japan which would surprise the world, and that this "war without a declaration of war" would do more temporarily to restore China's courage in the face of Japanese aggression than any moral sympathy which could be shown her by outside nations. Fortunately this unexpected episode did not clash but on the contrary worked in harmony with the long-distance policy which we believed in.[21] It showed that not only was the policy of respecting the integrity of China the honest and farsighted policy to pursue, but that China herself was more worthy of being the beneficiary of such a policy than some of her critics were fond of saying.

In the ensuing days of excitement we tried to keep this long-distance policy clearly in view and never to allow it to be obscured by the exigencies of the immediate present. We were constantly faced with the various problems of protective action in the violent scenes which followed. In coöperation with the other nations we worked energetically to avoid those dangers and to secure the withdrawal of the Japanese troops, but we never lost sight of the fact that behind this immediate objective there was another which in the long run would be far more important.

On that morning of January 24th I discussed all those matters with my assistants in the Department. I then laid them before the President. I found him, as usually was the case in such an emergency, keenly alive to the broad possibilities of the situation and fully in accord with our viewpoint. I then invited in the British Ambassador, laid before him our analysis of the situation and the forecast of possibilities which we feared, and told him that I was desirous of ascertaining whether his government would share our views and would coöperate in a harmonious policy to meet the situation. The immediate measures which I proposed were, first, a prompt message to Japan suggesting our concern as

[21] As a matter of fact I believe, had it been thoroughly availed of, it would have powerfully assisted in obtaining a successful result from the invocation of the Nine Power Treaty which I subsequently suggested to the British government.

to her making the International Settlement a base for her hostile action against China and pointing out to her that, in view of the efficient international police force which existed in the Settlement and the absence of violence which had thus far attended the boycott, any armed intervention on her part against China was at least premature. In the second place I told him that Japan's mobilization already had alarmed our representatives both in Shanghai and further up the river and that they were calling on us for additional vessels for protecting them in the emergency which they foresaw would be created by her intervention. I asked, if we should send such vessels, would the British do likewise. I pointed out that not only would it tend to tranquilize the fears of foreigners, but it would convince China that we were not oblivious to our responsibilities in the situation. Thus before that day was over and four days before the actual attack by Shiozawa we had not only formulated our general policies, but put under way the first steps towards a coöperative solution of the difficult problem. At the same time that we were thus formulating our plans to meet the emergency which was arising, by a fortuitous concurrence of events a movement of the American fleet took place which to a certain extent contributed to steady the situation and to strengthen the hands of those who were endeavoring to prevent the events at Shanghai from getting entirely out of control and possibly spreading to other far-distant localities.

B

The American Fleet at Hawaii

Under plans which had been made and published the preceding summer, long before the outbreak of the trouble in Manchuria, the American navy had been ordered to hold its annual maneuvers in the Pacific between the California coast and the Hawaiian Islands. The prosecution of these maneuvers brought the fleet in natural course to Hawaii. Soon after the outbreak in Manchuria we discussed whether the plans should be changed, but decided that, in view of the fact that it was so well known that they had not originated as a threat to Japan, the maneuvers would be allowed to continue. Thereafter, just when the Japanese were making their attack on Shanghai, the American fleet in the course of these maneuvers came to Hawaii on February 13th. After further careful consideration it was allowed to remain in that neighborhood and was not dispersed or sent back to the Atlantic on the conclusion of the maneuvers. During the tumultuous and uncertain times which followed we were glad of that decision. With events showing that the Japanese government was falling completely into the control of militaristic leaders, backed by a populace inflamed to a state of fanatical excitement by the events which had occurred, it was impossible to tell what coup might not be attempted. During that winter responsible foreign observers stationed in the Far East were informing their respective governments that in their opinion there was a real possibility of a Japanese attack being suddenly launched at the possessions of European and American governments in the neighborhood. In such a situation the presence of the entire American fleet assembled at a port which placed it on the flank of any such outbreak southward towards Hongkong, French Indo-China or the Philippines, undoubtedly exercised a steadying effect. It was a potent reminder of the ultimate military strength of peaceful America which could not be overlooked by anyone, however excited he might be.

C

The Defense of the International Settlement

For four days I awaited rather anxiously a reply from the British government to the inquiries as to future coöperation which I had made through Sir Ronald Lindsay on January 25th. The situation seemed to me to be getting more ominous each day with the demands and finally the ultimatum which the Japanese Consul and Admiral were making upon the Chinese Mayor. I was receiving every day reports and inquiries from our representatives on the spot. Mr. Edwin S. Cunningham, the American Consul General in Shanghai, was the senior consular officer in that port and under the traditional organization of the consular body a great deal of responsibility for advice and initiative rested upon him. He was being consulted by the local authorities of the Settlement as well as by the consuls of other powers, and of course was in turn reporting to us for instruction and assistance. Moreover, since the Chinese capital had been moved from Peking to Nanking, Shanghai, owing to its proximity to the latter place, was constantly resorted to by members of the Chinese government as well as by foreign ministers on their way to the capital. It was always a center of political activity and now it was filled with every possible current and cross-current of excitement and rumor.

On January 29th a reply finally came and was favorable in its tenor. But it was fairly submerged in the torrent of official and press reports which on the same morning flooded the wires with the news of Admiral Shiozawa's attack upon and bombardment of Chapei. Thereupon, as we had anticipated, our friends in the

London Foreign Office awoke with a rush. There was no need thereafter for any suggestions on our part of action or coöperation. They seemed to be even more anxious than we for vigorous measures to meet the emergency which was now upon us, and on all such measures, to my great gratification and relief, the two governments seemed again to be marching in full step and time with each other.

Before evening on January 29th the British government already had sent a sharp protest to the Japanese government in respect to the attack on Chapei and had requested us to do likewise. Although on January 27th, before the attack, I had sent a precautionary message to Tokyo urging that in view of the efficient police force already existing in the Settlement armed intervention by the Japanese government to protect its nationals would seem to be uncalled for, now in response to this request of the British and in order to confirm the spirit of full coöperation, I responded with another representation to Tokyo along the lines which they had suggested. On January 31st I learned by telephone from our Embassy in London that the British were sending two more eight-inch gun cruisers with additional marines and that they suggested that we do the same. On the same day after a conference with the President the cruiser *Houston* and the transport *Chaumont* with the Thirty-first Infantry aboard were ordered from Manila to Shanghai, together with our remaining destroyers, thus collecting in that port our entire Asiatic Squadron under the command of Rear Admiral Montgomery Taylor. On the same day the British suggested that a neutral zone should be created to protect the International Settlement and asked whether we would do our proportionate share to police such a zone if established.

To this we also consented, only cautioning them that the consent of the Chinese should first be obtained in order that there be no danger of such a step bringing our troops into conflict with them.

In addition to this direct coöperation between the two nations it was necessary also to coöperate with the League of Nations. The League still retained ultimate jurisdiction over the controversy between China and Japan. It was naturally deeply concerned by the outbreak of violence at Shanghai. On January 30th Sir Eric Drummond, the Secretary General of the League, proposed that the local representatives at Shanghai of the various League nations should be constituted a committee to send to him at Geneva reports of the conditions at Shanghai for consideration by the Council. On Sir Eric's invitation we at once authorized Mr. Cunningham, our Consul General, to coöperate with that committee. The subsequent reports of this committee upon the rapid sequence of events in Shanghai have become the chief source of the recorded history of those events. Mr. Cunningham assisted in their labors and concurred in general with their report.

On February 1st we instructed Mr. Hugh Wilson, our Minister to Switzerland, to keep constantly in touch with the handling of the Shanghai situation by the League and to constitute himself a liaison officer for the interchange of information between them and us.

I have already alluded to the difficulty of the task of defending the International Settlement under the best of circumstances.[22] Under the peculiar situation of 1932 these difficulties were immensely increased. The Japanese warships were anchored along the Whangpoo River fronting the International Settlement. Immedi-

[22] See p. 115.

ately beyond the Settlement the Chinese Nineteenth Route Army was occupying Chapei. Between these opposing forces extended the long thin strip of the Settlement. The boundary between it and Chapei in many places was purely artificial. On the river front of the Settlement the Japanese owned wharfs. For several weeks, in spite of the protests of the Settlement authorities, Japanese troops continually landed at these wharfs, from which they marched across the narrow strip of the Settlement to take up their positions in the operations against the Chinese. From the Japanese airplane-carrier anchored in the river bombing planes winged their way directly over the Settlement on their destructive missions against the Chinese in Chapei. Several times bombs dropped by them fell in the Settlement. One such bomb on the 11th of February fell on a Chinese mill in the American sector killing five of the Chinese employees and wounding fifteen. Naturally such actions attracted reprisals from the Chinese, which also endangered the Settlement. Shells from Chinese guns aimed either at bombing planes or Japanese vessels fell in the Settlement, and on February 17th two British sailors were fatally injured by such a shell. But the greatest danger of all was that these Japanese attacks originating from the Settlement would ultimately provoke the Chinese troops into an attempt to rush the International Settlement itself. Had they done so, their numbers were such that it would have been impossible to protect the inhabitants of the Settlement from disastrous consequences. In the face of this danger repeated representations were earnestly made by us and the other nations to the Japanese government against this use of the Settlement as a base. As I have pointed out in my description of the operations, it was not only unnecessary but it seemed strategically a mistaken procedure from the standpoint of the Japanese themselves. Yet the landing of Japanese troops in the Settlement continued until the latter part of February, when, perhaps in deference to a last vigorous and united protest made by all of us at Tokyo itself, it was discontinued, and the subsequent reënforcements landed further down the river at Woosung.

In the first few days of the operations the position of the American troops in their sector was still further endangered by the intrusion of detachments of Japanese troops and irregulars. The American and Japanese sectors were adjacent. On February 3rd the Defense Committee of the Settlement reported that the Japanese had placed no less than five hundred marines with twelve machine-guns in some mills in the American sector with the apparent intention of using this force offensively against the Chinese. There was manifest danger that such action would draw the Chinese attack directly upon our sector. On the same day the Japanese were reported as having planted two machine-guns in our sector close to an American marine post which was thus brought in line of their fire. There also came a long recital of outrages upon defenseless Chinese committed behind the lines in the American and British sectors by armed Japanese soldiers and ronin[23] and these actions were sometimes accompanied by provocative acts directed at our troops themselves. In fact, for the first two or three days it seemed as if many of the Japanese under the sting of their unexpected repulse by the Chinese had lost their heads and were getting completely beyond control. Very fortunately, the American

[23] A Japanese word for armed irregulars who often accompany or precede a Japanese attack.

and British commanders and men acted with exemplary patience, and at last on February 4th, under the pressure of very vigorous representations made by us to Tokyo, as well as by Admiral Taylor at Shanghai, all of the intruding troops in our sector were withdrawn by the Japanese commanders. But for nearly a week the situation had been like a tinder-box.

D

The Bombardment of Nanking

At Nanking, the seat of government of the Nationalist government of China, there were many Japanese merchants and their families. At the outbreak of the trouble at Shanghai two Japanese war vessels were lying in the Yangtze River opposite Nanking, presumably to afford protection to their Japanese nationals during the growing tension between the two countries. Immediately after the attack at Shanghai several more Japanese war vessels were sent up to Nanking. This movement of additional vessels accentuated the uneasiness of the Chinese population of the city. Late in the evening of February 1st these Japanese vessels bombarded the city for about an hour. This caused tremendous excitement not only in Nanking and throughout China, but throughout the world, and it added greatly to the tension already caused by the events at Shanghai. It seemed to confirm the fears of many that the action at Shanghai had been merely a prelude to a general Japanese invasion of the Yangtze Valley.

The facts as to the origin of this bombardment, as given respectively by the Chinese and the Japanese, are entirely conflicting. Fortunately, it did comparatively little damage and was followed by no further military activities. But in consequence of it the Chinese government removed itself temporarily from Nanking to Loyang.

At the State Department we were inclined to attribute the bombardment to the misjudgment of an excited Japanese naval commander, and that is the view now taken by historians.[24] The panic caused by the incident fortunately soon died down, but it served as an illustration of the irresponsibility with which the Japanese commanders, under the stress of apparent emergency, were inclined to use the destructive weapons placed in their hands. A more lamentable example of this occurred on February 6th when Japanese airplanes dropped bombs on one of the camps of flood refugees which had been established near Shanghai by Sir John Hope Simpson of the League of Nations, the Director General of the National Flood Relief Commission, to care for the victims of the great flood disaster on the Yangtze. Over fifty people were killed by these bombs or died of fright. The Japanese government expressed its deep regret for this incident, calling it a "deplorable mistake."

E

The Japanese Request for Our Good Offices

We soon began to receive evidence that the Japanese government was becoming worried at the result of Admiral Shiozawa's attack upon Chapei. The public

[24] See Royal Institute of International Affairs, *Survey* for 1932, p. 485. At the very time of the incident I had on my desk a message from one of the American oil companies having a plant on the Whangpoo River below Shanghai, reporting an incident illustrative of the "jumpiness" at that time of the Japanese naval commanders. Some Chinese citizens celebrating their New Year let off some cannon crackers just as a Japanese vessel was passing by, and the vessel at once opened fire on the oil plant with machine-guns, riddling the office.

reaction to that attack was very different from that occasioned by the aggressions in Manchuria. Partly from its comparative remoteness and isolation from observation, and partly, no doubt, because we had all held our hands in the attempt to employ the methods of conciliation between the two disputants and to allow the Japanese government to regain control of its army, the world had never received an adequate impression of the violent tactics which the Japanese army had adopted in Manchuria. But the atrocities at Shanghai had occurred in the blazing publicity of a cosmopolitan city. Certainly in America the feeling excited by the bombing and burning of a crowded, unwarned city population was very strong. On that subject Japan had no defenders. None of the explanations put forth by her carried for a minute with our press or our people. When it occurred, Ambassador Debuchi had been absent in Cuba. Upon his return on January 30th, he met the full blast of the expressions of public indignation which had been excited, and when he called upon me that day the shock to him was evident without words. I have no doubt that some of his impressions were transmitted to Tokyo.

On the afternoon of January 31st a flash from the Associated Press first brought the news that the Premier of Japan had suggested to the Ambassadors of several powers, including ourselves, that we offer our good offices to stop the fighting. The next morning this was confirmed by cable and later in the day by the Japanese Ambassador. We carefully awaited this double confirmation, but in the meanwhile prepared ourselves to act promptly. For it was not a simple proposition. The Japanese government undoubtedly had been startled and taken aback. Its Admiral clearly had made a bad mistake. He had attacked with insufficient forces

and received a severe military repulse. He had then
affronted the world by methods of terrorism employed
on a civilian population. His government undoubtedly
realized the mistake and wished to escape from its
embarrassing consequences. But was this feeling strong
enough to make them willing to accept mediation on
the real causes of the controversy out of which this
deplorable incident had arisen? Were they sufficiently
impressed by the adverse public opinion against them
to agree to a method of solution which would solve by
peaceful methods the entire controversy between themselves and China, or were they still determined to proceed by the methods of force which had been employed
since September? If not, their present request simply
might mean that they were seeking our assistance to
help them out of a bad hole into a position from which
they might again proceed in their course of aggression
against China. We could not afford to be a party to that.
In this latter case our efforts could not be productive of
lasting good. They might only reënforce a skillful but
determined aggressor.

As soon as the preliminary news flash was confirmed
by cable, I consulted with President Hoover and found
that he fully and strongly agreed with these views. Even
under the pressure of the dangerous situation in Shanghai he was unwilling to be made a cat's-paw for the
assistance of further Japanese aggression. Together we
drew up a proposition of five points which might be
presented by the intermediary powers as a basis of solution. By telephone I presénted these to the Prime Minister and Foreign Minister of Great Britain, the President listening in on the wire. In less than three hours
our points had been considered and with slight amendments had been approved by the British government,
which also agreed to obtain the concurrence of France

and Italy in presenting them to Japan. This was done and a time table arranged under which the propositions were presented by the four nations to Tokyo and Nanking on February 2nd and made public on February 3rd. The five points as thus agreed upon were as follows:

1. Cessation of all acts of violence on both sides forthwith on the following terms:
2. No further mobilization or preparation whatever for further hostilities between the two nations.
3. Withdrawal of both Japanese and Chinese combatants from all points of mutual contact in the Shanghai area.
4. Protection of the International Settlement by the establishment of neutral zones to divide the combatants; these zones to be policed by neutrals; the arrangements to be set up by the consular authorities.
5. Upon acceptance of these conditions prompt advances to be made in negotiations to settle all outstanding controversies between the two nations in the spirit of the Pact of Paris and the resolution of the League of Nations of December 10, without prior demand or reservation and with the aid of neutral observers or participants.

Even as we were talking over the telephone, cables were handed to us reporting the bombardment of Nanking and also other cables bringing rumors of the preparation of further troop movements by Japan. In the light of these reports, the importance of proposition 2 in the terms above-mentioned can be understood.

Under proposition 5 we insisted upon concurrent steps being taken towards the settlement of the controversy over Manchuria. The reason for this was obvious. The attack on Shanghai had originated as a result of that controversy. With that controversy unsettled we had no assurance of lasting peace between the two countries, but quite the reverse. Furthermore, in the protracted negotiations during the autumn the League of Nations, as well as we ourselves, had taken a definite position against Japan's action in Manchuria. Had we omitted proposition 5 from our present proposals the press all over the world would have announced, and Japan have believed, that we had abandoned the vital treaties for the vindication of which we had so long been working.

The Chinese government promptly accepted all of our five proposals. On February 4th the Japanese government curtly rejected the second and fifth, returning replies to the other three proposals, which contained conditions depriving them of any substantial value.[25]

[25] The Japanese reply was as follows (Willoughby, *op. cit.,* pp. 320-321):

1. The Japanese forces will cease hostile acts if it is assured that the Chinese forces will immediately and completely stop their disturbing and menacing activities. If, on the contrary, the Chinese (including both regular and plain clothes soldiers) persist in such activities, the Japanese government must reserve full freedom of action for its military forces.

2. In view of the unreliability of the Chinese in the past and of the gravity of the present situation, the Japanese government finds it impossible to renounce mobilization or preparations for hostilities.

3 and 4. The Japanese government has no objection to its Consul General and Commander entering into negotiations for an agreement concerning the separation of the respective forces and the establishment, if necessary, of a neutral zone in the district of Chapei.

5. While it is to be presumed that "all outstanding controversies" between Japan and China include the Manchurian question, the Japanese government regards this latter as entirely a separate question from the Shanghai affair, and, moreover, it is covered by the League action of December 10th. Furthermore, it is the settled policy of the Japanese government not to accept the assistance of neutral observers or participants in settlement of the question concerning Manchuria. For these reasons the conditions in Paragraph 5 of the powers' note are not acceptable to the Japanese government.

On the same day that the Japanese reply reached me, I made a careful study of all of the messages which had come in from any source bearing upon the situation at Shanghai and including not only the messages coming to the State Department, but those which were coming in from observers of the army and navy. I had the advice of the Chief of Staff of our army and the Chief of Operations of our navy. These messages taken as a whole and in connection with each other made it quite clear that during this period, while the Japanese Foreign Office was asking for our good offices, the Japanese army and navy were preparing the movement of large land forces from Japan to Shanghai to take over the situation at that place. From that time on I was convinced that the Japanese government felt that its prestige in Asia required it to obtain something in the nature of a military success at Shanghai in order to "save its face" after the defeat which it had received.

Several times during the following weeks suggestions again came in from one source or another that the Japanese government would consent to a termination of the hostilities and to the withdrawal of its troops. I could not put any faith in the sincerity of such suggestions. I felt confident that no termination by the intervention of the other powers would be accepted by Japan unless it involved a retreat by the Chinese, which would be equivalent to a victory for Japan and a humiliation for China. Such an intervention was manifestly one to which we could not lend our influence. Whenever such suggestions came to us, I was careful not to rebuff them. They were usually made at Shanghai through the local representatives of the various governments there who coöperatively handled the situation as far as possible. But in my instructions to our representatives I exercised special care to make certain that in acting upon any such request we should not be led into urging propositions which manifestly would do injustice to and rouse consequent hostility from the government of China.

Now that the passage of time has made it possible to collate the facts as to the military operations then taking place behind the screen of censorship and to compare them with these Japanese suggestions of mediation, we can see that each of such proposals was immediately followed by a new military movement, and thus was apparently designed merely to temper the effect of that movement upon the outside world.

Thus, on February 3rd and 4th, immediately after their diplomatic advances which I have just discussed, the Japanese with their naval forces made their first landing attack on the forts at Woosung and a renewed attack at Chapei. On February 6th a new suggestion for negotiations at Shanghai came from Japan through the local authorities at that port. Immediately afterwards, on February 8th, they made a determined but unsuccessful attack with their newly arrived land forces upon the Woosung forts. Again, two or three days prior to their main attack under General Uyeda at Kiangwan, new suggestions that they would welcome a truce came to us from Shanghai. They were immediately followed by General Uyeda's ultimatum and the attack of February 20th. Finally, in the last days of February just prior to their enveloping movement at Liuho and the renewal of their attack at Kiangwan, the now familiar suggestions came in the shape of a *démarche* at Geneva from the Japanese representative at that place, Mr. Matsudaira. By such a comparison it now seems clear that these olive branches were not intended to bear the fruits of peace.

Our proposal of the five points and the manner of

their reception by Japan had thus served to clarify my mind as to the course which she was bent on following in the fighting at Shanghai. In the interests of the ultimate objectives which our government tried to keep in view, I was not anxious for any termination of the fighting which would involve a real surrender of principle. I only foresaw greater eventual difficulties if Japan by our assistance got off without the moral condemnation of the world which she deserved. Every fresh repulse which the courageous Chinese infantry were able to administer to her forces and the greater and more expensive efforts to which she was thereby driven, only served to make it more certain that she would not escape such condemnation. The inadequate size of the successive reënforcements which she called to her aid and the difficulty in obtaining the financial authorization from her Diet for even such as she brought up, made it ever clearer to us that her militarists eventually would pay a high price for their adventure. The higher that price the better the hopes for an ultimate reign of law in the world. It seemed that one of those rare moments of history had arrived when the soldier can render better service to the future of law and order than can the negotiator.

F

The Nine Power Treaty and the Letter to Senator Borah

For a long time my mind had been seeking for some way in which the real interest of the American people in and the true policy of their government towards the controversy in the Far East might be clearly and fully stated. The proceedings during the autumn had been initiated and carried on by the League of Nations. To many Americans that seemed an artificial approach. We were not members of the League and many were inclined to be suspicious of it. Furthermore, to a great many of our people Manchuria was an unknown part of the earth and they wondered what we had to do with any controversy there at all. But when the issue shifted to the center of China at Shanghai, it aroused keen interest in a large portion of our countrymen. With the violence of the attack on Chapei and the picture of the Chinese soldiers defending their country against an invader, the attempt that the Japanese were making to exploit China became more clear. This touched a phase of American feeling which has not been thoroughly understood or described by writers in dealing with the Sino-Japanese controversies.

The most widespread interest of our people in China is not commercial, although our commerce with that country is of long standing and of late years has been rapidly growing. Our most general information of China has come through quite a different channel. It came through the great missionary movement—religious, educational and medical—which had been carried on in China for nearly a century by the churches and humanitarian organizations of this country. The breadth and influence of that movement have not always been adequately appreciated by historians. Throughout those years, in almost every fair-sized American community, particularly throughout our Northeastern and mid-Western states, there had been situated one or more churches, each of which was in whole or in part supporting one or more foreign missionaries, a large percentage of whom were working in China. The news of the work of these missionaries coming through their reports and letters reached a large number of our people living in almost every quarter of the land. To many of them the progress of this work was one of their keenest interests. They followed the details of Chinese progress as reported to them by their missionaries and thus acquired a humanitarian interest of a quite personal character in that land and its people. Side by side with this movement another smaller but very significant one had been carried on by the Chinese themselves when they had sent to the schools and colleges of this country for education a large number of their most promising young men and women. When I was a boy at Phillips Academy at Andover in the early 'eighties, several of those Chinese students were my schoolmates. They were respected and well liked at the school. One of them indeed became a school hero when, as center fielder of our baseball team, he won the annual game with our great rival school at Exeter by a timely three-base hit! In later years he returned to us as the Chinese Minister at Washington. Such Chinese students were being educated at schools and colleges throughout this country, and many of them have since become leaders in the Nationalist government of China or in key positions in its educational and professional life.[26]

Through these two channels of contact a quite unusual interest in China had been widely spread among

[26] For example, T. V. Soong, the former Finance Minister of China, is a graduate of Harvard; C. T. Wang, former Foreign Minister, and Wellington Koo, also of the Cabinet, are graduates of Yale; Mrs. Sun Yat-sen, the widow of the founder of the modern China, is a graduate of a seminary at Macon, Georgia, and her two sisters, one of them the wife of Chiang Kai-shek, general in chief and former President of China, are graduates of Wellesley; H. H. Kung, the present Finance Minister, is a graduate of Oberlin and Yale; Chiang Meng-lin, the Chancellor of the National University of China, is a graduate of California and Columbia, and Hu Shih, one of China's most prominent men of letters, of Cornell and Columbia. Dr. Alfred Sze and Dr. W. W. Yen who represented China's side in the Manchurian controversy before the League of Nations were both educated in America. All of these men have been prominent in the development of modern China.

our people. It was not rooted in our commercial in-
stincts, but rather in our political and humanitarian
idealism. It represented the same characteristic of our
people which had turned our colonial adventure in the
Philippines into a farsighted attempt to train an Oriental people in the art of self-government according
to the American model. It involved no antagonism
towards Japan, with whose people we had a somewhat
similar though less widespread educational experience.
But it was wholly opposed to any idea that Japan was
entitled to exploit China or that the Chinese were in
any way an inferior race to the Japanese. On this point
very many Americans not only had ideas, but felt that
those ideas were founded upon adequate experience
with both races.

It can be seen also that such an American feeling
towards the Chinese was quite different from that voiced
by the London *Times* in its articles on January 11, 1932,
to which I have alluded. It was free from prejudices
arising out of commercial intercourse with the Chinese
and from the grievances of the "Old Timer," and it
also was embarrassed by no sentiment for Japan arising
out of a former military alliance. It may have been
idealistic, but it was also free from any caste spirit,
whether military or otherwise. It was purely democratic and it was held by people who strongly believed
in self-government, in humanitarianism and in peace.
This interest in the progress of Chinese national development was much more keen and traditional on "Main
Street" in America than in the "City" in London.

I have no doubt that this historic American attitude
towards China, consciously or unconsciously, influenced
the efforts of John Hay and Charles Evans Hughes
when the one of them initiated the Open Door policy
and the other helped to crystallize it in the Nine

Power Treaty. That policy was based upon the postulate that China deserved a fair chance to develop herself in the modern world by a protection against violation of her administrative and territorial integrity. It was adopted with full appreciation of the size and duration of her task of development and was intended to give her a real chance to complete it. It had no sympathy with the doctrine that because her government was still imperfectly organized she could be forcibly dominated by a temporarily stronger nation. It had been expressly formulated in 1899 in order to put an end to the idea of special spheres of interest in China by all such nations.

This American feeling towards China was outraged by the burning of Chapei and was at once made keenly alive to and critical of any proposal to exploit or dominate that nation. It was now ready to follow with keen interest what was going on across the Pacific, and it was looking for some expression by its own government in vindication of a feeling which was so widespread in America and so deeply rooted in American traditions.

As I listened to the expressions of this feeling which came to me through the press and the people with whom I came in contact, there recurred to my mind the memories of the similar feeling which had been excited in the communities where I lived at the outbreak of the World War by the news of the violation of the neutrality of Belgium and the subsequent military terrorism imposed upon the people of that country as reported by the Bryce Commission. On that occasion the United States was not a party to the treaty which was violated in respect to Belgium, and the American government felt, in consequence, that it had no duty or right to express officially any censure for the international wrong which had been done. In the present case in the Far East at least two treaties were involved to which our government was a party. The aim and purpose of these treaties had been violated; a widespread feeling to that effect existed among our people, and no adequate expression in condemnation of that wrong had yet been made. As I reflected upon it, it seemed to me that in future years I should not like to face a verdict of history to the effect that a government to which I had belonged had failed to express itself adequately upon such a situation.

Just at this moment there came from Tokyo a message which sharply crystallized my feeling. The Reuter News Agency contained a dispatch on February 8th from Tokyo of the following tenor:

> What are admitted to be "feelers" aiming at a permanent solution of Shanghai problems in particular and the China problem in general were put out by the Japanese Foreign Office this morning. Briefly, the proposal is the establishment of demilitarized zones fifteen or twenty miles around the principal trading ports, notably Shanghai, Hankow, Tientsin, Canton and Tsingtao, while Manchuria, it is suggested, might also be demilitarized, although better disciplined Chinese troops might be utilized as police.
>
> The powers have not been sounded officially on these proposals, stated a Foreign Office spokesman, but Japanese diplomatic representatives abroad have been instructed to seek a suitable occasion to broach the idea either officially or unofficially.

The official spokesman was also reported as saying quite

frankly that such a proposal was contrary to the Nine Power Treaty, but that ten years' trial had proved the ineffectiveness of the policy which it laid down, and that the only policy that could result in benefit to Chinese as well as foreigners was a policy of intervention.

Here was a frank suggestion, albeit an unofficial one, from the Foreign Office at Tokyo that it was time to turn back the hands of the clock and revert to a policy of dismemberment of China similar to that which John Hay by the Open Door notes had succeeded in stopping in 1899. That policy of dismemberment had aroused the Boxer Rebellion; had brought about the siege of our Legation in Peking, and had brought China into open rebellion against the outside world. In less than two days I was receiving serious warnings of the effect which this new suggestion from Tokyo was already having upon the people of China. We had known for a long time that those people were discouraged by the ineffectiveness of the response to their appeals concerning the violation of these treaties. There was now evidence that this new provocation might turn their discouragement into explosive action against the outside world, similar to that which had occurred thirty years before.

This new crisis in Chinese feeling seemed to me to reënforce strongly the demand for a clear statement of our government's position. Not only did our own people require such a statement in order to understand their government's policy and to be reassured that it was doing its best to carry out American convictions as to international justice, but the people of China needed to be reassured that the international structure of solemn covenants upon which they had relied was now about to be abandoned by its framers.

The Nine Power Treaty stood out as manifestly the

most appropriate vehicle to convey both such assurances. It was true that the Covenant of the League of Nations contained in Article X an agreement "to respect and preserve against external aggression the territorial integrity and existing political independence" of its signatories, and the Pact of Paris contained in Article II an agreement that the settlement of all disputes should never be sought except by pacific means. But both of these covenants were entirely general and multilateral in their terms and had been made without reference to any specific country. On the other hand, the Nine Power Treaty had been drawn up expressly to apply to the case of China. Its first article providing an agreement by the signatory nations

(1) to respect the sovereignty, the independence and the territorial and administrative integrity of China and
(2) to provide the fullest and most unembarrassed opportunity to China to develop and maintain for herself an effective and stable government

was expressly designed to prevent just such a case as that now presented to the world by the action of Japan.

No human language seemed to be more explicitly applicable to the situation confronting us in both Manchuria and Shanghai than the words of these two covenants. In all of the steps which had been taken thus far, the nations had been proceeding only under the Covenant of the League and the Pact of Paris. The Nine Power Treaty had not yet been invoked. It seemed now that a situation had been reached which demanded that this step should be taken. The clearest way to explain to our own people the historic policy of their government would seem to lie in pointing to the terms of this treaty, supported by a statement of the facts out of which it had arisen. In the second place, the most effective way of reassuring China would be to make it clear to her that the signatories of that treaty still intended to respect their obligations thereunder.

These were the two motives which were impelling me to action. But if such action should be taken, if this clear and explicit treaty should be brought forward in a vigorous and whole-hearted way by its leading sponsors and signatories, was it not possible that even greater results might be accomplished? It was true that the Nine Power Treaty did not contain provisions authorizing any signatory to call a compulsory conference thereunder; but in Article VII it did contain a provision that

> whenever a situation arises which, in the opinion of any one of them [the signatory powers], involves the application of the stipulations of the present treaty, and renders desirable discussion of such application, there shall be full and frank communication between the contracting powers concerned.

Japan had not only put herself in the wrong, but she was now caught in an embarrassing position in the operations at Shanghai. She was on the defensive before the entire world. While she was evidently intent to force through her present operations until she obtained some measure of success, was it not possible that in this embarrassment, under a proper and sufficiently earnest approach, she might be willing to do what we had been trying to get her to do before her attack at Shanghai, namely to sit in a fair conference upon the subject of her controversy with China? Even if Japan refused such a conference, there were other possibilities in which an invocation of the Nine Power Treaty might possibly be extremely important. The possible use of economic sanctions against Japan was being more discussed in America since the Shanghai attack than it had been during the preceding autumn. It had become more of a practical possibility. Petitions looking to such use were now being circulated, assisted by such influential men as President Lowell of Harvard and Mr. Newton D. Baker. Congress was now in session and several bills to give the President power to impose such action had been introduced in the Congress by various members. If a situation should ultimately arise when the American government felt it necessary to recommend the imposition, in coöperation with the rest of the world, of an embargo upon Japanese goods, I believed that such a measure would have more chance of being adopted by Congress if it were recommended following the invocation of the Nine Power Treaty than if it had been recommended solely by the League of Nations.

On February 8th I broached the matter of the invocation of the Nine Power Treaty to the President. When, four days before, Japan had rejected the tender of good offices which she had invited from the four powers, we had made no response to her rather abrupt note. The President had expressed regret at this, feeling that some answer should have been made. I think a feeling to that effect was expressed in the press. But I had been unwilling to add to the interchange of notes until I had some new and constructive rejoinder to make. I told the President so on February 8th, adding that now I felt that I had such a constructive suggestion in the invocation of the Nine Power Treaty. He at once agreed with me as to the timeliness and importance of making such an invocation, and suggested that a notice of non-recognition like that contained in our note of January 7th might well be brought forward as an appropriate determination to be announced by the signatories of that treaty.

On February 9th I invited in the British Ambassador and told him that I was impressed with the importance at the present juncture of invoking the Nine Power Treaty, in order to clarify the thought and focus the moral support of the world upon the situation which had taken place in Shanghai, including the unjustified bombing of Chapei and the attack on Woosung forts. I told him that Article VII of that treaty seemed to give ample opportunity for such a statement as to this attack on Chinese sovereignty and independence.

Time was pressing; the Japanese were evidently preparing for a new and more powerful attack at Shanghai. On February 11th the President suggested that I call up the British Foreign Minister, Sir John Simon, directly on the telephone in order to hasten the matter and to have the best possible opportunity for fully discussing the proposition and ascertaining whether the British government would coöperate. I did so the same day. He was in Geneva at a meeting of the Council of the League of Nations. Coöperation between our two governments on all the steps being taken at Shanghai had been progressing with complete harmony, and on many such matters we had already consulted each other by telephone. I explained to him fully and at length the main reasons which actuated me in desiring to make such a *démarche* under the Nine Power Treaty—the importance of the clarification of our position, and the news which had reached me from China as to the dangerous effect upon the Chinese people of the Tokyo suggestion reported by Reuter on February 8th. I suggested that our two governments, together with any other signatories who might be willing to follow us, might act

under Article VII of that treaty in a joint statement as
to the attack thus made on the policy of the Nine Power
Treaty, and make it clear that we, as such signatories,
did not propose to acquiesce in any of the suggestions
for the abandonment of that treaty which were emanat-
ing from Tokyo. The following day, February 12th, I
talked with him again at Geneva after he had had an
opportunity to reflect upon the suggestion, and on that
day, at his request, I cabled him a proposed draft of
such a joint statement, which I had prepared with my
assistants in the Department. I made it clear to him that
this statement was, in form, merely a tentative draft
open for the fullest discussion and amendment. The proposal was obviously a matter of importance which
should be passed upon by the Cabinet and Prime Minister. Sir John Simon was returning to London the following day, February 13th, and the draft statement was
sent at his suggestion to enable him to consider and reflect upon it on his journey. There were complications,
obvious to anyone, arising out of the fact that Great
Britain was not only a signatory of the Nine Power
Treaty, but a member of the League of Nations which
was engaged in considering the same controversy. But
the League had already shown its readiness to seek the
support of the Pact of Paris in the earlier negotiations
during the autumn, and members of the League had
already discussed in informal talks with our Minister
at Geneva the possibility of also falling back on the
Nine Power Treaty. Therefore, such obstacles did not
seem insuperable. In the light of them, however, the
draft which I sent him was expressly drawn so as not
to prejudge the question of responsibility for the present situation as between China and Japan which was
pending for adjudication before the League of Nations.
As I explained to the British Foreign Minister, its

main purpose was to make clear our faith in and intention to live up to the covenants of the Nine Power Treaty respecting the future sovereignty and integrity of China.

I talked with the Foreign Minister again on the same subject at London on February 13th and February 15th and, while no explicit refusal to my suggestion was ever made, I finally became convinced from his attitude in those conversations that for reasons satisfactory to it, and which I certainly had no desire to inquire into or criticize, the British government felt reluctant to join in such a *démarche*.[27] I therefore pressed it no further.

The British nonjoinder obviously killed the possibility of any such *démarche*. The American government, in the circumstances, could not act alone in sending such a communication to the other signatories of the Nine Power Treaty without inviting the danger of receiving replies from some of them of such a nature as to destroy the effect of the *démarche*. My plan was therefore blocked. I had intended to take the matter up at once with Monsieur Claudel, the French Ambassador, but on learning the British attitude gave it up.

The Japanese were now launching their heavy concerted attack of February 20th. The fighting was going on from day to day, and the situation seemed more and more destructive and critical. The Chinese and the supporters of international law and order in the world at large seemed more than ever in need of encouragement and leadership. Moreover, the Chinese had, on February 12th, appealed their case from the Council of the League of Nations to the Assembly composed of

[27] A speech which Sir John Simon made in Geneva before the Anglo-America Press Association on February 12th and his reported replies to questions in the House of Commons on February 18th tended strongly to confirm me in the correctness of this diagnosis of his government's attitude.

all the nations who were members of the League, and the meeting of the Assembly to consider their case was called for March 3rd. In the confused situation which would obviously exist in such a meeting of so many nations, it was doubly important that if our government had any views which might assist to clarify the situation, it should promptly give them expression.

For several days I was deeply discouraged at my inability to carry out the coöperative plan which we had suggested. I seemed doomed to inaction, while a great tragedy was following its predestined course. But on February 21st a solution occurred to me by which I might state our views on the Nine Power Treaty without having them nullified by an expression of the doubts and fears of others. I had good precedent for my solution. I suddenly remembered that Elihu Root, when a member of President Theodore Roosevelt's Cabinet, was accustomed to say humorously that whenever his chief desired to get off an announcement of major policy without contradiction or discussion, he used to sit down and write a public letter on the subject to William Dudley Foulke! Mr. Foulke was then a member of the United States Civil Service Commission, a man of letters and prominent citizen of Indiana, and a devoted friend of Mr. Roosevelt. The latter could thus make an announcement without the slightest fear of an unfriendly rejoinder which might mar its effect! I thought I might even improve on Mr. Roosevelt's technique. Senator Borah was not only a friend who had been sympathetic and helpful throughout the Manchurian controversy, but he was Chairman of the Foreign Relations Committee of the Senate. So I decided to make the statement of our views on the Nine Power Treaty in the form of a letter to him.

The following day, February 22nd, was filled with official ceremony which kept me busy all day long. It was the 200th anniversary of the birth of George Washington. From morning until night the President and the members of his Cabinet were engaged in a memorial meeting at the Capitol, a visit to Mount Vernon, and the opening of the Washington Memorial Highway. But after dinner that evening, in company with Messrs. Rogers and Klots of the State Department and with the aid of historical memoranda which Dr. Hornbeck had prepared for me, I addressed myself to the task, and by midnight it was finished. The following day the President and Senator Borah gave it their approval, and on the morning of the 24th it was given to the press. It read as follows:

February 23, 1932.

My Dear Senator Borah:

You have asked my opinion whether, as has been sometimes recently suggested, present conditions in China have in any way indicated that the so-called Nine Power Treaty has become inapplicable or ineffective or rightly in need of modification, and if so, what I considered should be the policy of this Government.

This treaty, as you of course know, forms the legal basis upon which now rests the "open door" policy towards China. That policy, enunciated by John Hay in 1899, brought to an end the struggle among various powers for so-called spheres of interest in China which was threatening the dismemberment of that empire. To accomplish this Mr. Hay invoked two principles (1) equality of commercial opportunity among all nations in dealing with China, and (2) as necessary to that equality the preservation of China's territorial and administrative integrity. These principles were not new in the foreign policy of America. They had been the principles upon which it rested in its dealings with other nations for many years. In the case of China they were invoked to save a situation which not only threatened the future development and sovereignty of that great Asiatic people, but also threatened to create dangerous and constantly increasing rivalries between the other nations of the world. War had already taken place between Japan and China. At the close of that war three other nations intervened to prevent Japan from obtaining some of the results of that war claimed by her. Other nations sought and had obtained spheres of interest. Partly as a result of these actions a serious uprising had broken out in China which endangered the legations of all of the powers at Peking. While the attack on those legations was in progress, Mr. Hay made an announcement in respect to this policy as the principle upon which the powers should act in the settlement of the rebellion. He said:

"The policy of the Government of the United States is to seek a solution which may bring about permanent safety and peace to China, preserve Chinese territorial and administrative entity, protect all rights guaranteed to friendly powers by treaty and international law, and safeguard for the world the

principle of equal and impartial trade with all
parts of the Chinese Empire."

He was successful in obtaining the assent of
the other powers to the policy thus announced.

In taking these steps Mr. Hay acted with
the cordial support of the British Government. In responding to Mr. Hay's announcement, above set forth, Lord Salisbury, the
British Prime Minister, expressed himself
"most emphatically as concurring in the policy
of the United States."

For 20 years thereafter the "open door"
policy rested upon the informal commitments
thus made by the various powers. But in the
winter of 1921 to 1922, at a conference participated in by all of the principal powers
which had interests in the Pacific, the policy
was crystallized into the so-called Nine Power
Treaty, which gave definition and precision to
the principles upon which the policy rested.
In the first article of that treaty, the contracting powers, other than China, agreed:

"1. To respect the sovereignty, the independence and the territorial and administrative integrity of China.

"2. To provide the fullest and most unembarrassed opportunity to China to develop and
maintain for herself an effective and stable
government.

"3. To use their influence for the purpose of
effectually establishing and maintaining the
principle of equal opportunity for the commerce and industry of all nations throughout
the territory of China.

"4. To refrain from taking advantage of conditions in China in order to seek special rights or privileges which would abridge the rights of subjects or citizens of friendly states, and from countenancing action inimical to the security of such states."

This treaty thus represents a carefully developed and matured international policy intended, on the one hand, to assure to all of the contracting parties their rights and interests in and with regard to China, and on the other hand, to assure to the people of China the fullest opportunity to develop without molestation their sovereignty and independence according to the modern and enlightened standards believed to obtain among the peoples of this earth. At the time this treaty was signed, it was known that China was engaged in an attempt to develop the free institutions of a self-governing republic after her recent revolution from an autocratic form of government; that she would require many years of both economic and political effort to that end; and that her progress would necessarily be slow. The treaty was thus a covenant of self-denial among the signatory powers in deliberate renunciation of any policy of aggression which might tend to interfere with that development. It was believed—and the whole history of the development of the "open door" policy reveals that faith—that only by such a process, under the protection of such an agreement, could the fullest interests not only of China but of all nations which have intercourse with her best be served.

In its report to the President announcing this treaty, the American Delegation, headed by the then Secretary of State, Mr. Charles E. Hughes, said:

"It is believed that through this treaty the 'open door' in China has at last been made a fact."

During the course of the discussions which resulted in the treaty, the chairman of the British Delegation, Lord Balfour, had stated that—

"The British Empire Delegation understood that there was no representative of any power around the table who thought that the old practice of 'spheres of interest' was either advocated by any government or would be tolerable to this conference. So far as the British Government were concerned, they had, in the most formal manner, publicly announced that they regarded this practice as utterly inappropriate to the existing situation."

At the same time the representative of Japan, Baron Shidehara, announced the position of his Government as follows:

"No one denies to China her sacred right to govern herself. No one stands in the way of China to work out her own great national destiny."

The treaty was originally executed by the United States, Belgium, the British Empire, China, France, Italy, Japan, the Netherlands, and Portugal. Subsequently it was also executed by Norway, Bolivia, Sweden, Denmark, and Mexico. Germany has signed it, but her parliament has not yet ratified it.

It must be remembered also that this treaty was one of several treaties and agreements entered into at the Washington Conference by the various powers concerned, all of which were interrelated and interdependent. No one of these treaties can be disregarded without disturbing the general understanding and equilibrium which were intended to be accomplished and effected by the group of agreements arrived at in their entirety. The Washington Conference was essentially a disarmament conference, aimed to promote the possibility of peace in the world not only through the cessation of competition in naval armament but also by the solution of various other disturbing problems which threatened the peace of the world, particularly in the Far East. These problems were all interrelated. The willingness of the American Government to surrender its then commanding lead in battleship construction and to leave its positions at Guam and in the Philippines without further fortifications, was predicated upon, among other things, the self-denying covenants contained in the Nine Power Treaty, which assured the nations of the world not only of equal opportunity for their Eastern trade but also against the military aggrandizement of any other power at the expense of China. One cannot discuss the possibility of modifying or abrogating those provisions of the Nine Power Treaty without considering at the same time the other promises upon which they were really dependent.

Six years later the policy of self-denial against aggression by a stronger against a weaker power, upon which the Nine Power Treaty had been based, received a powerful reinforcement by the execution by substantially all the nations of the world of the Pact of Paris, the so-called Kellogg-Briand Pact. These two treaties represent independent but harmonious steps taken for the purpose of aligning the conscience and public opinion of the world in favor of a system of orderly development by the law of nations including the settlement of all controversies by methods of justice and peace instead of by arbitrary force. The program for the protection of China from outside aggression is an essential part of any such development. The signatories and adherents of the Nine Power Treaty rightly felt that the orderly and peaceful development of the 400,000,000 of people inhabiting China was necessary to the peaceful welfare of the entire world and that no program for the welfare of the world as a whole could afford to neglect the welfare and protection of China.

The recent events which have taken place in China, especially the hostilities which having been begun in Manchuria have latterly been extended to Shanghai, far from indicating the advisability of any modification of the treaties we have been discussing, have tended to bring home the vital importance of the faithful observance of the covenants therein to all of the nations interested in the

Far East. It is not necessary in that connection to inquire into the causes of the controversy or attempt to apportion the blame between the two nations which are unhappily involved; for regardless of cause or responsibility, it is clear beyond peradventure that a situation has developed which cannot, under any circumstances, be reconciled with the obligations of the covenants of these two treaties, and that if the treaties had been faithfully observed such a situation could not have arisen. The signatories of the Nine Power Treaty and of the Kellogg-Briand Pact who are not parties to that conflict are not likely to see any reason for modifying the terms of those treaties. To them the real value of the faithful performance of the treaties has been brought sharply home by the perils and losses to which their nationals have been subjected in Shanghai.

That is the view of this Government. We see no reason for abandoning the enlightened principles which are embodied in these treaties. We believe that this situation would have been avoided had these covenants been faithfully observed, and no evidence has come to us to indicate that a due compliance with them would have interfered with the adequate protection of the legitimate rights in China of the signatories of those treaties and their nationals.

On January 7th last, upon the instruction of the President, this Government formally notified Japan and China that it would not recognize any situation, treaty or agreement entered into by those Governments in violation of the covenants of these treaties, which affected the rights of our Government or its citizens in China. If a similar decision should be reached and a similar position taken by the other governments of the world, a caveat will be placed upon such action which, we believe, will effectively bar the legality hereafter of any title or right sought to be obtained by pressure or treaty violation, and which, as has been shown by history in the past, will eventually lead to the restoration to China of rights and titles of which she may have been deprived.

In the past our Government, as one of the leading powers on the Pacific Ocean, has rested its policy upon an abiding faith in the future of the people of China and upon the ultimate success in dealing with them of the principles of fair play, patience, and mutual goodwill. We appreciate the immensity of the task which lies before her statesmen in the development of her country and its Government. The delays in her progress, the instability of her attempts to secure a responsible government, were foreseen by Messrs. Hay and Hughes and their contemporaries and were the very obstacles which the policy of the "open door" was designed to meet. We concur with those statesmen, representing all the nations in the Washington Conference, who decided that China was entitled to the time necessary to accomplish her development. We are prepared to make that our policy for the future.

Very sincerely yours,

HENRY L. STIMSON

The Honorable
William E. Borah,
United States Senate

While this letter was based on the draft for the joint invocation of the Nine Power Treaty which I had sent to Sir John Simon, its informal nature afforded me a greater flexibility of expression and purpose. From its face it can easily be seen that it was intended for the perusal of at least five unnamed addressees. It was intended as a message of encouragement to China; as an explanation of policy to the public of the United States; as a suggestion of future possible action to the nations who were to be assembled at the coming meeting of the Assembly of the League of Nations; as a gentle reminder to the Conservative party, which was now in control of the British government, that they, through Lords Salisbury and Balfour, were joint authors with us of the Open Door policy and the Nine Power Treaty, and finally, as a reminder to Japan, that if she chose to break down one of the group of treaties arrived at at the Washington Conference, other nations might feel themselves released from some of those treaties which were as important to her as the Nine Power Treaty was to us.

My deepest interest of course was in the coming meeting of the Assembly of the League which was taking jurisdiction over the entire controversy between China and Japan. In that forum would be decided the fundamental policies which largely controlled all other questions. It was fortunate that on February 23rd, the day before the publication of my letter to Senator Borah, Japan had published her reply to the appeal of the League of Nations in respect to Shanghai. In that document she argued at length the thesis that China could not be considered "an organized people" within the meaning of the Covenant of the League. This reply of Japan and my simultaneous letter to Senator Borah thus placed in sharp antithesis before the attention of the Assembly the two contradictory policies which were opposing each other in the Far East—the policy of far-sighted self-control towards a weaker nation which was embodied in the Nine Power Treaty, and the policy of immediate exploitation put forward by Japan. In the Assembly of the League there were now represented as actors in this situation the smaller nations of Europe and America—not merely the great powers—and they were naturally a more sympathetic jury towards the first of these principles than had been the Council.

While the matter was thus pending, we were informally told that a resolution adopting a policy of non-recognition similar to that stated in our American note of January 7, 1932, would be proposed and probably passed by the Assembly. In fact on February 16th before the publication of my letter to Senator Borah, the Committee of Twelve of the Council in their appeal to the government of Japan had undertaken to remind that government of the terms of Article X of the Covenant "by which all the members of the League have undertaken to respect and preserve the territorial integrity and political independence of all other members," and they had then followed this reminder with a notice that it appeared to them (the Committee of Twelve) "to follow that no infringement of the territorial integrity and no change in the political independence of any member of the League brought about in disregard of this Article ought to be recognized as valid and effective by the members of the League of Nations." Nevertheless, this guarded appeal was quite different from a positive declaration by the entire body of nations, and as the time approached for the meeting of the Assembly there seemed to be danger that any resolution of non-recognition might be sidetracked at the last moment.

The General Disarmament Conference was sitting in Geneva simultaneously with the Assembly of the League and my letter to Senator Borah had been exciting the approval of some of the delegates from the smaller countries to that conference who wished to make speeches about it. I was warned that there was danger that effective action on the subject of recognition in the Assembly might be sidetracked by being transformed into a series of speeches and resolutions in the Disarmament Conference.

On the same day, March 4th, the press reported that in answer to questions in the British House of Commons an Under Secretary of the Foreign Office had indicated that it was doubtful whether the British government would support a resolution as to non-recognition. I was troubled by these rumors. It seemed to me that the leadership as to these matters of worldwide importance which were coming up in the Assembly was confused and that until that leadership should become clear we might well go a little slowly in our coöperation as to matters which seemed to me of much less general importance.

The fighting at Shanghai had stopped on March 3rd. The Japanese were anxious to withdraw their troops and get free of an embarrassing situation. Several of the governments with large commercial interests in Shanghai were pressing vigorously to have this accomplished as soon as possible. A conference of Ministers and other national representatives had been called at Shanghai for the purpose of working out the formulæ by which this could be done. As in all other matters relating to the various steps taken at Shanghai, we had been coöperating earnestly with the other nations in all these matters of immediate detail. It seemed to me now, however, that these details could wait at least until there was a clearer understanding about the questions of ultimate principle which had now come to the foreground at Geneva. On March 4th I instructed our Minister to China to abstain from attending the conferences in Shanghai until he received further notice from me. Through our Minister to Switzerland I next informed the British Foreign Minister who was then in Geneva of what I had done, and the reason. He replied to my message with a cordial reassurance as to Britain's intentions in the Assembly, and there was thereafter no further trouble.

G

Action by the Assembly

On March 7th in the Assembly of the League of Nations the British government proposed a resolution substantially to the effect of our note of January 7th and in the following terms:

> The Assembly . . . declares that it is incumbent upon the members of the League of Nations not to recognize any situation, treaty or agreement which may be brought about by means contrary to the Covenant of the League of Nations or to the Pact of Paris.

At the meeting of the Assembly on the 11th this

resolution was passed unanimously, the two parties to the controversy, China and Japan, not voting.[28]

On the following day at Washington I issued this statement to the press:

> The nations of the League at Geneva have united in a common attitude and purpose towards the perilous disturbances in the Far East. The action of the Assembly expresses the purpose for peace which is found both in the Pact of Paris and the Covenant of the League of Nations. In this expression all the nations of the world can speak with the same voice. This action will go far towards developing into terms of international law the principles of order and justice which underlie those treaties, and the government of the United States has been glad to coöperate earnestly in this effort.

There was another equally important reason for going carefully at Shanghai. There were many time-honored little grievances which the various nations had suffered in their relations with China at Shanghai, some of them inheritances of many years standing. The international settlements themselves represented an evolution of divergent interests and complex problems which, Topsy-like, had grown out of the past, often without logical reason or assent from all parties interested; problems usually representing some sort of an issue between the sovereignty of China and the interests of other nations which for various periods had been camping on her territory.

[28] An account of the debate on the resolution describing the attitude of the various powers, the motion of the British Foreign Secretary and the influence on the debate of the letter to Senator Borah is given in Royal Institute of International Affairs, *Survey* for 1932, pp. 575-578.

Now the dislocated conditions at Shanghai, where the Chinese government and its soldiers and citizens had been roughly handled by the forces of Japan and where a general conference was meeting to liquidate the situation and try to set the place going again in its normal life, seemed to many people to offer a Heaven-sent opportunity to settle some of these time-honored questions at the expense of China. Many of our own people, citizens and officials resident at Shanghai, felt the same way. They wanted to iron out and clinch according to our own interests various little questions which had been in dispute with China for many years. It was a strong temptation to do so, particularly to those who had lived and worked on the spot and long suffered from these illogical inconveniences. But basically it would have amounted to our profiting from the aggression of Japan.

So in my instructions to our representatives on the ground I cautioned them in the first place that China should not be urged into the conference unless she was ready to go, and should not be urged to submit to that conference any questions except those relating to the liquidation of the purely military situation. On the one side she should not be forced to discuss in this conference the surrender of her right to institute a peaceful boycott; such a broad question as that should be reserved for a general conference between China and Japan covering all matters of broad controversy between them, including Japan's action in Manchuria which had provoked the boycott. On the other side our representatives should take particular care not to join in any log-rolling between the representatives of the foreign powers at the expense of China which would result in taking advantage of the Japanese occupation to extort various favors each one for himself in respect to the International Settlement and its many little troubles. We must come out of that conference with absolutely clean hands; there must be no transactions which in the future might obscure our single-mindedness.

In these matters my rather difficult task was made easy by the absolutely straight vision of the President. I remember his telling me that, as he looked at it, if we took a dollar's worth of interest out of this coming conference in Shanghai while the Japanese troops were still there, it would put us in the position of violating the Kellogg Pact and of joining in a profit obtained under military pressure. We both were clear that yielding to such a temptation might destroy all our influence on the future great problem of holding the situation in the Far East fair for China and all others concerned.

The resolution of March 11th, of which the non-recognition provision was a part, provided for the appointment of a Committee of Nineteen composed of the President of the Assembly, the members of the Council (other than China and Japan) and six other members to be elected by secret ballot. This committee was to retain jurisdiction of the controversy on behalf of the Assembly with the duties, among other things, of following the process of the withdrawal of the Japanese forces from Shanghai, the execution of the Council's resolutions of September 30th and December 10th, 1931, and the conduct of further efforts at conciliation between the parties.[29] The Assembly itself recorded its intention of remaining in session and in ultimate control of the matter, instructing its president to convene it as soon as he deemed a meeting necessary.

[29] A full copy of this resolution is to be found in Willoughby, *Sino-Japanese Controversy*, p. 299; also in Royal Institute of International Affairs, *Documents on International Affairs, 1932.*

The Lytton Commission which had been appointed to investigate the controversy in December had reached the Far East and was engaged in the execution of its task. It was evidently anticipated that on the submission of its report, assuming no settlement was arrived at in the meanwhile, there would be further work for the Assembly to do.

Thus the process of liquidating the situation at Shanghai thereafter was supervised by two international bodies: first, the conference of Ministers acting locally at Shanghai on the evacuation of the Japanese troops and other local problems resulting from the contest; and second, the Committee of Nineteen, exercising general supervision for the League at Geneva. Many difficulties and delays naturally occurred requiring great skill and patience on the part of the local mediators. China, for example, kept pressing for a time limit in which the evacuation should be accomplished. Japan, in retiring, was anxious to save as much face as possible in the shape of assurances for the protection of her nationals on whose behalf the intervention ostensibly had been made. A successful formula was finally devised on April 26th[30] through the patience of the

[30] By a curious accident I myself may have been helpful in securing the acceptance of this formula. As will be hereafter narrated, I was in Geneva in the latter part of April while the formula was under discussion. While there I was visited by a Japanese friend; a man of conspicuous fairness and good judgment and of great influence in his own government. He called upon me on April 25th and mentioned the trouble which the Japanese government was having with the proposed formula, fearing that it violated the Japanese Constitution, which placed all authority for the movement of Japanese troops in the Emperor. I told him that I could quite understand that Japan could not consent to any resolution which would deprive her of the ultimate authority to give orders to her own troops, but that this resolution seemed to me to provide only that the local neutral commission should make a report confined solely to the question of whether at a given time the evacuation might take place without peril to life and property, etc., leaving the ultimate decision still in the Emperor and merely giving to him the benefit of a neutral unbiased opinion on the facts. My friend seemed struck by this suggestion and said that if that were so he thought it would

local mediators, supported by the efforts of the Committee of Nineteen, and a formal armistice agreement was signed on May 5th. The last of the Japanese troops left Shanghai on the 31st of May, leaving thereafter merely the customary quota of 2,500 marines for garrison duty. Japan's unsuccessful effort at intervention at Shanghai was ended.[31]

---

remove the objection of his government. The acceptance by his government followed soon afterwards.

[31] "It remains to state that the Japanese attempt to cut the knot at Shanghai with the sword did not achieve its purpose. Anti-Japanese activities continued; and at the end of August 1932, simultaneously with the Japanese recognition of 'Manchukuo,' there were rumours of further trouble impending at Shanghai and of the despatch of a Japanese naval squadron to the Whangpoo for the protection of Japanese nationals in case the continued boycott should lead to further outbreaks of violence." Royal Institute of International Affairs, *Survey* for 1932, p. 514.

"Whatever may have been the reasons which moved Japan to extend her military operations to the Shanghai region, it is certain that, for her, the whole enterprise was a disastrous one. In final result, she did lessen the severity of the organized boycott against herself, but paid an enormous price for it. She lost the lives of many of her marines and soldiers; the money cost to her must have been very great; the resistance of China to her aggressions was strengthened rather than weakened; and, above all, she made more plain than even the invasion of Manchuria had done, the extent and character of her policies *vis-à-vis* China." Willoughby, *op. cit.,* p. 362.

PART FOUR

THE ADJUDICATION OF RESPONSIBILITY

THE ADJUDICATION OF
RESPONSIBILITY

I

THE NATURE OF THE ADJUDICATION AND THE IMPORTANCE THEREOF TO THE AMERICAN GOVERNMENT

WHILE the action taken at the March meeting of the Assembly marked a step forward in international action and served morally to clear the atmosphere which surrounded this controversy between China and Japan, it was in no sense a decision upon the rights and the wrongs of the issues between them. The adoption of the resolution not to recognize the fruits of an aggression was not such a decision. It was intended to mark out a standard determined upon by the fifty nations in the Assembly which would guide their conduct thereafter when a legal case calling for it should be presented. It did not attempt to adjudicate on the merits of this particular controversy between China and Japan.

China claimed that Japan had been guilty of unjustified aggression in Manchuria. Japan denied this and claimed that her action had been taken solely in self-defense and in the protection of her nationals. Other steps were being taken to form a new state in Manchuria, and as to these there was arising a

new controversy between the two nations. China
claimed that the new state was being created solely
by the action of Japan and in violation of her duties under the various treaties towards China; Japan
claimed that the new state was the result of autonomous
and independent action of the local population. On
none of these issues had there been any step taken by
the other nations of the world in the nature of a trial of
the facts and an adjudication of the responsibility.

But, unlike America, the nations who were united
in the League had ready at their hands machinery
by which they were entitled to hold a trial on these
issues and to decide them. Both Japan and China were
members of the League and by becoming members had
agreed to submit to such machinery. This machinery
had already been set in motion. Under the authority of
the resolution of the Council of December 10th, which
in turn was based upon the Council's powers under
Article XI, an impartial commission had been appointed with the full assent of Japan to go to Manchuria, investigate the facts of these controversies and
report its recommendations thereon to the League.
When this commission should report as to these facts
and each of the respective parties should have been
heard, the Assembly of the League of Nations would
be in a position to render a decision on the merits, and
such a decision when rendered would have conformed
to the conditions recognized throughout the world as
constituting the basic elements of a judicial process. A
similar investigation and report also could be made
under other articles of the Covenant, notably Article
XV, which might in a similar way result in a fair
determination according to such a judicial process.

These considerations may serve to show the reader
the advantage in such a situation as the Sino-Japanese

controversy, which the nations belonging to the League possessed over the position occupied by the United States. It was a great advantage. It represented a long step forward in the evolution of government in our present world. Many times during the preceding months this difference had been brought home to President Hoover and myself in the consideration of this dispute. In our efforts to protect the interests of the United States in this tangled controversy we had constantly faced it. The integrity of treaties was involved, which were of great consequence to our government and our people, as I have already pointed out. Changes of status were being made in the Far East which not only immediately affected our citizens doing business there, but which might to a far greater extent affect our future interests in the years to come. Actions were being taken by Japan and claims being made by her which seemed to us to affect vitally those treaties and the interests which we possessed under them. Some of these acts seemed to us to be plainly violative of the treaties, and some of the defenses put up seemed to us quite untenable. Yet neither in the Pact of Paris nor in the Nine Power Treaty was machinery provided which gave us a right to insist upon an investigation and decision as to these acts and claims. Such machinery existed for all of the members of the League of Nations as to the rights given by their Covenant. In short, they lived in a world purporting to be governed by law and its methods. We still lived in what was little better than a world of anarchy, governed by force or the threat of force.

If Japan was willing to agree, conceivably it might have been arranged to arbitrate some of her claims, but arbitration is a very slow and cumbrous method and it depends wholly upon the consent of both sides whether any such arbitration shall be undertaken. If a nation refuses to arbitrate, saying, as Japan did here, that it was nobody's business except hers what she did in Manchuria, there was no peaceful way by which we could obtain an investigation and a decision as to whether she was right or wrong. On the other hand, the League Covenant provided such a method. It also provided a system of sanctions by which in some cases and under some conditions economic pressure could be brought to bear upon a country in case she was found to be in the wrong. But even if one did not propose to resort to sanctions other than the moral pressure of public opinion, and simply sought a fair determination of the issue in order to bring such public opinion to bear, there was no way in which the American government could peacefully obtain such a determination.

Looked at in its ultimate possibilities, this Far Eastern controversy was one of the most far-reaching in the present world, affecting the development and growth of hundreds of millions of people dwelling on the Pacific immediately opposite our own country. Next to these people themselves and to their neighbors, the Russians, the American people were those who probably in the long run would be most vitally affected. The issues of law and order as well as economic development for years to come seemed to us to be involved. Yet we were one of the very few nations in the world which had no right to participate in any way except as a friendly observer of the determination by others of these issues which were facing us across the way.[1]

We therefore were very keenly interested in follow-

---

[1] It was true that General McCoy, an American, was a member of the Lytton Commission; but he was a member solely because he had been appointed as such by the League. We had no right to participate as a government in the inquiry. In what he did, General McCoy was responsible to the League, not to us.

ing the course of the determinative proceedings which had been instituted by the League in the appointment of the Lytton Commission and we were very anxious by our moral support, so far as was properly possible, to aid them in coming to a fair decision upon the facts. We were deeply interested in having this controversy rightfully settled, and this was the only way in which such a decision could be peacefully reached.

II

STEPS TAKEN BY JAPANESE GOVERNMENT TO MAKE DIFFICULT SUCH AN ADJUDICATION AND TO FRUSTRATE ANY EFFECTIVE RESULT THEREFROM

Almost immediately after its army had overthrown the Chinese government of Manchuria, the Japanese government began a succession of steps to establish the political and economic control of Japan over that country. This was by the forcible creation of an ostensibly independent but really puppet state controlled by Japan and known as "Manchukuo."

Thereafter, as soon as the other nations of the world had announced their intention not to recognize as valid any fruits of this conquest, the Japanese government proceeded to take further steps designed to make this policy of the rest of the world as difficult and ineffective as possible. By these steps Japan sought first to frustrate the rendering of an adjudication upon the real facts of the situation and, if such an adjudication was made, to thwart its enforcement. These successive steps have been made the subject of a thorough investigation by the Lytton Commission. Its unanimous report thereon is clear and authoritative.[2] It is necessary for

[2] See Lytton Report, Chap. VI.

In the American State Department we were placed in a position of

me here only to give cursorily a description of the steps taken.

A

Formation of "Manchukuo" and the Recognition of Its Independence by Japan

In the formation of "Manchukuo" Japan followed generally the plan which she had followed two decades before in regard to Korea. Korea had been originally subject to the titular sovereignty of China. By military action in the war of 1895 Japan destroyed China's sovereignty and forced China to recognize Korea's independence. A puppet Korean emperor and government, acting under the guidance and direction of Japan, was then installed and finally in 1910 Japan formally annexed Korea as a part of her own territory. In the case of Manchuria, on account of the greater wisdom of the Chinese government in refusing to be forced into war as well as owing to the critical opposition of the League of Nations, Japan was obliged to proceed more cautiously. Her military operations not having resulted in a recognized state of war, she was not in a position to force the recognition of Manchuria's independence by China, but by military action her army succeeded in forcibly overthrowing the preëxisting Chinese government and putting to flight all of the loyal Chinese officials. Thereupon, under the pressure of the Japanese army and beginning in the latter part of October, 1931, nominal municipal

---

unusual advantage in this matter by the reports which we had received during the autumn of 1931 (See *supra* Part II, pp. 44-45). These reports gave us very detailed accounts of the measures taken by Japanese officers and emissaries to "promote" the "autonomous" formation of "Manchukuo" and to accomplish the "voluntary" acceptance of office in the new government by such Chinese as did so coöperate.

governments were erected in the different cities and nominal provincial governments in the different provinces.

These governments were organized and in large part officered by Japanese, such Chinese officials as took part being usually compelled to do so by the pressure of Japanese force. These local governments were then invited into an All-Manchuria organization created in the same fashion out of similar materials. This central government then enacted a "declaration of independence" from China on the 18th of February, 1932, and on the following day decided to establish a republic and invited Mr. Henry Pu Yi to become the chief executive. This gentleman was the deposed Emperor of the former Manchu Empire in China and for some years had been living under the protection of the Japanese, at first in the Japanese concession in Tientsin and later in their leased territory of Kwantung (Port Arthur). By the 9th of March he had accepted and been installed as Regent of the new state, announcing that he undertook to found the policy of the new state upon the basis of the principles of "morality, benevolence and love"!

In the light of her former actions in Korea it had not been difficult for us in the State Department to forecast what would be Japan's course in Manchuria. When the Japanese government was emphatically pledging itself against the annexation of a single foot of China's territory, I find that in a meeting with my Cabinet colleagues on November 17, 1931, I prophesied that she would for the present set up a puppet Manchurian government under her control. On account of such an anticipation, in drafting our note of January 7, 1932, I was careful to make its language broad enough to exclude from recognition any such "situation *de facto*" as actually was established. The Assembly of the League in its resolution of March 11th prudently followed the same course.

But, although it was easy to forecast the fiction and during the course of its operation to penetrate the subterfuges which were adopted, and although the fact of Japanese authorship and control were clear to any impartial observer, yet there was no doubt that this method of procedure would produce a situation much more difficult to be dealt with by an international tribunal of investigation than would have been the case if Japan had at once formally annexed Manchuria. It would not only involve a mass of conflicting testimony before that tribunal itself, but it would make it very easy for the Japanese government by *ex parte* statements and announcements to deceive its own people and to arouse among them a passionate belief that no wrong had been committed by Japan. It undoubtedly was a shrewd method of digging themselves in for the defense of their forcibly acquired gains. On the threshold it threw difficulties in the path of the investigation of the Lytton Commission. It presented questions which required more careful work and greater courage by that Commission as well as greater courage and persistence by the Assembly of the League of Nations when the matter came before that body. The steps taken by Japan were well calculated to promote a spirit of defeatism and dissension in the future action of her judges.

B

Subsequent Steps Taken to Thwart an Adjudication upon "Manchukuo"

Just as soon as the Japanese government realized that its action in creating "Manchukuo" was not to escape challenge by the rest of the world, it set on foot a series of moves to force the thing through; to warn the nations of the difficulties which such a challenge would involve for them in case they persisted in it, and finally to present them with a *fait accompli* before the report of the tribunal, which had been appointed with Japan's own consent to investigate the situation, could be rendered. These steps are all a matter of record and I shall only briefly allude to them.

1. *Demand for recognition by "Manchukuo" officials.* Within ten days after the Assembly had met to consider China's appeal, and the very day after the resolution of non-recognition had been passed, the "Minister for Foreign Affairs of Manchukuo" on March 12th addressed communications to seventeen countries which had consular officials in Manchuria and also to the governments of some thirty-five other countries, announcing the establishment of the independent State of "Manchukuo" and expressing the "earnest desire of this government" for the establishment of formal diplomatic relations between the addressees of the note and "Manchukuo."

2. *Seizure of the customs and salt revenues.* The total customs revenues from Manchuria and a portion of the salt revenues, prior to the Japanese coup of September 18, 1931, had belonged to and been forwarded to the National government of China at Nanking. Both of these revenues had been pledged as security for foreign loans made to China and their collection had been administered by foreign personnel employed by the Chinese government. The Inspector General of the salt gabelle, for example, was an Englishman. All of these revenues were now claimed by the new government of "Manchukuo" and in June, 1932, were forcibly seized and control by the Chinese government was ended.

3. *Japan threatens to withdraw from the Assembly if it investigates further in Manchuria.* Warning to this effect was given to me on April 4th and I was informed that similar warnings had been addressed to other powers, including Great Britain, France, Italy, Germany, Czechoslovakia, Greece and Belgium. I was also informed that the particular basis of Japanese objection was that Japan's peculiar position in Manchuria and her interests there would not allow her to permit outside intrusions into such questions; in particular she could not permit the application of Article XV of the League Covenant to questions in Manchuria. Similar objections to the application of Article XV had been taken by the Japanese representative at the Assembly meeting in March.

4. *Recognition of "Manchukuo" by Japan.* In August, 1932, the Lytton Commission had finished its field investigations and was engaged in the examination of the evidence taken and the drafting of its report. While this was going on and with direct reference to it, if not for the express purpose of influencing it, the Foreign Minister, Count Uchida, in an address delivered before the Diet at Tokyo on August 25th, stated that he regarded the recognition by Japan of "Manchukuo" as being "the sole effective means of solving the Manchurian problem"; and in the same speech he declared that the Japanese people could "never consent" to "a solution by patching up matters for the moment by investing China proper in one form or another with authority over Manchuria" on the lines of "a plan which was being considered in certain quarters" (evidently meaning the Lytton Commission). Thereupon the Japanese government proceeded rapidly to the execution of a treaty of recognition with the new state of "Manchukuo." This treaty was approved by the Japanese Privy

Council on September 13th and signed at Changchung in Manchuria on September 15th. Article 2 of this treaty provides:

2. Japan and Manchukuo, recognizing that any threat to the territory or to the peace and order of either of the High Contracting Parties constitutes at the same time a threat to the safety and existence of the other, agree to coöperate in the maintenance of their national security; it being understood that such Japanese forces as may be necessary for this purpose shall be stationed in Manchukuo.[3]

The report of the Lytton Commission was signed at Peking September 4, 1932. It was not, however, to be made public until it was presented to the Council of the League at Geneva on October 1st.

At the meeting of the Council of the League on September 24th its President, Mr. DeValera of the Irish Free State, said:

I should . . . be lacking in frankness, both to the Japanese government and to the members of the League as a whole . . . [did I not give] expression to the regret which I am sure is felt by the generality of the members of the Council that before the discussion of the report of the Commission, before even the publication of that report, Japan has, not only by

[3] "In deliberately forestalling the publication of the Lytton Report by clinching the erection of 'Manchukuo' through a diplomatic *fait accompli*, from which Japan could hardly recede without some 'loss of face,' the Japanese Government were, as it were, 'nailing their colours to the mast' as a preliminary to 'going into action' at Geneva. They were intentionally creating a state of affairs in which they would not be able to abandon their puppet without evoking an overwhelming opposition in the hearts of the Japanese people." Royal Institute of International Affairs, *Survey* for 1932, p. 463.

recognizing, but also by signing a treaty with what is known as the Manchukuo government, taken steps which cannot but be regarded as calculated to prejudice the settlement of the dispute. For almost a year the Council in its collective capacity, and the individual governments which compose it, have scrupulously refrained from uttering any word of judgment on the merits of this grave dispute, on the grounds that a Commission had been set up to investigate the dispute in all its bearings, and that, until that Commission had reported and its report been considered by the organs of the League, the whole question is still to be regarded as *sub judice*.

It can be easily appreciated even from this brief enumeration of the steps which were being taken in Manchuria during this period how many opportunities were thus created for differences of opinion and action between the various governments interested in commerce with that country; also how important it was, if the collective action which had been initiated by the League with our support was to be carried through without dislocation and failure, that every effort should be made by personal conference and discussion to avoid all misunderstandings.

In January I had been appointed by the President the chairman of the American delegation to the General Disarmament Conference, but owing to the pressure of my duties at Washington had been unable to leave for that conference with the other members of the delegation when they sailed for Geneva. It was important that I should attend that conference at least for a brief period during the spring for the purpose of conferring with the remainder of the delegation on certain proposals which had arisen. The sessions of the Assembly of the League of Nations were being carried on in Geneva simultaneously with the meetings of the Disarmament Conference and both bodies were composed of substantially the same nations. I therefore decided to visit Geneva in April in order to be able to attend to both of these duties.

III

MY TRIP TO GENEVA

I sailed on April 8th and returned to America again on May 14th. Landing at Havre in the morning of April 15th, I spent the day at Paris where I saw the Premier, M. Tardieu, and M. Berthelot, the Under Secretary at the Foreign Office. Going on to Geneva that night, I spent the rest of my time there. While I was in Geneva Prime Ministers MacDonald of Great Britain and Tardieu of France, Chancellor Bruening of Germany, Signor Grandi, the Foreign Minister of Italy, and Mr. Tsuneo Matsudaira, the Japanese Ambassador at London, all came from their respective posts to Geneva for conference. In addition to them the representatives of many other countries were already at Geneva for the purpose of either the meeting of the Assembly or of the Disarmament Conference. Among these were M. Hymans of Belgium, the President of the Assembly, Sir Eric Drummond, its permanent Secretary, and as delegates or representatives Sir John Simon, the British Foreign Minister, with Lords Hailsham and Londonderry of Great Britain; Messrs. Paul-Boncour, Aubert and Massigli of France; Signor Rosso of Italy; Dr. Nadolny and Dr. Von Buelow of Germany; Dr. W. W. Yen, the representative of China before the Assembly; M. Motta, the President of the Swiss Republic; Prime Minister Beneš of Czechoslovakia; Count Apponyi of Hungary; Messrs. te Water of the Union of South Africa and Wilford of New Zealand.

With all of these gentlemen, as well as with my colleagues on the American delegation, and many others, I had conferences—with some of them repeated conferences. These conferences were very valuable. They confirmed my long-held conviction that in the realm of international relations more than in any other realm of human activities, personal conference is indispensable to mutual understanding. It immensely reënforces that which can be achieved through the ordinary channels of cables, dispatches and ambassadors. To talk face to face with the chiefs of other governments greatly facilitates a mutual grasp of the respective difficulties and points of view of each government. Such regular and direct contact between the officers of governments is the greatest innovation which has been established by the organization of the League of Nations and is in my opinion one of its most signal contributions to the conduct of international relations.

The picture of the League's Sino-Japanese problem was seen in better perspective and my comprehension of it clarified. The small powers had a much livelier sense of the importance of vindicating the general principles for which the League was striving than their larger colleagues and were naturally less troubled by the difficulties of detail that lay in the path. They were the chief beneficiaries of the principles and were less open to the hazards and difficulties. Even they, however, were impressed with the obstacles presented by Japan's unyielding attitude. But in spite of that they had a firm grasp of the ethical significance of the controversy and had no thought of flinching from pressing it through to a logical conclusion.

There were very frank expressions from them as to the importance of vigorous leadership in such a matter on the part of the great powers and also to the effect that thus far such leadership had not been manifested. On the latter point the criticism of the press correspondents at Geneva was open and almost universal. The whole picture confirmed one's impression of the misfortune it had been for the world that this first great test of the strength of the collective structure, in which the war-torn Caucasian nations were so terrifically interested, should have come to a head in an issue between other races on the opposite side of the world.

I also had repeated conferences with the gentlemen representing Great Britain, France, Germany, Italy, China, and Japan. With Mr. MacDonald and Sir John Simon, in repeated talks of the most frank and informal nature, I went over almost every detail of what had occurred in the past and what might be anticipated in the future in the Far Eastern controversy. Earnest anxiety for complete coöperation in the future conduct of the matter was expressed by all. In order to minimize the possibility of misunderstandings, we held one conference at which not only Mr. MacDonald, Sir John Simon and I were present but at which we had with us on each side career representatives of the respective departments and at which it was attempted to cover all future matters of policy concerning which any such misunderstanding could be anticipated. When I finished my visit at Geneva, I felt that so far as my earnest effort could accomplish it I had made clear to my friends in the British government the purposes and policies upon which we were acting in America.

My conversations with the gentlemen representing

France were equally frank, though less in detail. M.
Tardieu was an old friend and is always direct and
outspoken. His supervision of Far Eastern matters,
however, evidently had been through others. M. Berthelot, the permanent Under Secretary, was familiar
with them in detail and evinced a sympathetic and intelligent point of view in our conversation. I was able
to tell him with truth that the reports on the Far Eastern situation which I had received from French sources
through M. Claudel at Washington had seemed to me
to be often the most accurate that came to me from any
foreign source.

IV

FURTHER EFFORTS TO AVOID MISUNDERSTANDINGS AND TO ENCOURAGE EUROPE AS TO THE SINCERITY AND CONTINUANCE OF AMERICAN COÖPERATION

The spring of 1932 was not an easy time in which to
labor in America for international farsightedness or
good will. It was the year of a presidential election. It
was also the precise period when the depression in
America had struck the nadir of discouragement and
before the upward movement of the early summer had
commenced. The question of the payment to the United
States of the foreign debts hung like a cloud over the
landscape, poisoning our relations with all of the great
European powers; and, to make our position more difficult, the Congress in its joint resolution of December,
1931, had imposed a peremptory mandate upon us
against any attempt to solve that problem by negotiation and remove that cloud.

When I was in Geneva the European nations were
on the point of meeting at Lausanne in June for the
purpose of taking up and settling the question of Ger-

man reparations due to them—a question which they regarded as intimately connected with the payment of their debts to us. They were probably most desirous to discuss the matter with me; and yet, for fear of possible misunderstanding both there and at home, I could not permit the subject to be even broached. Finally, by way of a special touch, just as I was embarking for Europe, the American House of Representatives passed by an enormous majority, against the recommendations of the President, the bill providing for speedy and complete independence of the Philippine Islands. The effect which such an abandonment of protection of our Filipino wards, as well as of American responsibility in general in the Far East, would inevitably have upon our prestige with Far Eastern countries can be imagined.

Yet there were steps even then which could be taken and which it was important to take in order that the governments which were handling their difficult Far Eastern problem in the League might realize that we were still sincerely anxious to help and coöperate.

During the past two or three years there had been several times suggested by European leaders as a step toward intelligent coöperation, the proposal that the United States should enter into a pact to consult with the other nations in case of emergency threatening the peace. Unfortunately, it had been advanced first at the time of the London Naval Conference under circumstances when it easily might have been misunderstood. If then adopted, it might have been taken as a commitment on our part to render armed naval assistance in case of war. For that reason it had been attacked then by some of the members of the American Senate. Under different circumstances there was no such danger. In fact the United States was already a party to covenants of that kind in specific treaties. The disappointment caused in Europe by our refusal to consider the matter in 1930, however, was widespread and constituted ammunition against us on the part of critics who charged us with a spirit of total non-helpfulness. The matter was now taken up again by us and carried forward with the aid of members of both of the American national parties, with the result that in June, 1932, a plank in favor of such consultation was inserted in both the Republican and Democratic platforms.[4]

Later on in the summer, on August 8th, I made an address before the Council on Foreign Relations in New York in which I pointed out that even without any explicit covenant to that effect the actions taken by the American government under the Pact of Paris since its ratification, conveyed the necessary implication that we would consult with the other signatories in case of any threat of its violation.[5]

In the same speech I also took occasion to point out that the growing interdependence of the modern world was rapidly rendering isolationism obsolete in that world, and I called attention to the inevitable effect of such a development upon the traditional doctrine of neutrality.

In Latin America there also occurred an opportunity to carry forward the development of collective action

[4] I think the first suggestion came from Senator Swanson, who was one of the American delegates at the Disarmament Conference at Geneva. The plank in the Democratic platform was as follows:

"We advocate . . . the Pact of Paris abolishing war as an instrument of national policy, to be made effective by provisions for consultation and conference in case of threatened violation of treaties."

The plank in the Republican platform was as follows:

"We favor enactment by Congress of a measure that will authorize our government to call or participate in an international conference in case of any threat of non-fulfillment of Article 2 of the Treaty of Paris (Kellogg-Briand Pact)."

[5] The text of this speech was printed as a special supplement to Vol. XI, No. 1 of *Foreign Affairs* (October, 1932).

in support of peace. For nearly four years a dispute followed by armed hostilities had been going on between Bolivia and Paraguay concerning the boundaries of their respective territories. The locality of the dispute was in a remote and almost uninhabited wilderness. The two countries themselves were secluded from the outside world in the heart of the South American continent, where neither of them possessed any access to the sea. The difficulties of this geographical situation and the stubborn bitterness of the contestants had resisted long and patient efforts by neutral nations to induce a settlement by peaceful means.

On August 3, 1932, all the independent republics of the Western World under the lead of the United States united in an unprecedented appeal to the two quarreling nations. They declared the Chaco dispute to be susceptible of a peaceful solution. They earnestly requested Bolivia and Paraguay to submit it immediately to arbitration or such other peaceful means of solution as might be acceptable to both; they invited them at once to stop the movements of troops in the disputed territories, and they ended their appeal by a declaration following the precedent set by the Assembly of the League of Nations at Geneva on March 11th in the following terms:

> The American nations further declare that they will not recognize any territorial arrangement in this controversy which has not been obtained by peaceful means nor the validity of territorial acquisitions which may be obtained through occupation or conquest by force of arms.

By each of these steps we sought to let our friends in the League know that regardless of the discouraging atmosphere and general spirit of defeatism in the world, the American government was prepared to carry on the spirit of coöperation to which it had committed itself.

V

THE LYTTON REPORT

A

Arrival and Publication of the Report

The Lytton Report was to be made public on Sunday, October 2nd. A sealed copy had been sent to us by the League of Nations with authority to open it on that morning at 7 A.M. There was no doubt in our minds as to the importance which our countrymen attached to the decision contained in this document. The time of its arrival, its probable contents, and their probable effect had been a matter of constant speculation in the press. The Department of State, therefore, made every effort to assure a prompt and wide publicity for its contents. Early that morning Dr. Hornbeck, the head of the Far Eastern Division, was on hand ready to open it at the appointed hour, and with the stenographic staff of the Department organized to make immediate copies. By that afternoon the entire document had been transcribed and mimeographed and was in the hands of the press. As a consequence the press were not obliged to depend upon the excerpts cabled from Geneva, but had the entire document available for their use. It thus received wide publicity throughout the country, even in the height of a bitter presidential campaign—probably a far wider publicity than it received in any other country.

B

The Character of the Report

The report when received was found well worthy of these anticipations. It became at once and remains today the outstanding impartial authority upon the subjects which it covers. Its terseness and the finish of its language made it easily readable, and this added greatly to its value. It contained not merely an impartial decision of the issues which had already arisen, but also constructive suggestions for the eventual solution of the whole problem.

Above all, it was unanimous. There were no minority opinions or recommendations. Five eminent and specially qualified citizens[6] of the five great powers of Great Britain, France, Germany, Italy and the United States had collected and studied the evidence and reached a unanimous conclusion as to the facts of and the consequent responsibility for a bitterly complicated controversy between two other great powers. Furthermore, this was accomplished in a case where their judg-

[6] Lord Lytton had had many years of experience in the East as Governor of Bengal and as Viceroy and acting Governor-General of India.

General McCoy had served for many years in the Philippines and was familiar with Japan and China through many visits to those countries. He had been the head of the American Relief Mission to Japan on the occasion of the great earthquake of 1923. He had also rendered important foreign service as supervisor of the presidential election in Nicaragua in 1928 and as chairman of the Commission of Inquiry and Conciliation between Bolivia and Paraguay in 1929.

General Claudel was a French officer who had rendered much foreign service in West Africa and other colonies of France and was a member of the Higher Council of War.

Count Aldrovandi-Marescotti was an Italian diplomatist of wide experience and had been chief of Cabinet for the Italian Minister of Foreign Affairs.

Dr. Schnee had had executive and diplomatic experience in foreign countries. He had been a member of the Reichstag as well as the German Colonial Office.

ment did not involve a pecuniary award but where it might be made the basis of political action under the organization of the League against a great nation. Such a report was not only momentous; it was unprecedented.

C

The Contents of the Report

For the Lytton Report to be understood and appreciated it must be read in its entirety. I can refer here only to the general character of its contents and to the findings upon certain vital issues of fact which bear upon the diplomatic events which I have described. The Commission did not flinch from drawing the conclusions necessary to reach *ultimate* facts out of the mass of *evidentiary* facts which the Commission had collected. It felt, however, that it was the duty of the Assembly of the League itself to adjudicate whether the facts thus presented amounted to a breach of the Covenant of the League, the Kellogg-Briand Pact and the Nine Power Treaty of Washington. But it reported without equivocation its view that the preservation of the sanctity of each of those three treaties was necessary to the international relations of the world in general and particularly to the situation existing in Manchuria. Thus it said in its Chapter IX on the principles and conditions of the settlement:

Apart from China and Japan, other powers of the world have also important interests to defend in this Sino-Japanese conflict. We have already referred to existing multilateral treaties, and any real and lasting solution by agreement must be compatible with the stipulations of these fundamental agreements, on which is based the peace organisation of the world. *The considerations which actuated the representatives of the powers at the Washington Conference are still valid. It is quite as much in the interests of the powers now as it was in 1922 to assist the reconstruction of China and to maintain her sovereignty and her territorial and administrative integrity as indispensable to the maintenance of peace.* Any disintegration of China might lead, perhaps rapidly, to serious international rivalries, which would become all the more bitter if they should happen to coincide with rivalries between divergent social systems. Finally, the interests of peace are the same the world over. Any loss of confidence in the application of the principles of the Covenant and of the Pact of Paris in any part of the world diminishes the value and efficacy of those principles everywhere. (Italics mine.)

The report was divided into ten chapters, the first eight consisting of an historical description of the events and issues up to date, and the last two being devoted to the broad conditions and specific suggestions as to a settlement. These chapters are enumerated as follows:

Chapter I —Outline of Recent Developments in China.

Chapter II —Manchuria.

Chapter III —Manchurian Issues between Japan and China.

Chapter IV —Narrative of Events in Manchuria on and subsequent to September 18, 1931.

Chapter V —Shanghai.

In the course of its report on the facts it disposed adversely of a number of claims which had been made by Japan.

First: As to the position of China as an organized state. It stated:

> The dominating factor in China is the modernisation of the nation itself which is slowly taking place. China today is a nation in evolution, showing evidence of transition in all aspects of its national life.

The report discussed without any attempt to minimize them the evils resulting to China and to other nations from China's political, social and economic unrest during recent years. It indicated that present conditions in China were better than at the time of the Washington Conference and that, if not checked by Japan's aggression, the future outlook was hopeful. It stated:

> Although the spectacle of China's transitional period, with its unavoidable political, social, intellectual and moral disorder, is disappointing to her impatient friends and has created enmities which have become a danger to peace, it is nevertheless true that, in spite of difficulties, delays and failures, consider-

able progress has in fact been made. An argument which constantly reappears in the polemics of the present controversy is that China is 'not an organised State' or 'is in a condition of complete chaos and incredible anarchy,' and that her present-day conditions should disqualify her from membership of the League of Nations and deprive her of the protective clauses of the Covenant. In this connection, it may be useful to remember that an altogether different attitude was taken at the time of the Washington Conference by all the participating Powers. Yet, even at that time, China had two completely separate Governments, one at Peking and one at Canton, and was disturbed by large bandit forces which frequently interfered with communications in the interior, while preparations were being made for a civil war involving all China. As a result of this war, which was preceded by an ultimatum sent to the Central Government on January 13th, 1922, when the Washington Conference was still in session, the Central Government was overthrown in May, and the independence of Manchuria from the Government installed at Peking in its place was declared in July by Marshal Chang Tso-lin. Thus, there existed no fewer than three Governments professing to be independent, not to mention the virtually autonomous status of a number of provinces or parts of provinces. Although, at present, the Central Government's authority is still weak in a number of provinces, the central authority is not, at least openly, repudiated, and there is reason to hope that, if the Central Government as such can be maintained, provincial administration, military forces and finance will acquire an increasingly national character. Those, among others, were doubtless the reasons which induced the Assembly of the League of Nations last September to elect China to the Council.

By these findings the Commission disposed not only of Japan's argument that China, not being an organized state, was not entitled to be treated by the other powers as a sovereign political body under the multilateral treaties, but also of Japan's argument that the Nine Power Treaty was obsolete and the Washington Conference mistaken in its policy.

Second: The relations between China and Manchuria. The report not only found that China was entitled to the titular sovereignty over Manchuria, but it stated that, in view of the great subsequent immigration of millions of Chinese farmers, "Manchuria is now unalterably Chinese" (Chap. II, subhead 1).

Again it found that until the Japanese intervention these ties were being strengthened:

> Thus during the period preceding the conflict between China and Japan, both the political and economic ties between Manchuria and the rest of China were gradually strengthened (Chap. II, subhead 2).

Again it found as to the attitude of the Chinese people in the remainder of China toward Manchuria:

> The Chinese people regard Manchuria as an integral part of China and deeply resent any attempt to separate it from the rest of their

country. Hitherto, these Three Eastern Provinces have always been considered both by China and by foreign powers as a part of China, and the *de jure* authority of the Chinese Government there has been unquestioned. This is evidenced in many Sino-Japanese treaties and agreements, as well as in other international conventions, and has been reiterated in numerous statements issued officially by Foreign Offices, including that of Japan.

The report then recited the reasons why the Chinese regard Manchuria as their "first line of defense" in the shape of a buffer against Japan and Russia; as a granary or food supply, and as a region furnishing both seasonal employment and an opportunity for permanent immigration for Chinese from other more overcrowded portions of China.

Third: Japan's argument of self-defense. It directly disposed of Japan's original argument that her occupation of Mukden and south Manchuria had been an act of self-defense. As to this, after a careful and well-poised narration of the incident, it concludes:

The military operations of the Japanese troops during this night [September 18–19] which have been described above, cannot be regarded as measures of legitimate self-defense. In saying this, the Commission does not exclude the hypothesis that the officers on the spot may have thought they were acting in self-defense (Chap. IV).

Fourth: The alleged autonomous origin and present condition of "Manchukuo." As to these points the historical account given by the Commission is particularly strong. Its terse statement of the ultimate facts is as follows:

> The evidence received from all sources has satisfied the Commission that, while there were a number of factors which contributed to the creation of "Manchukuo," the two which, in combination, were most effective, and without which, in our judgment, the new State could not have been formed, were the presence of Japanese troops and the activities of Japanese officials, both civil and military. For this reason, the present régime cannot be considered to have been called into existence by a genuine and spontaneous independence movement (Chap. VI, Part 1).
>
> Such are the opinions of the local population conveyed to us during our tour in Manchuria. After careful study of the evidence presented to us in public and private interviews, in letters and written statements, we have come to the conclusion that there is no general Chinese support for the "Manchukuo Government," which is regarded by the local Chinese as an instrument of the Japanese. (Chap. VI, Part 3).

Fifth: Ultimate finding as a basis for adjudication upon Japan's responsibility. This basic ultimate finding is contained in Chapter IX entitled "The Principles and Conditions of Settlement." It is as follows:

> These facts must be considered by those who debate the issues [viz., the League of Nations]. It is a fact that, without declaration of war, a large area of what was indisputably the

Chinese territory has been forcibly seized and occupied by the armed forces of Japan and has, in consequence of this operation, been separated from and declared independent of the rest of China (Chap. IX, 5th paragraph).

The foregoing are merely excerpts from a powerful and convincing report which should be read as a whole. I do not believe that any impartial reader can peruse its pages and not be convinced that Japan has violated her obligation contained in Article X of the Covenant of the League "to respect and preserve as against external aggression the territorial integrity and existing political independence" of her fellow-member of the League of Nations, China; that she has also violated her obligation under Article II of the Pact of Paris to the effect that the settlement or solution of all disputes or conflicts between the signatories of that treaty, of whatever nature or origin they might be, "shall never be sought except by pacific means;" finally that she also violated her obligations under Article I of the Nine Power Treaty (1) "to respect the sovereignty, the independence and the territorial and administrative integrity of China; (2) to provide the fullest and most unembarrassed opportunity to China to develop and maintain for herself an effective and stable government."

The report, however, did not stop with these findings as to past occurrences. It went much further into the realm of constructive statesmanship. Recognizing that the constantly developing requirements of international life cannot be fully satisfied by the mere adjudication of the rights and wrongs of a past dispute, it proceeded to work out and present to the League its suggestions for a practical solution of the Sino-Japanese problem.

It based these suggestions upon the general principles and conditions which it deduced from the basic facts found in the first eight chapters of its report.

The Commission frankly recognized that a mere restoration of the *status quo ante* would be no solution of the underlying problems out of which the existing conflict had arisen and would merely invite a repetition of the quarrel. It also recognized with irrefutable clarity that a continuance of the present Japanese control in "Manchukuo" would be equally unsatisfactory; that it violated the fundamental principles of existing international obligations as well as the good understanding between the two countries upon which peace in the Far East depends. It was opposed to the interests of China. It disregarded the wishes of the people of Manchuria, and the Commission doubted whether it would ultimately serve the permanent interests of Japan.

The Commission therefore presented a proposed solution designed to conform with the interests of both China and Japan and also with those of Russia; which would conform with the existing multilateral world treaties; which at the same time would recognize China's sovereignty and Japan's legitimate interests in Manchuria; which would maintain general order and security against external aggression; and which would provide for the settlement of future disputes. The solution was to be one which would make for permanence by encouraging an economic rapprochement between China and Japan in place of the present economic warfare, and it also contained a far-reaching provision for international assistance in the reconstruction of China herself.

The League was thus presented not merely with the ascertained facts upon which it could enter a moral judgment as to the past; it was placed in possession of a carefully studied plan for a program of conciliation, devised by a commission of experts which had made itself master of the facts of the situation to an extent unprecedented in Sino-Japanese affairs. By this plan the League might proceed to work out constructively a solution of the problem which might bid fair to be satisfactory to the honor and national requirements of both China and Japan and have a chance of being permanently lasting and effective. This in itself was an immense accomplishment. So far as I am aware, it surpassed anything which has ever been done in a dispute of similar difficulty and importance between two great nations. It represented a great advance in the collective peace efforts of the nations of the world.

VI

ACTION IN THE LEAGUE OF NATIONS UPON THE LYTTON REPORT

A

General Nature of the League's Task and Outside Factors Bearing on It

Even before the report was made public Japan, on September 24th, asked for a six weeks' postponement of the date set for its consideration in order that she might have an opportunity to study it. This request might have been considered a little malapropos in view of Japan's haste in recognizing "Manchukuo" in an evident attempt to forestall League action on the report. Nevertheless it was granted by the League, and in fact every effort to avoid hasty action by the nations and to give opportunity for sober reflection and possible reconsideration by Japan was afforded in the subsequent steps which took place in the League.

The Lytton Commission originally having been appointed by the Council of the League, its report was rendered to that body. But during the period while the Commission was carrying out its investigation, the entire controversy had been transferred from the Council to the Assembly. When, therefore, the Council, after the expiration of Japan's period for study, took up the matter, it transferred the report on November 28th to the Assembly for action. Thereafter the Council ceased to play any active part in the consideration of the dispute.

The Assembly met on December 6, 1932, to consider and take action upon the report. Roughly speaking, the Assembly was then in the position of a court of equity which, having referred a complicated question of fact to a special master or referee to investigate it and make a report of his findings upon the essential facts, had now received from the master his report and findings for action thereon. In such a situation the normal procedure would be for the court, after hearing the argument of the parties upon the master's report, to decide the matter in the light of those findings and, if the findings are approved by the court, to enter judgment accordingly, making the findings its own and decreeing the action, if any, to be taken thereon. Thus in essence the procedure was simple and according to standards which were well understood at least throughout the English-speaking world.

But in a great international transaction such as this there were also other things to be considered. In the first place, the whole situation was a novel one. More than fifty nations were working under machinery for which there were no exact precedents, and in a matter so serious it was important that they should proceed in close conformity to the regulations provided in the Covenant of the League. The Assembly was acting under the powers of Article XV of the Covenant which had been invoked the preceding February by China. Japan had challenged their right to proceed under that Article, and this made it important that their procedure should be careful and consistent with their powers.

Furthermore, the proceeding originally had been begun not under Article XV but under Article XI, and the Lytton Commission of Enquiry had been created under a resolution of the Council adopted while it was acting under Article XI. Article XV, paragraph 4, provides for the making and publication of a report on the facts of the case by the League itself (acting through either the Council or Assembly as the case may be).

There was no reason why the League should not avail itself of the report of the Lytton Commission (if it approved of it) as a basis upon which to make its own report. But Article XV provided under subdivision 3 that before the making of such a report the Assembly should endeavor to effect a settlement of the dispute between the parties. This provision evidently was intended to apply normally to cases arising *ab initio* under Article XV. But in the present case the Council of the League had already spent at least four months of earnest effort under Article XI in trying to effect such a settlement by conciliation. The further those efforts had progressed, the more defiant and contumacious had become the conduct of Japan which, as has already been pointed out, had been steadily extending its conquest over Manchuria in disregard of the repeated requests of the League, and had finally engi-

neered a segregation of this territory of China into a
new state called "Manchukuo." There were, therefore,
very few reasons of merit or hopes of success in any
further efforts at conciliation.

It was true that the Lytton Report had brought up a
new and carefully-worked-out suggestion of a solution
which was now presented to the parties for a peaceful
settlement of their quarrel, but there was no basis in the
experiences of the past year upon which to found any
reasonable hope of success. Every recent act of Japan or
statement by her representatives indicated that she was
still entirely obdurate and determined to pursue her
own course.

Looking at the matter, therefore, from the standpoint
of an observer from outside, it seemed to me that the
principal objective to be kept in mind was that the
League should proceed promptly and decisively to a
judgment on these facts against Japan, thereby bringing
to bear upon that single nation, in addition to the opinion of the Commission, all the momentum of public
opinion that would go with the moral condemnation of
the entire organized world in which she lived.

I felt that while it might be important from the
standpoint of regularity under the provisions of Article
XV for the League to make a new gesture at conciliation, it was very unlikely that it would amount to more
than a gesture and the main thing was for this great
group of nations to keep their resolution steeled up to
the ultimate momentous step of a formal judgment
in respect to Japan.

Furthermore, there were dangers inherent in the very
offer of conciliation. It was very likely to be taken as
an evidence of weakness on the part of the League. It
might well be blazoned out in the press, which necessarily issued its reports hastily and without catching the

procedural reasons for the step, as proof that the League was not going to back up the report of the Lytton Commission. Any delay in pressing steadily the successive steps in the drama, any words of weakness or wavering, were sure to be taken as proof of indecision and thus to mar the effect of the unity of world opinion which alone could be hoped to produce any effect upon the course of Japan.

Other factors had also entered the situation which were likely to affect the resolution of the Assembly. The American election had taken place on November 8th and had resulted in an overwhelming defeat for the administration of President Hoover. The new administration was coming in in March and no one knew what its policy would be in regard to this controversy. The policy of our administration had been for coöperation with the League to an extent exceeding that of any of our predecessors. Since January 1st we had even taken the lead in certain steps which thereafter had been followed by the other nations. Our policy had been made clear in repeated statements. The leaders of the European countries knew by this time what we could be depended upon to do. They necessarily had no such assurance as to what would be the American policy after March 4th. Already rumors were flying about, zealously fostered by propagandists for Japan, that the new administration would completely change the policy of the United States. If such a change should occur, it would necessarily make the position of the Assembly much more difficult.

In addition to this, at the very time when this matter came up for debate before the Assembly the question of the payment of the foreign debts owed to the United States by several of the most important nations of Europe reached its most acute stage. The Assembly of the League began its debate on the Lytton Report on December 6th. A semiannual instalment of interest on these debts fell due on December 15th. The two subjects, therefore, were under consideration coincidently.

A tentative settlement of the reparations due from Germany to these European countries had been reached the preceding June, under which those creditor nations surrendered their right to receive the major part of the reparations which they had been receiving from Germany. They felt that this materially affected their ability to make their own interest payments on their debts to the United States, and that concessions to them should be made by us. Our own Congress, as I have already narrated, had the preceding December announced that no such concession should be made and it refused to authorize negotiations to that end on the part of the American Executive. A very painful impasse on a most delicate subject had thus arisen between us and some of the most influential nations in the League. In spite of a courageous speech by the French Premier, M. Herriot, urging payment of the instalment, the Chamber of Deputies of France had decided to default on their payment due on December 15th. Belgium and other nations made similar defaults. By these occurrences the whole atmosphere of the relations between the United States and these nations of Europe was thoroughly poisoned. Not only the press and people, but many of the leading statesmen on both sides of the Atlantic, were filled with a spirit of mutual resentment and recrimination. It was about as difficult a set of conditions for the carrying through of a great international transaction requiring poise and judicial judgment as could well be conceived. Under such circumstances the Assembly began its debate on the Lytton Report, which had been referred to it.

B

The Debate in the Assembly

The debate was opened by the arguments of China and Japan, made by Dr. Yen and Mr. Matsuoka, respectively. These arguments were then followed by a general debate in the Assembly. Nine of the smaller powers spoke first.[7] They emphasized the worldwide character of the issues involved and the effect which the issue in the Far East would have upon the general cause of peace throughout the world and the future of the League itself. They recognized the difficulties under which the League was acting, but urged that it should stand definitely and with courage and determination behind the Covenant and its own former decisions. They had evidently been deeply impressed by the Lytton Report and many of them at once announced themselves in favor of adopting that report and refusing to recognize the state of "Manchukuo." In short, these smaller powers, while recognizing the desirability of a solution by conciliation if such a solution were possible without surrender of principle, emphasized as of paramount importance the vindication of the great principles which had been violated by Japan.

There then followed the representatives of the large powers, France, Great Britain, Italy and Germany in the order named. The tenor of these speeches all showed a perceptible cleavage from those of their predecessors in that they were more cautious and emphasized the desirability of conciliation as distinguished from judgment. They also all indicated a certain indulgence towards the conduct of Japan in one way or another.

[7] The Irish Free State, Czechoslovakia, Sweden, Norway, Spain, Switzerland, Greece, Guatemala, Uruguay.

The speech of the British Foreign Minister in particular emphasized the arguments in favor of Japan to such an extent that it was at once reported by the American press as a strongly pro-Japanese speech and as evidence that the Assembly would shelve the Lytton Report.[8] Though I was troubled at first, a careful study of our incoming reports and cables reassured me that the press were mistaken in their prophecies as to the ultimate action of the Assembly, and that the speeches apparently favorable to Japan were actuated by a desire to offer conciliation in a genuinely conciliatory atmosphere.

Following the four great powers, representatives of Turkey, Mexico, Poland, Canada, Panama, Chile, Rumania, Hungary, Australia and Colombia spoke in that order and the debate was then concluded by the closing speeches of representatives of China and Japan. Most of the ten smaller powers followed substantially the views of the nine who had preceded the large powers.

The debate was closed on December 9th and the Assembly thereupon adopted a resolution referring the Lytton Report to the Special Committee of Nineteen appointed the preceding March 11th. This committee was directed to study the report, the arguments of parties and the opinions and suggestions expressed in

[8] "In other words, were one to judge of the Report wholly from what Sir John Simon said, he would gain the idea that, so far from bringing a strong indictment against Japan, it was critical of China." Willoughby, *op. cit.*, p. 451.

"As for Sir John Simon, he held out a helping hand to Mr. Matsuoka by drawing attention to certain passages in the Lytton Report which brought out the complicated character of the circumstances of the dispute and the weak points in the Chinese case, and which submitted, *à propos* of future action in Manchuria, that 'a mere restoration of the *status quo ante* would be no solution.' . . . After listening to Sir John Simon's speech, Mr. Matsuoka was reported to have remarked that 'Sir John Simon had said in half an hour, in a few well-chosen phrases, what he—Mr. Matsuoka—had been trying to say in his bad English for the last ten days'." Royal Institute of International Affairs, *Survey* for 1933, p. 492.

the debate, and to draw proposals with a view to the settlement of the dispute which were to be submitted at the earliest possible moment to the Assembly.

Thereafter the Assembly itself did not hold a plenary session until February 21, 1933. In the meantime this special Committee of Nineteen endeavored to perform its duty of seeking a solution by conciliation of the controversy between China and Japan. For this purpose certain draft resolutions were drawn up accompanied by a proposed explanatory statement of the special committee. It was proposed in these papers that the United States and the government of Russia should be invited to become parties in these efforts at conciliation, and copies of these proposed documents were informally submitted to us in Washington and to the government in Moscow. They were of course also submitted to the two disputants, Japan and China. It was a trying time. There was much informal discussion. For the reasons I have already given I had small hope of the successful outcome of any solution by conciliation; I was afraid it would result in an appearance of weakness and vacillation and I was not at all desirous of having our government join in that effort. Yet I did not wish to decline the offer, for fear of discouraging the others in their difficult task. I was saved from the necessity of decision by Japan herself objecting to the extension of such an invitation to either the American government or the government of Russia.

Before the meeting of the Assembly on February 21st the Committee of Nineteen and the members of the Assembly themselves had reached the conclusion that further efforts at conciliation were futile. Japan herself had made this decision inevitable. Her representative at the December meeting of the Assembly had maintained a quite unyielding attitude on all the cardinal issues of the controversy. Among other things he absolutely insisted that no settlement was possible which did not include a recognition by the world of the independence of "Manchukuo." In addition to this, on the 3rd of January Japan's army proceeded to a fresh attack upon hitherto unconquered portions of China. The province of Jehol was invaded. The entrance at Shanhaikwan leading from Manchuria into the main portion of China was attacked and captured. In the clearest way Japan made it evident that her policy would be to extend further the plans of her militarists to acquire dominion not only over Manchuria, but over large additional portions of northeastern China.

The action of the League was further facilitated by the receipt of information as to the future policy of the American government. In the latter part of December I quite unexpectedly received an invitation from Mr. Roosevelt, the President-elect, to visit him for a discussion of foreign policy. On January 9th I went to Hyde Park and spent the day with Mr. Roosevelt discussing with him the matters of our foreign policies in which he was interested. Among these we discussed the events which had taken place in the Far East. Thereafter and before the middle of January, through various unofficial channels, assurance was conveyed to inquirers in Europe that a change in American policy towards the Far Eastern controversy on the part of the new administration need not be apprehended. On January 17th Mr. Roosevelt made a statement in the press which had the effect of confirming these assurances.

Doubts were now resolved on two points: it was clear that Japan would accept no solution except that of a full recognition of the fruits of her conquest, and the fear of a change of American policy was eliminated. The Assembly then proceeded resolutely to its task. The Committee of Nineteen proceeded to prepare a report containing a statement of the facts of the dispute and the recommendations deemed just and proper in regard thereto, as is provided for under Article XV of the Covenant. This momentous report was adopted on February 24th by a unanimous vote of all the nations sitting in the Assembly, Japan only dissenting. It is so voluminous that I cannot refer to it *in extenso*. Yet it is so important that for anyone interested in the controversy it should be read in full. In substance it adopted fully and without modification the findings of the Lytton Commission of Enquiry and it recommended a solution following the lines of the report of that Commission. It recognized China's sovereignty over Manchuria. It found that neither the initial military operations of the Japanese troops at Mukden and South Manchuria nor the subsequent military measures of Japan developed in the course of the dispute could be regarded as measures of self-defense. While recognizing that legitimate grievances by each party against the other had existed prior to September 18, 1931, creating tension between them on that date, it held that no question of Chinese responsibility could arise for the development of events since September 18, 1931. It found the organization of Manchuria into the new state of "Manchukuo" to have been due to the activities of Japanese officials acting with the assistance and direction of the Japanese General Staff and under the support of the presence of the Japanese troops, and it held that "Manchukuo" could not be considered as the result of a spontaneous and genuine independence movement, and that it was not supported by the Chinese population of Manchuria. It found that "Manchukuo" had not been recognized by any other state than Japan and that such recognition was incompatible with the spirit of the resolution of the League of March 11, 1932. It provided that the nations which were members of the League "in adopting the present report . . . will continue not to recognize this régime [Manchukuo] either *de jure* or *de facto*."

The report in short thus amounted to a judgment against Japan as to her responsibility for the controversy which had been brought before the Assembly. In its recommendations for future action it provided

(1) for the evacuation of the Japanese troops from their positions outside of their original zone of the South Manchuria Railway, and

(2) for the establishment of a governmental organization in Manchuria under the sovereignty and compatible with the administrative integrity of China, and yet which should provide a wide measure of autonomy consistent with its historic traditions, with the rights and interests of Japan and other outside nations, and in general with the principles of the multilateral treaties.

It then recommended the opening of negotiations between the two parties for the attainment of this solution along the lines recommended by the Lytton Commission. As a sanction to assist in effectuating its decision it pledged its membership not to recognize the existing state of "Manchukuo."[9]

[9] The findings of fact of the Assembly upon the controversy and the statement of its recommendations for the future are printed as Appendix IV. A full copy of the report can be found among the records of the League of Nations. It is also printed in full as an appendix to Willoughby, *The Sino-Japanese Controversy and the League of Nations*, p. 689 *et seq.*

On February 25th, the day following the adoption of this report by the Assembly, I gave out the following statement to the press:

In the situation which has developed out of the controversy between China and Japan, the purpose of the United States has coincided in general with that of the League of Nations, the common objective being maintenance of peace and settlement of international disputes by pacific means. In pursuance of that objective, while the League of Nations has been exercising jurisdiction over a controversy between two of its members, the Government of the United States has endeavored to give support, reserving to itself independence of judgment with regard to method and scope, to the efforts of the League on behalf of peace.

The findings of fact arrived at by the League and the understanding of the facts derived by the American Government from reports made to it by its own representatives are in substantial accord. In the light of its findings of fact the Assembly of the League has formulated a measured statement of conclusions. With those conclusions the American Government is in general accord. In their affirmations, respectively of the principle of non-recognition and their attitude in regard thereto, the League and the United States are on common ground. The League has recommended principles of settlement. In so far as appropriate under the treaties to which it is a party, the American Government expresses its general endorsement of the principles thus recommended.

The American Government earnestly hopes that the two nations now engaged in controversy, both of which have been long in friendly relationship with our own and other peoples, may find it possible in the light of world opinion to conform their policies to the need and the desire of the family of nations that disputes between nations shall be settled by none but pacific means.

On March 4, 1933, a week after this judgment of the Assembly on February 24th, my own term of office as Secretary of State terminated.

On March 27, 1933, Japan gave notice of her intention to withdraw from the League of Nations. This, however regrettable, was a logical result of Japan's preceding action. Her continuance of association with an international society whose principles and rules she had deliberately and flagrantly broken could have been nothing but an embarrassment and a likelihood of future danger to the other members of that society as well as to the rest of the world.

PART FIVE

SOME CONCLUSIONS

SOME CONCLUSIONS

DURING the foregoing controversy between China and Japan, which I have portrayed in this book, the two main purposes of the American government may be described as follows:

First: The purpose of preserving our future relations with China by adequately fulfilling our obligations to that country under enlightened treaties heretofore entered into by our government.

Second: The purpose of preserving from destruction the foundations of a system of coöperative action for the preservation of peace which had been established under certain post-war multilateral treaties, to two of which we were parties.

These two purposes have sometimes been criticized as being idealistic and as transcending the usual objectives of diplomatic action, such as the preservation of commercial rights. I am quite ready to face such criticism. Even in normal times a Foreign Minister must never permit his vision of the future permanent welfare of his country to become obscured by the pressure of immediate interests. But in times like the present, when new developments are rapidly taking place in the world and crises are arising almost every day which may enormously affect the long-distance future, the danger of a narrow vision and a short-range objective is greatly increased.

A

THE OBJECTIVE OF FULFILLING OUR OBLIGATIONS TO CHINA

Taking up then the first of these two objectives: The relations of the United States towards China and the Far Eastern world in one vital respect are different from those of any European power towards that world. Several European powers have far larger commercial and territorial interests in China than we, but geographically they are remote; we are adjacent. They are in a sense absentee landlords; we, a neighbor. The repercussions which are possible in a modernization of the Far East can directly affect us in ways which would not affect them. The Pacific Ocean is no longer a barrier but a means of communication.

That there was a fundamental difference in the viewpoint of our country towards China from that of even those of the European nations whose normal attitude towards government and international relations is most similar to ours, was forced upon my attention continually through the long drawn out diplomatic efforts recorded in these pages. But its roots and reasons were at first not adequately realized even when I was confronted by their manifestations.

I kept feeling the difference between our view and that of the British Foreign Office long before I had time to reflect and analyze the reasons for it. Recently there has taken place a movement in British opinion itself, an allusion to which may help explain to British readers what I refer to in respect to the Far East. The American feeling as to the Far East which gradually gathered in force and influenced the attitude of its government in 1932 was in character not unlike the feeling of those elements of the British people who expressed themselves so forcibly in the "Peace Ballot" concerning coöperation with the League of Nations in June, 1935. This latter view has been described as representing a deep-seated "instinctive" feeling of the "British democracy." Such a description might well fit the character of the American feeling towards stability and fair play in the Far East. It is not measured by the volume of our trade nor by a desire to extend our commerce. We are near enough to Oriental peoples to have felt the impact of their immigration. We have had to defend ourselves vigorously against that impact. Sometimes we have done so by methods which have seemed to them to be harsh and irritating. But by that same token it is demonstrated that we recognize that they are near enough to us and sufficiently in our world to make it important that international relations in the Far East shall be upon a basis of stability.

Japan's attack upon China in September, 1931, was of interest to the American people not only because it was an attack upon the fundamental basis of collective action in the modern world—fidelity to treaty obligations—but because it was also a destructive assault upon the good relations which must exist between neighbor nations if order and stability are to be preserved in the North Pacific. In other words, the shock to our interest in collective fidelity was much accentuated because the trouble was in our part of the world. The intrusion into that world of a militaristic adventure on the part of a nation as thoroughly armed as Japan, and the recrudescence of theories of colonial markets which, so far as the Western Hemisphere is concerned, had passed away with the colonial power of

Spain, was a shock to us of the same nature as the exploitation by a rearmed Germany of one of her European neighbors would be to Great Britain. In passing, I may observe that this analogy will serve as an explanation to European readers of the difference between the so-called "Japanese Monroe Doctrine" and the original American doctrine. To liken the aggressive policy now being pushed by Japan under the name of the "Monroe Doctrine in Asia" to that defensive bulwark of local independence and self-government among the South American republics which was provided by the announcement in 1823 of the American doctrine, should be fantastic enough to be seen through by any impartial observer.

The future of China is one of the great problems of the ages. But one thing is clear—she must develop in her own way. She cannot be dominated or driven by outside force into an alien or undesired form of evolution. Hers is the most persistent national culture in the world. Forty centuries have demonstrated that fact. Also the essentially peaceful character of her domestic and internal culture is now the main stabilizing factor of Asia. Its loss would be a blow which would directly affect the peace of her neighbors, including America. It would be a very shortsighted policy if that loss should come through a disregard of its treaty obligations by the American government.

Those Americans who think that all that is necessary to solve the Manchurian problem is for the United States and Japan to patch up a *modus vivendi* which will be agreeable to Japan, forget this far more important underlying problem of China. At the present moment no agreement or arrangement which would be consented to by Japan would be other than destructive and repugnant to China.

Before the ultimate solution of this problem is arrived at, we may be faced with an intermediate period of stress and storm. This, however, is not a necessarily hopeless attitude or view, nor is it inconsistent with the ultimate development of American friendship with Japan. But the elements of such friendship necessarily are (1) that it must not involve the sacrifice of our friendship with China, and (2) that it must not involve the cynical abandonment of treaties which are important to our own development along with the rest of the world.

It is my belief that we are entitled to look forward with hope to an eventual development of Japan which will be consistent with both these obligations. Some of her greatest leaders have shown an appreciation of the duties of good citizenship in the world equal to those of any other country. I am well aware of the difficulty of the problem by which these leaders were faced in 1931 as well as the earnest efforts which they made to preserve the better order of international life. The problem in Japan was not that of a voluntary reversion on the part of her entire people to militarism and the methods of past ages. It was far more complex than that. The worldwide economic depression produced similar suffering and unsettlement in Japan to that which it produced elsewhere and there resulted from it among the younger generations of her stricken people the same restlessness against those who were representative of the old order.

For ten years prior to 1931 she had been providing for her growing population by developing her foreign trade and by pursuing a general policy of peace, in harmony with the general purpose of the outside world. But under the effect of the great depression in 1930 and 1931 her foreign trade fell off nearly fifty per cent and the pressure of that change resulted in the suffering and restlessness which I have just mentioned. Her discontented youth then turned to and availed themselves of the army leadership and its theories of forcible exploitation in Manchuria as a means of successfully overthrowing the conservative statesmen at home, against whom their animus had been excited. Thus in Japan in 1931 militarism and imperialism were reënforced by the same radical movement which had come from economic unrest. That unusual combination in a people as naturally patriotic as the Japanese has greatly accentuated the difficulties of those who were striving for moderation and peace and the preservation of international responsibility.

But reckless action against China did not remedy the condition of Japan's commerce or balance her budget and thus reduce the suffering of her people. It produced exactly the contrary effect. It plunged her balance sheet still deeper into the red and it resulted in a disastrous boycott of her goods by the second best customer which she had in the world—China. Japan's internal troubles could not be remedied or alleviated by unlawfully hacking away at the Young Marshal's government in Mukden. On the contrary, those steps were certain immediately to react adversely to Japan's financial condition, and they did. When several years later she began to recover rapidly from her depression, it was due to the expansion of her foreign trade elsewhere and not to her adventure in Manchuria.

There is today this much ground for encouragement: one of the factors in the shape of her economic depression which produced the original overthrow of Japan's conservative international policy has been alleviated. True, her imperialistic military leaders, having been placed in the saddle, are still eager to push their adven-

ture in China further and further. But there is beginning to appear evidence that they have not behind them
today the same pressure caused by popular discontent
as they had five years ago. The recent elections showed
decided gains among the anti-militarist elements in the
Japanese Diet. The recent outbreak of terrorism among
certain units of the army was curbed with more courageous decision than was manifested four years ago. In
spite of lamentable assassinations, most of Japan's conservative leaders as well as the moderate elements of
her people still exist. Sooner or later they will again
come into power. They have believed that the welfare
of their own country depended on the cultivation of
good will and friendly trade with China and not upon
the forcible dismemberment and exploitation of that
country. They have believed, like us and like most of
the rest of the world, that the world is so bound together today that no one nation can permanently pros-
per at the expense of peace and friendly relations
throughout that world. The unanimous condemnation
of aggressive policy which took place at Geneva in
1933; the unanimous condemnation of the forcible exploitation of Manchuria and the creation of "Manchukuo" will, I believe, play powerfully into the hands
of these conservative forces in their efforts to terminate
the military adventure.

During the past eighty years no nation has shown
itself more sensitive towards the good opinion of the
outside world than has Japan. In every step of her
rapid development into modernism she has been keenly
alive to praise or criticism from abroad. Her recent
efforts to explain her action in Manchuria by continued
propaganda is evidence that this feeling still persists.
With such a people the non-recognition of "Manchukuo" stands as a constant public reminder of the moral

condemnation by the rest of the world of Japan's aggressive action towards China. On such a nation that
reminder is certain to have lasting effect. When the
moderate elements of her population who are now
under terroristic restraint again come into their own,
the judgment at Geneva may be a strong influence tend-
ing to bring Japan back into her normal position in
international life.

Such a result will be promoted and made more certain by the fact that China, in spite of the blows which
she has received, is still progressing towards economic
and administrative unity. Despite the advances of
Japan's military expeditions in the north, despite the
defection of an occasional provincial Chinese leader or
general, and despite the financial hardships brought
about by the unsettlement of her finances through foreign purchases of silver, the economic development of
China through the improvement of her lines of communication has been going on under an orderly and
systematic program. In spite of the handicaps under
which she has labored, she is showing in this fundamental method more economic progress towards national unity than at any previous time.

Therefore I believe that there is rational ground to
hope that much sooner than now seems likely Japan
will again realize that her own lasting interest is more
dependent upon friendly commercial and political relations with China than with any other nation; that such
relations cannot be cultivated by a forcible exploitation
of China; and that, in the equitable settlement which
may then be attained, the opinion and judgment of the
world as expressed unanimously in 1933 will be,
whether publicly admitted or not, a potent factor. If
that occurs, the strong position taken by the American

government in the Manchurian crisis of 1931 will be thoroughly justified.

B

THE OBJECTIVE OF PRESERVING A SYSTEM OF COÖPERATIVE ACTION FOR THE MAINTENANCE OF PEACE

We who worked in the State Department in 1931 realized that in the interconnected and industrialized world of today war has become immeasurably more destructive and likely to spread than in former ages, and that, unless it is controlled, our civilization will be in real peril. We believed that it can be effectively controlled only by the coöperative action of all the nations. We also recognized that if war came no nation, however powerful and isolated, could be immune from economic damage or from the possibility of actual involvement. In the world before us the League of Nations represented the only existing and general system for such coöperative war prevention. In the crisis which confronted us manifestly the only course for us to follow was one of the heartiest coöperation with the League directed towards the common objective of preventing a spread of the hostilities and eventually of restoring peace.

If we had not done this; if we had stood aside in a problem which was in our part of the world and where Europe naturally would feel that we should be peculiarly interested, the League's effort would have been hamstrung from the beginning and the two other great peace treaties, which our government had initiated and to which we were signatories, inevitably would have become dead letters. So, under the conditions with which we were faced, we endeavored to do our best to coöperate with the action of the League.

In the present frightened and discouraged world it is being questioned—was the effort worthwhile? Is the League system faulty and futile? Is the whole conception of collective action a fundamental error? Is it utterly impossible to unite mankind into a war preventive system? Is there anything left for us to do but to go back to the old methods of defensive armaments alone even if those methods have shown themselves so faulty and destructive in the modern world? These are far-reaching questions and in the space at my disposal here I can only undertake to sketch the answers as I myself see them.

The history of the Sino-Japanese controversy of 1931 is the record of the arraignment, the trial and the condemnation of a great power for the violation of certain new standards of conduct aimed at preventing international aggression. This was the first time in man's history that such an attempt had been made. These standards of conduct which the trial enforced had been in existence for less than a dozen years.[1] Nevertheless the proceeding was carried through with dignity and firmness to the final step of condemnation by the forty-two nations sitting in the Assembly of the League, and their verdict was unanimous. Following the example set by the January 7th note of the American government, this verdict was also reënforced by the concurrent agreement of these forty-two nations not to recognize "Manchukuo."

The coöperative action of the nations very possibly prevented a declaration of war in the Far East, a blockade of China's coast, and a direct annexation of Manchuria by Japan. For a time it even restricted and slowed up some of the movements of the Japanese

[1] The Covenant of the League of Nations had been signed in 1919, the Nine Power Treaty in 1922 and the Pact of Paris in 1928.

army, notably the advance on Chinchow. But it failed to halt Japan's aggression against China. This may have been for a variety of reasons which prevented more effective results from the coöperative proceeding. The great depression, the remoteness of the *locus in quo* from the nations which were the natural leaders of the League, the promptness with which the Japanese army acted and presented the world with a *fait accompli*, and especially the novelty of the situation and of the remedial machinery which rendered coöperative action slow and difficult and was responsible in part for the cautiousness with which the nations acted and the differences of policy which arose between them, all served as powerful restrictions upon the vigor of action and the effectiveness of results.

The subsequent Japanese advances in North China took place after it became evident that the League was entangled in complications over the unsettled conditions in Germany and Italy; in other words, after the League's united front against Japan had become divided on other questions of greater immediate moment to the principal European powers. Yet, as I write these lines, the bond of non-recognition of "Manchukuo" which helped to hold together the former united front still stands loyally adhered to by practically all the nations which entered into it. Hence that covenant may still serve to promote an ultimate just settlement of the Sino-Japanese controversy.

We are too prone to be unduly influenced and discouraged by the shadows of events which are near at hand. Measured by the ordinary progress of human evolution in international conduct, the achievement of the League of Nations in the Manchurian controversy was a signal and momentous event marking a great step forward from previous conditions. We have only to look back seventeen years to measure that contrast. In July, 1914, we witnessed the spectacle of a high-minded British Foreign Minister seeking to avert a world disaster and yet unable to persuade the representatives of the interested nations even to sit down at a table with him and talk the matter over. There was no machinery in existence by which he could compel such a consultation. Kings and emperors wrote futile telegrams to each other while their governments drifted into a suicidal war. The alleged complicity of the Serbian government in the murders at Serajevo was clearly a justiciable issue of fact, but the world lacked even the most rudimentary machinery by which the truth as to such allegations compulsorily could be determined. Surely the Manchurian controversy showed an enormous advance in the construction of the elements of international judicial procedure, and surely the existence of such a procedure marks an important and necessary progress in the international world.

Another measure of the soundness of the conception of collective action in war prevention is afforded by the fact that mankind itself apparently is coming to believe in such a system and that the movement for it has had a growing popular support throughout the world. Evidence of this has been forcing itself upon our attention in various ways and from quite different quarters.

In the first place there is the intelligent and loyal support which has been given to the collective system of the League by the peoples of the small powers throughout the world. These nations ever since the formation of the League have steadily supported it and in the debates on the subject of the controversy between China and Japan their leaders were preëminent. In fact it was not until the Assembly of the League, with its predominant membership of smaller nations, took jurisdiction of the controversy that the judicial procedure began to move with firmness and precision. These smaller nations have shown throughout the history of the League their firm belief in the necessity as well as the possibility of establishing a reign of law in the world as distinguished from what has been called "power diplomacy." It is beside the mark to criticize their decision as an irresponsible one. It doubtless has been influenced by the fact that being smaller and weaker than the great powers, they have recognized more readily the need of the protection which can only come from collective strength in support of a reign of law. But this is really proof that their vision is free from some of the obstacles which serve to distort the vision of representatives of some of the larger powers. The sooner the leaders of the great powers recognize that there is no safety even for their own countries from at least the economic damage of a modern war in an interdependent world, the sooner will accuracy of vision in this respect become general.[2]

So I think it is safe to say that one of the most cogent proofs of the soundness of the movement for collective action is the unwavering popular support which it has received from substantially all the small powers of the world.

Furthermore, during the progress of the Manchurian controversy proof of a growing interest and support for our policy of frank coöperation with the League was evident within the United States. We had embarked upon that policy with apprehension but we found behind us a constantly growing interest and support. Even today when the threat of war and the chaotic conditions in Europe have appalled America, there is neverthe-

[2] In saying this I have in mind very particularly some of the leaders of my own country.

less a greater interest and a more intelligent study of foreign relations going on in many new centers of international education throughout our country than ever before in our history. Included within those studies is a constantly growing interest in the importance and possibilities of coöperative action.

Finally, after the Manchurian episode was ended, there was given what was perhaps the most striking demonstration of all. This was when the British people having in June, 1935, voted by enormous majorities in favor of supporting the system of the League of Nations, thereafter in December when the hand of official leadership had slipped, successfully insisted by the voice of public opinion that the experiment of economic sanctions be continued. In the light of such demonstrations of popular interest, I think it is not rash to say that in all those countries where public opinion is influential and is not suppressed by autocratic government, there is a steadily accelerating movement to seek a method of limiting and preventing war through the coöperation of the nations of the earth.

Why should this not be so? We have witnessed a similar evolution of man's treatment of individual combat within domestic communities. A thousand years ago in European communities the ordeal by battle settled the private quarrels of our ancestors and responsibility for the punishment of homicide rested not upon the community but upon the relatives of the victim. Private war in the shape of the duel in affairs of honor lasted into modern times. Yet the irrepressible development of mankind has terminated such methods of violence and has substituted the peaceful methods of law.

Can it be doubted that the same transition must eventually follow in the larger organizations of mankind until finally it becomes universal? The dangerous feature in the situation is that the new organization of the world has rendered speed necessary in an evolution of character which might otherwise await the leisurely progress of the centuries. We have recently created a civilization so fragile and weapons of war so dangerous that unless we speed up the development of the organized self-control of humanity, which hitherto has been notoriously slow in its growth, our entire civilization may be in peril. Personally I am not worried lest the new order do not come. I am only worried lest it be so delayed in coming that we suffer irreparable damage in the meantime.

I believe, therefore, that we need not be troubled as to the soundness of the theory of collective action in general for the solution of our problem of war prevention. There remains the question of the methods of the systems which have been attempted. Can we place our finger upon any defects in those systems which have brought about the failures by which we are now so greatly disturbed? To a certain extent I think we can.

The League of Nations is the principal existing machinery for collective action in war prevention. The provisions of that Covenant have been chiefly directed to the conciliation and adjudication of controversies and to the restraint of aggression. In those directions even its critics have admitted the progress which has been made and the wisdom of the gradual and careful growth which has been obtained. The League has developed a technique which has been most valuable in the solution of minor but dangerous controversies. It has discovered and revealed the value of constant face to face discussion as a safety valve for incipient international irritations. It has also shown a capacity for setting on foot the solution of economic international problems which may lead to immensely important results. It has been a medium for invoking and using the help of experts. Its assistance to the restoration of stable currency and exchanges in Central Europe in 1926 was admirable; likewise the economic rescues of Austria, Hungary, Estonia, Greece and Bulgaria.

But recently the League has been confronted with major problems arising out of the discontent of powerful nations, which have asserted that their political rights were unjustly treated or their economic necessities suppressed and thwarted. On these problems the war-preventive functions of the League seem in a fair way to break down. Not only have the provisions of the Covenant designed to meet the necessity for economic or political changes in the world been narrow and imperfect, but from the beginning the League itself has been tied up to the Treaty of Versailles and has thus been made the agency for an attempt to preserve the *status quo* in a situation which required change and growth. This seems to me the chief defect in the League's constitution, and I believe it to be a very serious one.[3]

This world of ours is a growing, developing community. In it there are great inequalities among the nations in respect to population, land and resources; some of long standing, others arising out of recent political changes as a result of war. In such a world a reign of law, however desirable, cannot be used as a strait-jacket to prevent growth and change and still less to protect injustice and preserve hardship. Any attempt to make such use of a system of war prevention will ultimately cause explosions which may well destroy the entire system.

[3] On this point see the interesting address of Mr. John Foster Dulles entitled "Peaceful Change Within the Society of Nations," delivered at Princeton University March 19, 1936, as one of the Stafford Little Foundation series.

As I have pointed out, this was not the case in the Manchurian controversy where Japan, though suffering from economic discontent and hardship, took violent action not at all designed to alleviate her pressure and suffering. Her need was commerce; she did not either seek or obtain that when she attacked, dismembered and angered her best customer. But I think it may be the case in other situations now exciting apprehension in Europe, and I fear that Europe will never achieve a permanent system of war prevention, no matter how sound a judicial system she may devise, until she has provided methods of relieving fundamental causes of pressure resulting in discontent.

Take a single example: Between 1870 and 1914 Germany acquired a surplus population exceeding by approximately twenty-eight million people the number which had ever been supported by the soil of Germany alone. During that period this population was supported by international trade, a very large proportion of Germany's food and other supplies being imported from the outside world. Today that population remains but the trade which supported it is largely gone—cut off by the new system of tariffs and barriers and the uncertainties of a fluctuating exchange which together prevent the development of her former commerce. The same is true of other European nations.[4]

Such a situation necessarily calls for readjustments. What is true in the sudden changes made by war in the condition of certain European countries is true in lesser degree throughout the world. World organization has never been rigid. National boundaries and national trade routes have always been subject to change. In the past those changes have commonly been

[4] See *Democracy and Nationalism in Europe* by the author, Chap. II, where this subject is treated.

made by war. Any attempt therefore to organize a world system so as to prevent war must provide for the necessary peaceful changes in a world which has always been dynamic and not static.

On its face and in its entire scope such a problem of providing constructive machinery to meet the changing conditions of a changeful world is most difficult. Peaceful changes of national boundaries are traditionally difficult. But fortunately in the modern world there is a safety valve which will relieve most of the pressure arising from inequalities in world organization. That is freedom of commercial intercourse. Americans may well recall the early example of their own history which, while differing in many respects from the dangerous situation in modern Europe, yet has sufficient similarity to be helpful and significant. The close of the Revolutionary War left thirteen discontented and quarrelsome sovereign states in North America. They had plenty of land and the memories of a successful foreign war, but they were war-torn, impoverished and in a desperately bad economic condition. Inflation was rife. Their commerce and industry were prostrate. Their respective natural resources and occupations were widely variant. During the seven years following the cessation of hostilities with Great Britain they drifted rapidly into discord and anarchy. They had acute boundary and tariff troubles. They began to develop separatist national feeling and even drifted towards actual hostility one with another.

Eventually they found their remedy in two fundamental economic reforms. They adopted a system of no tariffs and free trade between the thirteen states and they established a stable and uniform currency. The necessity of these reforms was the chief impelling cause which induced these thirteen jealous little sovereignties

to frame and ratify the Federal Constitution. Within a
very few years prosperity, credit and contentment were
acquired. Boundary troubles completely ceased. The
economic foundations were laid upon which it was
possible to build a successful structure for the peaceful
judicial solution of their interstate controversies.
Had it been possible at the close of the Great War
mandatorily to provide a similar prohibition against
the erection of tariff barriers between the war-torn
successor states of Central Europe, I believe that industrial recovery would have followed and that the pressure now threatening Europe with a new war might
have been avoided. Under more difficult conditions the
task of providing some such remedy must be begun
now.[5] At all events provisions must be made in any collective system, by which just grievances, economic and
political, may be prevented from provoking an irrepressible outbreak of violence. The preventive hygiene
of opening trade relations may prove far more effective
than the surgery of a judicial determination of controversies after they have arisen.

I believe that this subject has a direct bearing upon
the much mooted problem of sanctions. Whether an
attempt to enforce sanctions will lead to an irrepressible
war depends as much upon the nature of other factors
as it does upon the nature of the sanctions. Upon the
justice of the controversy, for example, will depend the
strength of the united front against the recalcitrant
nation. And a front perfectly united behind a just cause
will in all probability carry further with very mild
sanctions than a weak or vacillating front trying to apply the strongest sanctions. In a thoroughly organized

[5] A suggestion of such action underlay the proposal by M. Briand of France
for a "United States of Europe" in 1930. Progress on it was frustrated by
the coming of the great depression.

union, like the federation of the United States, the decisions of the Supreme Court upon the controversies of the sovereign states are uniformly obeyed under the sanction of public opinion alone. Somewhere between the conceivable extremes a successful collective system for the preservation of peace in the world at large, I believe, will gradually find its own system of sanctions. But it will be greatly assisted in so doing when it also provides for a constructive solution of those economic problems which lead men to desperation.

In the intervening period problems are being faced by those in authority as to which no critic can afford to be either dogmatic or uncharitable. My own tendency is to believe that in cases of doubt it is usually safer as well as wiser to steer by the steady objective of a reign of law than to trust to the varying compromises of "power diplomacy."

In any system of sanctions much will depend upon the wisdom and vigor of leadership with which the first international tests of the system are carried through to completion. Ultimate success will greatly be facilitated by momentum. Almost any form of collective action, provided it has been shown to command the faith of its members and to have been capable of being carried through to a beneficent and successful conclusion, would be accepted in a world which is looking anxiously for a solution of the problem of putting restraint on war. The influence of success would not be confined to the League of Nations itself. It would be very potent, I believe, in America. My observation of public opinion in America, while the League was proceeding unfalteringly with its program of sanctions during the autumn of 1935, confirmed me in this view. Coöperation between the United States and a League which had shown itself steadfast and successful in carrying through to the end its organized machinery of war prevention, I believe would be a comparatively easy matter.

In this book I have emphasized our experiences in coöperation with the government of Great Britain because of my confident feeling that in the ultimate development of collective action in Europe, whether through the present League of Nations or otherwise, it is inevitable that upon the government of Great Britain and her dominions will fall great responsibilities of leadership. I believe it is vital that the course of such leadership shall not be hampered by the fear that collective action will be stabbed in the back by states which, like the American government, are not members. To assure such security, coöperation between the two governments in all those executive steps which constitute so much the major part of international action should become frank, efficient and traditional. If I have made any statement herein which seems critical, it is not because I do not fully realize the difficulties under which the British government has labored or that I believe that my own government has been free from error. I have written as I have because I believe that frankness is possible between our two countries, and that in frankness alone can a permanent tradition of genuine coöperation between us be built up. I am happy to say, from my own experience in attempting it, that I believe that it is not only possible but easy, and I further believe that my own feeling as to the importance of Anglo-American coöperation in the solution of the problems of this troubled world is shared by the great majority of my countrymen.

In conclusion, and writing at what may seem the nadir of the world's post-war hopes, I believe that the vital qualities needed today are faith in the historic traditions of our race; fairmindedness towards each other's difficulties; and above all, courage. There is ample basis for intelligent hope. Our world may seem to be falling into ruins about us. Our progress may seem to have been set back to the old starting point. Even the task of beginning over again may seem to have been rendered impossible by the mistakes of the present. But such feelings are the common incidents of every prolonged struggle. Every soldier has met them on every hard-fought battle-field, and knows that they will evaporate before sustained courage.

We may none of us be able, from our restricted viewpoints, accurately to forecast the immediate future. But we at least know that the long progress in freedom, in tolerance and in justice which for literally millions of years our race has been gradually making—including that growth in organized self-control which we call popular government—will not be permanently destroyed. Our present world, however imperfect, will not wholly dissolve into chaos. The very inventions which have made that world interdependent and apparently fragile, and which have thus laid upon us our present difficulties, at the same time have rendered impossible any general destruction of knowledge and experience.

Our overwhelming problems will ultimately be solved; they will be solved by progress on the course already charted by mankind, and according to the principles for which the wise, the liberal, and the brave of all ages have labored. It is our business to see to it, through the exercise of faith and courage, that the intervening period of doubt and uncertainty be rendered as brief and innocuous as possible.

THE COVENANT OF THE LEAGUE OF NATIONS[1]

THE HIGH CONTRACTING PARTIES,

In order to promote international coöperation and to achieve international peace and security

by the acceptance of obligations not to resort to war,

by the prescription of open, just and honourable relations between nations,

by the firm establishment of the understandings of international law as the actual rule of conduct among Governments, and

by the maintenance of justice and a scrupulous respect for all treaty obligations in the dealings of organised peoples with one another,

Agree to this Covenant of the League of Nations.

ARTICLE I

1. The original Members of the League of Nations shall be those of the Signatories which are named in the Annex to this Covenant and also such of those other States named in the Annex as shall accede without reservation to this Covenant. Such accession shall be effected by a Declaration deposited with the Secretariat within two months of the coming into force of the Covenant. Notice thereof shall be sent to all other Members of the League.

2. Any fully self-governing State, Dominion or Colony not named in the Annex may become a Member of the League if its admission is agreed to by two-thirds of the Assembly, provided that it shall give

[1] The text is that published by the Secretariat of the League of Nations. It is numbered in conformity with the resolution adopted by the seventh ordinary session of the Assembly on September 16, 1926, and containing Article 6 as amended, in force since August 13, 1924, Articles 12, 13 and 15 as amended, in force since September 26, 1924, and Article 4 as amended, in force since July 29, 1926. The texts printed in italics indicate the amendments.

effective guarantees of its sincere intention to observe its international obligations, and shall accept such regulations as may be prescribed by the League in regard to its military, naval and air forces and armaments.

3. Any Member of the League may, after two years' notice of its intention so to do, withdraw from the League, provided that all its international obligations and all its obligations under this Covenant shall have been fulfilled at the time of its withdrawal.

ARTICLE 2

The action of the League under this Covenant shall be effected through the instrumentality of an Assembly and of a Council, with a permanent Secretariat.

ARTICLE 3

1. The Assembly shall consist of Representatives of the Members of the League.

2. The Assembly shall meet at stated intervals and from time to time, as occasion may require at the Seat of the League or at such other place as may be decided upon.

3. The Assembly may deal at its meetings with any matter within the sphere of action of the League or affecting the peace of the world.

4. At meetings of the Assembly each Member of the League shall have one vote, and may have not more than three Representatives.

ARTICLE 4

1. The Council shall consist of representatives of the Principal Allied and Associated Powers, together with Representatives of four other Members of the League. These four Members of the League shall be selected by the Assembly from time to time in its discretion. Until the appointment of the Representatives of the four Members of the League first selected by the Assembly, Representatives of Belgium, Brazil, Greece and Spain shall be members of the Council.

2. With the approval of the majority of the Assembly, the Council may name additional Members of the League, whose Representatives shall always be Members of the Council; the Council with like approval may increase the number of Members of the League to be selected by the Assembly for representation on the Council.

2. *bis. The Assembly shall fix by a two-thirds majority the rules dealing with the election of the non-permanent Members of the*

Council, and particularly such regulations as relate to their term of office and the conditions of re-eligibility.

3. The Council shall meet from time to time as occasion may require, and at least once a year, at the Seat of the League, or at such other place as may be decided upon.

4. The Council may deal at its meetings with any matter within the sphere of action of the League or affecting the peace of the world.

5. Any Member of the League not represented on the Council shall be invited to send a Representative to sit as a member at any meeting of the Council during the consideration of matters specially affecting the interests of that Member of the League.

6. At meetings of the Council, each Member of the League represented on the Council shall have one vote, and may have not more than one Representative.

ARTICLE 5

1. Except where otherwise expressly provided in this Covenant or by the terms of the present Treaty, decisions at any meeting of the Assembly or of the Council shall require the agreement of all the Members of the League represented at the meeting.

2. All matters of procedure at meetings of the Assembly or of the Council, including the appointment of Committees to investigate particular matters, shall be regulated by the Assembly or by the Council and may be decided by a majority of the Members of the League represented at the meeting.

3. The first meeting of the Assembly and the first meeting of the Council shall be summoned by the President of the United States of America.

ARTICLE 6

1. The permanent Secretariat shall be established at the Seat of the League. The Secretariat shall comprise a Secretary-General and such secretaries and staff as may be required.

2. The first Secretary-General shall be the person named in the Annex; thereafter the Secretary-General shall be appointed by the Council with the approval of the majority of the Assembly.

3. The secretaries and the staff of the Secretariat shall be appointed by the Secretary-General with the approval of the Council.

4. The Secretary-General shall act in that capacity at all meetings of the Assembly and of the Council.

5. *The expenses of the League shall be borne by the Members of the League in the proportion decided by the Assembly.*

ARTICLE 7

1. The Seat of the League is established at Geneva.

2. The Council may at any time decide that the Seat of the League shall be established elsewhere.

3. All positions under or in connection with the League, including the Secretariat, shall be open equally to men and women.

4. Representatives of the Members of the League and officials of the League when engaged on the business of the League shall enjoy diplomatic privileges and immunities.

5. The buildings and other property occupied by the League or its officials or by Representatives attending its meetings shall be inviolable.

ARTICLE 8

1. The Members of the League recognise that the maintenance of peace requires the reduction of national armaments to the lowest point consistent with national safety and the enforcement by common action of international obligations.

2. The Council, taking account of the geographical situation and circumstances of each State, shall formulate plans for such reduction for the consideration and action of the several Governments.

3. Such plans shall be subject to reconsideration and revision at least every 10 years.

4. After these plans shall have been adopted by the several Governments, the limits of armaments therein fixed shall not be exceeded without the concurrence of the Council.

5. The Members of the League agree that the manufacture by private enterprise of munitions and implements of war is open to grave objections. The Council shall advise how the evil effects attendant upon such manufacture can be prevented, due regard being had to the necessities of those Members of the League which are not able to manufacture the munitions and implements of war necessary for their safety.

6. The Members of the League undertake to interchange full and frank information as to the scale of their armaments, their military, naval and air programmes and the condition of such of their industries as are adaptable to warlike purposes.

ARTICLE 9

A permanent Commission shall be constituted to advise the Council on the execution of the provisions of Articles 1 and 8 and on military, naval and air questions generally.

ARTICLE 10

The Members of the League undertake to respect and preserve as against external aggression the territorial integrity and existing political independence of all Members of the League. In case of any such aggression or in case of any threat or danger of such aggression the Council shall advise upon the means by which this obligation shall be fulfilled.

ARTICLE 11

1. Any war or threat of war, whether immediately affecting any of the Members of the League or not, is hereby declared a matter of concern to the whole League, and the League shall take any action that may be deemed wise and effectual to safeguard the peace of nations. In case any such emergency should arise the Secretary-General shall on the request of any Member of the League, forthwith summon a meeting of the Council.

2. It is also declared to be the friendly right of each Member of the League to bring to the attention of the Assembly or of the Council any circumstance whatever affecting international relations which threatens to disturb international peace or the good understanding between nations upon which peace depends.

ARTICLE 12

1. The Members of the League agree that if there should arise between them any dispute likely to lead to a rupture, they will submit the matter either to arbitration *or judicial settlement* or to enquiry by the Council, and they agree in no case to resort to war until three months after the award by the arbitrators *or the judicial decision* or the report by the Council.

2. In any case under this Article the award of the arbitrators *or the judicial decision* shall be made within a reasonable time, and the report of the Council shall be made within six months after the submission of the dispute.

ARTICLE 13

1. The Members of the League agree that whenever any dispute shall arise between them which they recognise to be suitable for submission to arbitration *or judicial settlement*, and which can not be satisfactorily settled by diplomacy, they will submit the whole subject-matter to arbitration *or judicial settlement*.

2. Disputes as to the interpretation of a treaty, as to any question of international law, as to the existence of any fact which, if established, would constitute a breach of any international obligation, or as to the extent and nature of the reparation to be made for any such breach, are declared to be among those which are generally suitable for submission to arbitration *or judicial settlement*.

3. *For the consideration of any such dispute, the court to which the case is referred shall be the Permanent Court of International Justice, established in accordance with Article 14; or any tribunal agreed on by the parties to the dispute or stipulated in any convention existing between them.*

4. The Members of the League agree that they will carry out in full good faith any award *or decision* that may be rendered, and that they will not resort to war against a Member of the League which complies therewith. In the event of any failure to carry out such an award *or decision*, the Council shall propose what steps should be taken to give effect thereto.

ARTICLE 14

The Council shall formulate and submit to the Members of the League for adoption plans for the establishment of a Permanent Court of International Justice. The Court shall be competent to hear and determine any dispute of an international character which the parties thereto submit to it. The Court may also give an advisory opinion upon any dispute or question referred to it by the Council or by the Assembly.

ARTICLE 15

1. If there should arise between Members of the League any dispute likely to lead to a rupture, which is not submitted to arbitration *or judicial settlement* in accordance with Article 13, the Members of the League agree that they will submit the matter to the Council. Any party to the dispute may effect such submission by giving notice of the existence of the dispute to the Secretary-General, who will

make all necessary arrangements for a full investigation and consideration thereof.

2. For this purpose, the parties to the dispute will communicate to the Secretary-General, as promptly as possible, statements of their case with all the relevant facts and papers, and the Council may forthwith direct the publication thereof.

3. The Council shall endeavour to effect a settlement of the dispute, and if such efforts are successful, a statement shall be made public giving such facts and explanations regarding the dispute and the terms of settlement thereof as the Council may deem appropriate.

4. If the dispute is not thus settled, the Council either unanimously or by a majority vote shall make and publish a report containing a statement of the facts of the dispute and the recommendations which are deemed just and proper in regard thereto.

5. Any Member of the League represented on the Council may make public a statement of the facts of the dispute and of its conclusions regarding the same.

6. If a report by the Council is unanimously agreed to by the members thereof other than the Representatives of one or more of the parties to the dispute, the Members of the League agree that they will not go to war with any party to the dispute which complies with the recommendations of the report.

7. If the Council fails to reach a report which is unanimously agreed to by the members thereof, other than the Representatives of one or more of the parties to the dispute, the Members of the League reserve to themselves the right to take such action as they shall consider necessary for the maintenance of right and justice.

8. If the dispute between the parties is claimed by one of them, and is found by the Council, to arise out of a matter which by international law is solely within the domestic jurisdiction of that party, the Council shall so report, and shall make no recommendation as to its settlement.

9. The Council may in any case under this Article refer the dispute to the Assembly. The dispute shall be so referred at the request of either party to the dispute, provided that such request be made within 14 days after the submission of the dispute to the Council.

10. In any case referred to the Assembly, all the provisions of this Article and of Article 12 relating to the action and powers of the Council shall apply to the action and powers of the Assembly, provided that a report made by the Assembly, if concurred in by the Representatives of those Members of the League represented on the

Council and of a majority of the other Members of the League, exclusive in each case of the Representatives of the parties to the dispute, shall have the same force as a report by the Council concurred in by all the members thereof other than the Representatives of one or more of the parties to the dispute.

ARTICLE 16

1. Should any Member of the League resort to war in disregard of its covenants under Articles 12, 13 or 15, it shall *ipso facto* be deemed to have committed an act of war against all other Members of the League, which hereby undertake immediately to subject it to the severance of all trade or financial relations, the prohibition of all intercourse between their nationals and the nationals of the covenant-breaking State, and the prevention of all financial, commercial or personal intercourse between the nationals of the covenant-breaking State and the nationals of any other State, whether a Member of the League or not.

2. It shall be the duty of the Council in such case to recommend to the several Governments concerned what effective military, naval or air force the Members of the League shall severally contribute to the armed forces to be used to protect the covenants of the League.

3. The Members of the League agree, further, that they will mutually support one another in the financial and economic measures which are taken under this Article, in order to minimise the loss and inconvenience resulting from the above measures, and that they will mutually support one another in resisting any special measures aimed at one of their number by the covenant-breaking State, and that they will take the necessary steps to afford passage through their territory to the forces of any of the Members of the League which are co-operating to protect the covenants of the League.

4. Any Member of the League which has violated any covenant of the League may be declared to be no longer a Member of the League by a vote of the Council concurred in by the Representatives of all the other Members of the League represented thereon.

ARTICLE 17

1. In the event of a dispute between a Member of the League and a State which is not a Member of the League, or between States not Members of the League, the State or States not Members of the League shall be invited to accept the obligations of membership in the League for the purposes of such dispute, upon such conditions as the

Council may deem just. If such invitation is accepted, the provisions of Articles 12 to 16, inclusive, shall be applied with such modifications as may be deemed necessary by the Council.

2. Upon such invitation being given, the Council shall immediately institute an enquiry into the circumstances of the dispute and recommend such action as may seem best and most effectual in the circumstances.

3. If a State so invited shall refuse to accept the obligations of membership in the League for the purposes of such dispute, and shall resort to war against a Member of the League, the provisions of Article 16 shall be applicable as against the State taking such action.

4. If both parties to the dispute when so invited refuse to accept the obligations of membership in the League for the purposes of such dispute, the Council may take such measures and make such recommendations as will prevent hostilities and will result in the settlement of the dispute.

ARTICLE 18

Every treaty or international engagement entered into hereafter by any Member of the League shall be forthwith registered with the Secretariat and shall as soon as possible be published by it. No such treaty or international engagement shall be binding until so registered.

ARTICLE 19

The Assembly may from time to time advise the reconsideration by Members of the League of treaties which have become inapplicable, and the consideration of international conditions whose continuance might endanger the peace of the world.

ARTICLE 20

1. The Members of the League severally agree that this Covenant is accepted as abrogating all obligations or understandings *inter se* which are inconsistent with the terms thereof, and solemnly undertake that they will not hereafter enter into any engagements inconsistent with the terms thereof.

2. In case any Member of the League shall, before becoming a Member of the League, have undertaken any obligations inconsistent with the terms of this Covenant, it shall be the duty of such Member to take immediate steps to procure its release from such obligations.

ARTICLE 21

Nothing in this Covenant shall be deemed to affect the validity of international engagements, such as treaties of arbitration or regional understandings like the Monroe doctrine, for securing the maintenance of peace.

ARTICLE 22

1. To those colonies and territories which as a consequence of the late war have ceased to be under the sovereignty of the States which formerly governed them and which are inhabited by peoples not yet able to stand by themselves under the strenuous conditions of the modern world, there should be applied the principle that the well-being and development of such peoples form a sacred trust of civilisation and that securities for the performance of this trust should be embodied in this Covenant.

2. The best method of giving practical effect to this principle is that the tutelage of such peoples should be entrusted to advanced nations who, by reason of their resources, their experience or their geographical position, can best undertake this responsibility, and who are willing to accept it, and that this tutelage should be exercised by them as Mandatories on behalf of the League.

3. The character of the mandate must differ according to the stage of the development of the people, the geographical situation of the territory, its economic conditions and other similar circumstances.

4. Certain communities formerly belonging to the Turkish Empire have reached a stage of development where their existence as independent nations can be provisionally recognised subject to the rendering of administrative advice and assistance by a Mandatory until such time as they are able to stand alone. The wishes of these communities must be a principal consideration in the selection of the Mandatory.

5. Other peoples, especially those of Central Africa, are at such a stage that the Mandatory must be responsible for the administration of the territory under conditions which will guarantee freedom of conscience and religion, subject only to the maintenance of public order and morals, the prohibition of abuses such as the slave trade, the arms traffic and the liquor traffic, and the prevention of the establishment of fortifications or military and naval bases and of military training of the natives for other than police purposes and the defense of territory, and will also secure equal opportunities for the trade and commerce of other Members of the League.

6. There are territories, such as South West Africa and certain of the South Pacific islands, which, owing to the sparseness of their population, or their small size, or their remoteness from the centers of civilisation, or their geographical contiguity to the territory of the Mandatory, and other circumstances, can be best administered under the laws of the Mandatory as integral portions of its territory, subject to the safeguards above mentioned in the interests of the indigenous population.

7. In every case of mandate, the Mandatory shall render to the Council an annual report in reference to the territory committed to its charge.

8. The degree of authority, control or administration to be exercised by the Mandatory shall, if not previously agreed upon by the Members of the League, be explicitly defined in each case by the Council.

9. A permanent Commission shall be constituted to receive and examine the annual reports of the Mandatories and to advise the Council on all matters relating to the observance of the mandates.

ARTICLE 23

Subject to and in accordance with the provisions of international conventions existing or hereafter to be agreed upon, the Members of the League:

(a) will endeavour to secure and maintain fair and humane conditions of labour for men, women and children, both in their own countries and in all countries to which their commercial and industrial relations extend, and for that purpose will establish and maintain the necessary international organisations;

(b) undertake to secure just treatment of the native inhabitants of territories under their control;

(c) will entrust the League with the general supervision over the execution of agreements with regard to the traffic in women and children, and the traffic in opium and other dangerous drugs;

(d) will entrust the League with the general supervision of the trade in arms and ammunition with the countries in which the control of this traffic is necessary in the common interest;

(e) will make provision to secure and maintain freedom of communications and of transit and equitable treatment for the commerce of all Members of the League. In this connection, the special necessities of the regions devastated during the war of 1914-1918 shall be borne in mind;

(*f*) will endeavour to take steps in matters of international concern for the prevention and control of disease.

ARTICLE 24

1. There shall be placed under the direction of the League all international bureaux already established by general treaties if the parties to such treaties consent. All such international bureaux and all commissions for the regulation of matters of international interest hereafter constituted shall be placed under the direction of the League.

2. In all matters of international interest which are regulated by general conventions but which are not placed under the control of international bureaux or commissions, the Secretariat of the League shall, subject to the consent of the Council and if desired by the parties, collect and distribute all relevant information and shall render any other assistance which may be necessary or desirable.

3. The Council may include as part of the expenses of the Secretariat the expenses of any bureau or commission which is placed under the direction of the League.

ARTICLE 25

The Members of the League agree to encourage and promote the establishment and coöperation of duly authorised voluntary national Red Cross organisations having as purposes the improvement of health, the prevention of disease and the mitigation of suffering throughout the world.

ARTICLE 26

1. Amendments to this Covenant will take effect when ratified by the Members of the League whose Representatives compose the Council and by a majority of the Members of the League whose Representatives compose the Assembly.

2. No such amendment shall bind any Member of the League which signifies its dissent therefrom, but in that case it shall cease to be a Member of the League.

THE NINE-POWER TREATY[1]

The United States of America, Belgium, the British Empire, China, France, Italy, Japan, the Netherlands and Portugal:

Desiring to adopt a policy designed to stabilize conditions in the Far East, to safeguard the rights and interests of China, and to promote intercourse between China and the other Powers upon the basis of equality of opportunity;

Have resolved to conclude a treaty for that purpose and to that end have appointed as their respective Plenipotentiaries [here follow the names and official titles of the Plenipotentiaries].

ARTICLE I

The Contracting Powers, other than China, agree:

(1) To respect the sovereignty, the independence, and the territorial and administrative integrity of China;

(2) To provide the fullest and most unembarrassed opportunity to China to develop and maintain for herself an effective and stable government;

(3) To use their influence for the purpose of effectually establishing and maintaining the principle of equal opportunity for the commerce and industry of all nations throughout the territory of China;

(4) To refrain from taking advantage of conditions in China in order to seek special rights or privileges which would abridge the rights of subjects or citizens of friendly States, and from countenancing action inimical to the security of such States.

ARTICLE II

The Contracting Powers agree not to enter into any treaty, agreement, arrangement, or understanding, either with one another, or,

[1] The text is that published by the Department of State, *Treaty Series*, No. 723.

individually or collectively, with any Power or Powers, which would infringe or impair the principles stated in Article I.

ARTICLE III

With a view to applying more effectually the principles of the Open Door or equality of opportunity in China for the trade and industry of all nations, the Contracting Powers, other than China, agree that they will not seek, nor support their respective nationals in seeking—

(*a*) any arrangement which might purport to establish in favor of their interests any general superiority of rights with respect to commercial or economic development in any designated region of China;

(*b*) any such monopoly or preference as would deprive the nationals of any other Power of the right of undertaking any legitimate trade or industry in China, or of participating with the Chinese Government, or with any local authority, in any category of public enterprise, or which by reason of its scope, duration or geographical extent is calculated to frustrate the practical application of the principle of equal opportunity.

It is understood that the foregoing stipulations of this Article are not to be so construed as to prohibit the acquisition of such properties or rights as may be necessary to the conduct of a particular commercial, industrial, or financial undertaking or to the encouragement of invention and research.

China undertakes to be guided by the principles stated in the foregoing stipulations of this Article in dealing with applications for economic rights and privileges from Governments and nationals of all foreign countries, whether parties to the present Treaty or not.

ARTICLE IV

The Contracting Powers agree not to support any agreements by their respective nationals with each other designed to create Spheres of Influence or to provide for the enjoyment of mutually exclusive opportunities in designated parts of Chinese territory.

ARTICLE V

China agrees that, throughout the whole of the railways in China, she will not exercise or permit unfair discrimination of any kind. In particular there shall be no discrimination whatever, direct or indirect, in respect of charges or of facilities on the ground of the nationality of passengers or the countries from which or to which they are proceeding, or the origin or ownership of goods or the country from which or to which they are consigned, or the nationality or ownership of the ship or other means of conveying such passengers or goods before or after their transport on the Chinese Railways.

The Contracting Powers, other than China, assume a corresponding obligation in respect of any of the aforesaid railways over which they or their nationals are in a position to exercise any control in virtue of any concession, special agreement or otherwise.

ARTICLE VI

The Contracting Powers, other than China, agree fully to respect China's rights as a neutral in time of war to which China is not a party; and China declares that when she is a neutral she will observe the obligations of neutrality.

ARTICLE VII

The Contracting Powers agree that, whenever a situation arises which in the opinion of any one of them involves the application of the stipulations of the present Treaty, and renders desirable discussion of such application, there shall be full and frank communication between the Contracting Powers concerned.

ARTICLE VIII

Powers not signatory to the present Treaty, which have Governments recognized by the Signatory Powers and which have treaty relations with China, shall be invited to adhere to the present Treaty. To this end the Government of the United States will make the necessary communications to nonsignatory Powers and will inform the Contracting Powers of the replies received. Adherence by any Power shall become effective on receipt of notice thereof by the Government of the United States.

ARTICLE IX

The present Treaty shall be ratified by the Contracting Powers in accordance with their respective constitutional methods and shall take effect on the date of the deposit of all the ratifications, which shall take place at Washington as soon as possible. The Government of the United States will transmit to the other Contracting Powers a certified copy of the procès-verbal of the deposit of ratifications.

The present Treaty, of which the French and English texts are both authentic, shall remain deposited in the archives of the Government of the United States, and duly certified copies thereof shall be transmitted by that Government to the other Contracting Powers.

In faith whereof the above-named Plenipotentiaries have signed the present Treaty.

Done at the City of Washington the Sixth day of February, One Thousand Nine Hundred and Twenty-Two.

[SIGNATURES]

THE PACT OF PARIS
(KELLOGG-BRIAND PACT)

The President of the German Reich, the President of the United States of America, His Majesty the King of the Belgians, the President of the French Republic, His Majesty the King of Great Britain, Ireland and the British Dominions beyond the Seas, Emperor of India, His Majesty the King of Italy, His Majesty the Emperor of Japan, the President of the Republic of Poland, the President of the Czechoslovak Republic,

Deeply sensible of their solemn duty to promote the welfare of mankind;

Persuaded that the time has come when a frank renunciation of war as an instrument of national policy should be made to the end that the peaceful and friendly relations now existing between their peoples may be perpetuated;

Convinced that all changes in their relations with one another should be sought only by pacific means and be the result of a peaceful and orderly process, and that any signatory Power which shall hereafter seek to promote its national interests by resort to war should be denied the benefits furnished by this Treaty;

Hopeful that, encouraged by their example, all the other nations of the world will join in this humane endeavor and by adhering to the present Treaty as soon as it comes into force bring their peoples within the scope of its beneficent provisions, thus uniting the civilized nations of the world in a common renunciation of war as an instrument of their national policy;

Have decided to conclude a Treaty and for that purpose have appointed as their respective Plenipotentiaries [here follow the names and official titles of the Plenipotentiaries] who, having communicated to one another their full powers found in good and due form, have agreed upon the following articles:

ARTICLE I

The High Contracting Parties solemnly declare in the names of their respective peoples that they condemn recourse to war for the solution of international controversies, and renounce it as an instrument of national policy in their relations with one another.

ARTICLE II

The High Contracting Parties agree that the settlement or solution of all disputes or conflicts of whatever nature or of whatever origin they may be, which may arise among them, shall never be sought except by pacific means.

ARTICLE III

The present Treaty shall be ratified by the High Contracting Parties named in the Preamble in accordance with their respective constitutional requirements, and shall take effect as between them as soon as all their several instruments of ratification shall have been deposited at Washington.

This Treaty shall, when it has come into effect as prescribed in the preceding paragraph, remain open as long as may be necessary for adherence by all the other Powers of the world. Every instrument evidencing the adherence of a Power shall be deposited at Washington and the Treaty shall immediately upon such deposit become effective as between the Power thus adhering and the other Powers parties hereto.

It shall be the duty of the Government of the United States to furnish each Government named in the Preamble and every Government subsequently adhering to this Treaty with a certified copy of the Treaty and of every instrument of ratification or adherence. It shall also be the duty of the Government of the United States telegraphically to notify such Governments immediately upon the deposit with it of each instrument of ratification or adherence.

IN FAITH WHEREOF the respective Plenipotentiaries have signed this Treaty in the French and English languages both texts having equal force, and hereunto affix their seals.

DONE at Paris, the twenty-seventh day of August in the year one thousand nine hundred and twenty-eight.

[SIGNATURES]

FINDINGS AND RECOMMENDATIONS OF THE LEAGUE ASSEMBLY ON THE LYTTON REPORT, FEBRUARY 24, 1933

The Assembly, in view of the failure of the efforts which, under Article 15, paragraph 3, of the Covenant, it was its duty to make with a view to effecting a settlement of the dispute submitted for its consideration under paragraph 9 of the said article, adopts, in virtue of paragraph 4 of that article, the following report containing a statement of the facts of the dispute and the recommendations which are deemed just and proper in regard thereto.

[Parts I and II of the Report, giving a brief historical summary of the development of the Sino-Japanese dispute, are omitted.]

PART III

Chief Characteristics of the Dispute

It will be seen from this review that for more than sixteen months the Council or Assembly has continuously tried to find a solution for the Sino-Japanese dispute. Numerous resolutions have been adopted based on various articles of the Covenant and other international agreements. The complexity, to which reference has already been made, of the historical background of the events; the special legal situation of Manchuria, where Japan, as will be noted later, exercised within Chinese territory extensive rights; finally, the involved and delicate relations existing in fact between the Chinese and Japanese authorities in certain parts of Manchuria justified and rendered necessary the prolonged efforts of negotiation and enquiry made by the League. However, the hopes entertained by the Council and the Assembly of an improvement in the situation, arising from the declarations of the parties and the resolutions adopted with their participation, were disappointed. The situation, on the contrary, tended to grow constantly worse. In Manchuria, or other parts of the territory of a Member of the League, military operations, which the report of the Commission of Enquiry has described as "war in disguise," continued and still continue.

Having considered the principal features of the dispute, the Assembly has reached, in particular, the following conclusions and noted the following facts:

1. The dispute between China and Japan which is submitted to the Assembly originated in Manchuria, which China and foreign Powers have always regarded as an integral part of China under Chinese sovereignty. In its observations on the report of the Commission of Enquiry,[1] the Japanese Government contests the argument that the rights conferred on Russia and subsequently acquired by Japan "in the extremely limited area known as the Southern Manchuria Railway zone" conflict with Chinese sovereignty. "They were, on the contrary, derived from the sovereignty of China."

The rights conferred by China on Russia and subsequently on Japan derive from the sovereignty of China. Under the Treaty of Pekin in 1905, "the Imperial Chinese Government consented to all the transfers and assignments made by Russia to Japan" under the Treaty of Portsmouth. In 1915, it was to China that Japan addressed demands for the extension of her rights in Manchuria and it was with the Government of the Chinese Republic that, following on these demands, the Treaty of May 25, 1915, was concluded concerning South Manchuria and Eastern Inner Mongolia. At the Washington Conference, the Japanese delegation stated, on February 2, 1922, that Japan renounced certain preferential rights in South Manchuria and Eastern Inner Mongolia and explained that, "in coming to this decision, Japan had been guided by a spirit of fairness and moderation, having always in view China's sovereign rights and the principle of equal opportunity."[2] The Nine-Power Treaty, concluded at the Washington Conference, applies to Manchuria as to every other part of China. Finally, during the first phase of the present conflict, Japan never argued that Manchuria was not an integral part of China.

2. Past experience shows that those who control Manchuria exercise a considerable influence on the affairs of the rest of China—at least of North China—and possess unquestionable strategic and po-

---

[1] Document C. 775. 1932 VII; *Official Journal,* Special Supplement No. 111, page 99.
[2] Conference on the Limitation of Armaments, Washington, 1922, page 1512.

litical advantages. To cut off these provinces from the rest of China cannot but create a serious irredentist problem likely to endanger peace.

3. The Assembly, in noting these facts, is not unmindful of the tradition of autonomy existing in Manchuria. That tradition, in one extreme case, and in a period of particular weakness on the part of the Central Government of China, made it possible, for instance, for the plenipotentiaries of Marshal Chang Tso-lin to conclude, in the name of the "Government of the autonomous three Eastern Provinces of the Republic of China," the agreement of September 20, 1924, with the Union of Soviet Socialist Republics concerning the Chinese Eastern Railway, navigation, the delimitation of frontiers, etc. It is obvious from the provisions of that agreement, however, that the Government of the autonomous three Eastern Provinces did not regard itself as the Government of a State independent of China, but believed that it might itself negotiate with the Union of Soviet Socialist Republics on questions affecting the interests of China in the three provinces, though the Central Government had, a few months previously, concluded an agreement on these questions with the self-same Power.

This autonomy of Manchuria was also shown by the fact that, first, Marshal Chang Tso-lin and later Marshal Chang Hsueh-liang were the heads both of the civil and military administration and exercised the effective power in the three provinces through their armies and their officials. The independence proclaimed by Marshal Chang Tso-lin at different times never meant that either he or the people of Manchuria wished to be separated from China. His armies did not invade China as if it were a foreign country but merely as participants in the civil war. Through all its wars and periods of "independence," Manchuria remained an integral part of China. Further, since 1928, Marshal Chang Hsueh-liang has recognised the authority of the Chinese National Government.

4. During the quarter of a century ending in September, 1931, the political and economic ties uniting Manchuria with the rest of China grew stronger, while, at the same time, the interests of Japan in Manchuria did not cease to develop. Under the Chinese Republic, the "three Eastern provinces" constituting Manchuria were thrown wide to the immigration of Chinese from the other provinces who, by taking possession of the land, have made Manchuria in many respects a simple extension of China north of the Great Wall. In a population of about 30 millions, it is estimated that the Chinese or

assimilated Manchus number 28 millions. Moreover, under the administration of Marshals Chang Tso-lin and Chang Hsueh-liang, the Chinese population and Chinese interests have played a much more important part than formerly in the development and organisation of the economic resources of Manchuria.

On the other hand, Japan had acquired or claimed in Manchuria rights the effect of which was to restrict the exercise of sovereignty by China in a manner and to a degree quite exceptional. Japan governed the leased territory of Kwantung, exercising therein what amounted in practice to full sovereignty. Through the medium of the South Manchuria Railway, she administered the railway zones, including several towns and important parts of populous cities, such as Mukden and Changchun. In these areas, she had control of the police, taxes, education, and public utilities. She maintained armed forces in certain parts of the country: the army of Kwantung in the leased territory; railway guards in the railway zones; consular police in the various districts. Such a state of affairs might perhaps have continued without leading to complications and incessant disputes if it had been freely desired or accepted by both parties and it had been the expression and manifestation of a well-understood policy of close economic and political coöperation. But, in the absence of such conditions, it was bound to lead to mutual misunderstandings and conflicts. The interconnection of respective rights, the uncertainty at times of the legal situation, the increasing opposition between the conception held by the Japanese of their "special position" in Manchuria, and the claims of Chinese nationalism were a further source of numerous incidents and disputes.

5. Before September 18, 1931, each of the two parties had legitimate grievances against the other in Manchuria, Japan taking advantage of rights open to question and the Chinese authorities putting obstacles in the way of the exercise of rights which could not be contested. During the period immediately preceding the events of September 18, various efforts were made to settle the questions outstanding between the two parties by the normal method of diplomatic negotiations and pacific means, and these means had not been exhausted. Nevertheless, the tension between Chinese and Japanese in Manchuria increased, and a movement of opinion in Japan advocated the settlement of all outstanding questions—if necessary, by force.

6. The present period of transition and national reconstruction in China, despite the efforts of the Central Government and the con-

siderable progress already achieved, necessarily involves political disturbances, social disorder and disruptive tendencies inseparable from a state of transition. It calls for the employment of a policy of international coöperation. One of the methods of that policy would be that the League of Nations would continue to afford China the technical assistance in modernising her institutions which her Government might request with a view to enabling the Chinese people to reorganise and consolidate the Chinese State.

The full application of the policy of international coöperation initiated at the Washington Conference, the principles of which are still valid, has been delayed, chiefly by the violence of the anti-foreign propaganda carried on in China from time to time. In two respects—the use of the economic boycott and anti-foreign teaching in schools—this propaganda has been pushed to such lengths that it has contributed to creating the atmosphere in which the present dispute broke out.

7. The use of the boycott by the Chinese previous to the events of September 18, 1931, to express their indignation at certain incidents or to support certain claims could not fail to make a situation which was already tense still more tense.

The use of the boycott by China, subsequent to the events of September 18, 1931, falls under the category of reprisals.

8. The object of the provisions of the Covenant of the League of Nations regarding the settlement of disputes is to prevent the tension between nations becoming such that a rupture appears to be inevitable. The Commission of Enquiry found that each of the issues between China and Japan was in itself capable of settlement by arbitral procedure. It is precisely because the accumulation of these issues increased the tension between the two nations that it was incumbent on the nation which regarded itself as injured to draw the attention of the League of Nations to the situation when diplomatic negotiations were unduly protracted.

Article 12 of the Covenant contains formal obligations as regards the pacific settlement of disputes.

9. Without excluding the possibility that, on the night of September 18-19, 1931, the Japanese officers on the spot may have believed that they were acting in self-defence, the Assembly cannot regard as measures of self-defence the military operations carried out on that night by the Japanese troops at Mukden and other places in Manchuria. Nor can the military measures of Japan as a whole,

developed in the course of the dispute, be regarded as measures of self-defence. Moreover, the adoption of measures of self-defence does not exempt a State from complying with the provisions of Article 12 of the Covenant.

10. Since September 18, 1931, the activities of the Japanese military authorities, in civil as well as in military matters, have been marked by essentially political considerations. The progressive military occupation of the Three Eastern Provinces removed in succession all the important towns in Manchuria from the control of the Chinese authorities, and, following each occupation, the civil administration was reorganised. A group of Japanese civil and military officials conceived, organised and carried through the Manchurian independence movement as a solution to the situation in Manchuria as it existed after the events of September 18, and, with this object, made use of the names and actions of certain Chinese individuals and took advantage of certain minorities and native communities that had grievances against the Chinese administration. This movement, which rapidly received assistance and direction from the Japanese General Staff, could only be carried through owing to the presence of the Japanese troops. It cannot be considered as a spontaneous and genuine independence movement.

11. The main political and administrative power in the "Government" of "Manchukuo," the result of the movement described in the previous paragraph, rests in the hands of Japanese officials and advisers, who are in a position actually to direct and control the administration; in general, the Chinese in Manchuria, who, as already mentioned, form the vast majority of the population, do not support this "Government" and regard it as an instrument of the Japanese. It should also be noted that, after the Commission of Enquiry completed its report and before the report was considered by the Council and the Assembly, "Manchukuo" was recognised by Japan. It has not been recognised by any other State, the Members of the League in particular being of opinion that such recognition was incompatible with the spirit of the resolution of March 11, 1932.

* * * *

The situation which led to the events of September 18, 1931, presents certain special features. It was subsequently aggravated by the development of the Japanese military operations, the creation of the "Manchukuo Government" and the recognition of that "Government" by Japan. Undoubtedly the present case is not that of a country which has declared war on another country without previously exhausting the opportunities for conciliation provided in the Covenant of the League of Nations; neither is it a simple case of the violation of the frontier of one country by the armed forces of a neighboring country, because in Manchuria, as shown by the circumstances noted above, there are many features without an exact parallel in other parts of the world. It is, however, indisputable that, without any declaration of war, a large part of Chinese territory has been forcibly seized and occupied by Japanese troops and that, in consequence of this operation, it has been separated from and declared independent of the rest of China.

The Council, in its resolution of September 30, 1931, noted the declaration of the Japanese representative that his Government would continue, as rapidly as possible, the withdrawal of its troops, which had already been begun, into the railway zone in proportion as the safety of the lives and property of Japanese nationals was effectively ensured, and that it hoped to carry out this intention in full as speedily as might be. Further, in its resolution of December 10, 1931, the Council, re-affirming its resolution of September 30, noted the undertaking of the two parties to adopt all measures necessary to avoid any further aggravation of the situation and to refrain from any initiative which might lead to further fighting and loss of life.

It should be pointed out in connection with these events that, under Article 10 of the Covenant, the Members of the League undertake to respect the territorial integrity and existing political independence of all Members of the League.

Lastly, under Article 12 of the Covenant, the Members of the League agree that, if there should arise between them any dispute likely to lead to a rupture, they will submit the matter either to arbitration or judicial settlement or to enquiry by the Council.

While at the origin of the state of tension that existed before September 18, 1931, certain responsibilities would appear to lie on one side and the other, no question of Chinese responsibility can arise for the development of events since September 18, 1931.

PART IV

Statement of the Recommendations

This part sets forth the recommendations which the Assembly deems just and proper in regard to the dispute.

The recommendations of the Assembly take into account the very special circumstances of this case and are based on the following principles, conditions and considerations:

(*a*) The settlement of the dispute should observe the provisions of the Covenant of the League, the Pact of Paris, and the Nine-Power Treaty of Washington.

Article 10 of the Covenant of the League provides that "the Members of the League undertake to respect and preserve as against external aggression the territorial integrity and existing political independence of all Members of the League."

According to Article II of the Pact of Paris, "the High Contracting Parties agree that the settlement or solution of all disputes or conflicts of whatever nature, or of whatever origin they may be, which may arise among them, shall never be sought except by pacific means."

According to Article I of the Nine-Power Treaty of Washington, "the Contracting Powers, other than China, agree to respect the sovereignty, the independence, and the territorial and administrative integrity of China."

(*b*) The settlement of the dispute should observe the provisions of Parts I and II of the Assembly resolution of March 11, 1932.

In that resolution, which has already been quoted in this report, the Assembly considered that the provisions of the Covenant were entirely applicable to the present dispute, more particularly as regards:

(1) The principle of a scrupulous respect for treaties;

(2) The undertaking entered into by Members of the League of Nations to respect and preserve as against external aggression the territorial integrity and existing political independence of all the Members of the League;

(3) Their obligation to submit any dispute which may arise between them to procedures for peaceful settlement.

The Assembly has adopted the principles laid down by the President-in-Office of the Council in his declaration of December 10, 1931, and has recalled the fact that twelve Members of the Council had again invoked those principles in their appeal to the Japanese Government on February 16, 1932, when they declared that no infringement of the territorial integrity and no change in the political independence of any Member of the League brought about in disregard of Article 10 of the Covenant ought to be recognised as valid and effectual by Members of the League.

The Assembly has stated its opinion that the principles governing international relations and the peaceful settlement of disputes between Members of the League above referred to are in full harmony with the Pact of Paris. Pending the steps which it might ultimately take for the settlement of the dispute which had been referred to it, it has proclaimed the binding nature of the principles and provisions referred to above and declared that it was incumbent upon the Members of the League not to recognise any situation, treaty or agreement which might be brought about by means contrary to the Covenant of the League of Nations or to the Pact of Paris.

Lastly, the Assembly has affirmed that it is contrary to the spirit of the Covenant that the settlement of the Sino-Japanese dispute should be sought under the stress of military pressure on the part of either party, and has recalled the resolutions adopted by the Council on September 30 and December 10, 1931, in agreement with the parties.

(c) In order that a lasting understanding may be established between China and Japan on the basis of respect for the international undertakings mentioned above, the settlement of the dispute must conform to the principles and conditions laid down by the Commission of Enquiry in the following terms:

"1. *Compatibility with the interests of both China and Japan.*

"Both countries are Members of the League and each is entitled to claim the same consideration from the League. A solution from which both did not derive benefit would not be a gain to the cause of peace.

"2. *Consideration for the interests of the Union of Soviet Socialist Republics.*

"To make peace between two of the neighbouring countries without regard for the interests of the third would be neither just nor wise, nor in the interests of peace.

"3. *Conformity with existing multilateral treaties.*

"Any solution should conform to the provisions of the Covenant of the League of Nations, the Pact of Paris, and the Nine-Power Treaty of Washington.

"4. *Recognition of Japan's interests in Manchuria.*

"The rights and interests of Japan in Manchuria are facts which cannot be ignored, and any solution which failed to recognise them and to take into account also the historical associations of Japan with that country would not be satisfactory.

"5. *The establishment of new treaty relations between China and Japan.*

"A re-statement of the respective rights, interests and responsibilities of both countries in Manchuria in new treaties, which shall be part of the settlement by agreement, is desirable if future friction is to be avoided and mutual confidence and coöperation are to be restored.

"6. *Effective provision for the settlement of future disputes.*

"As a corollary to the above, it is necessary that provision should be made for facilitating the prompt settlement of minor disputes as they arise.

"7. *Manchurian autonomy.*

"The Government in Manchuria should be modified in such a way as to secure, consistently with the sovereignty and administrative integrity of China, a large measure of autonomy designed to meet the local conditions and special characteristics of the Three Provinces. The new civil regime must be so constituted and conducted as to satisfy the essential requirements of good government.

"8. *Internal order and security against external aggression.*

"The internal order of the country should be secured by an effective local gendarmerie force, and security against external aggression should be provided by the withdrawal of all armed forces other than gendarmerie, and by the conclusion of a treaty of non-aggression between the countries interested.

"9. *Encouragement of an economic* rapprochement *between China and Japan.*

"For this purpose a new commercial treaty between the two countries is desirable. Such a treaty should aim at placing on an equitable basis the commercial relations between the two countries and bringing them into conformity with their improved political relations.

"10. *International coöperation in Chinese reconstruction.*

"Since the present political instability in China is an obstacle to friendship with Japan and an anxiety to the rest of the world (as the maintenance of peace in the Far East is a matter of international concern), and since the conditions enumerated above cannot be fulfilled without a strong Central Government in China, the final requisite for a satisfactory solution is temporary international coöperation in the internal reconstruction of China, as suggested by the late Dr. Sun Yat-sen."

The provisions of this section constitute the recommendations of the Assembly under Article 15, paragraph 4, of the Covenant.

Having defined the principles, conditions and considerations applicable to the settlement of the dispute,

THE ASSEMBLY RECOMMENDS AS FOLLOWS:

1. Whereas the sovereignty over Manchuria belongs to China,

A. Considering that the presence of Japanese troops outside the zone of the South Manchuria Railway and their operations outside this zone are incompatible with the legal principles which should govern the settlement of the dispute, and that it is necessary to establish as soon as possible a situation consistent with these principles,

The Assembly recommends the evacuation of these troops. In view of the special circumstances of the case, the first object of the negotiations recommended hereinafter should be to organise this evacuation and to determine the methods, stages and time-limits thereof.

B. Having regard to the local conditions special to Manchuria, the particular rights and interests possessed by Japan therein, and the rights and interests of third States,

The Assembly recommends the establishment in Manchuria, within a reasonable period, of an organisation under the sovereignty of, and compatible with the administrative integrity of, China. This organisation should provide a wide measure of autonomy, should be in harmony with local conditions and should take account of the multilateral treaties in force, the particular rights and interests of Japan, the rights and interests of third States, and, in general, the principles and conditions reproduced in Section 1 (c) above; the determination of the respective powers of and relations between the Chinese Central Government and the local authorities should be made the subject of a Declaration by the Chinese Government having the force of an international undertaking.

2. Whereas, in addition to the questions dealt with in the two recommendations 1A and 1B, the report of the Commission of Enquiry mentions in the principles and conditions for a settlement of the dispute set out in Section 1 (c) above certain other questions affecting the good understanding between China and Japan, on which peace in the Far East depends,

The Assembly recommends the parties to settle these questions on the basis of the said principles and conditions.

3. Whereas the negotiations necessary for giving effect to the foregoing recommendations should be carried on by means of a suitable organ,

The Assembly recommends the opening of negotiations between the two parties in accordance with the method specified hereinafter.

Each of the parties is invited to inform the Secretary-General whether it accepts, so far as it is concerned, the recommendations of the Assembly, subject to the sole condition that the other party also accepts them.

The negotiations between the parties should take place with the assistance of a Committee set up by the Assembly as follows: The Assembly hereby invites the Governments of Belgium, Great Britain, Canada, Czechoslovakia, France, Germany, the Irish Free State, Italy, The Netherlands, Portugal, Spain and Turkey each to appoint a member to the Committee as soon as the Secretary-General shall have informed them that the two parties accept the Assembly's recommendations. The Secretary-General shall also notify the Governments of the United States of America and of the Union of Soviet Socialist Republics of this acceptance and invite each of them to appoint a member of the Committee should it so desire. Within one month after having been informed of the acceptance of the two parties, the Secretary-General shall take all suitable steps for the opening of negotiations.

In order to enable the Members of the League, after the opening of negotiations, to judge whether each of the parties is acting in conformity with the Assembly's recommendations:

(a) The Committee will, whenever it thinks fit, report on the state of the negotiations, and particularly on the negotiations with regard to the carrying out of the recommendations 1A and B above; as regards recommendation 1A, the Committee will in any case report within three months of the opening of negotiations. These reports shall be communicated by the Secretary-General to the Members of the League and to the non-member States represented on the Committee;

(b) The Committee may submit to the Assembly all questions relating to the interpretation of Section II of Part IV of the present report. The Assembly shall give this interpretation in the same conditions as those in which the present report is adopted, in conformity with Article 15, paragraph 10, of the Covenant.

In view of the special circumstances of the case, the recommendations made do not provide for a mere return to the *status quo* existing before September, 1931. They likewise exclude the maintenance and recognition of the existing regime in Manchuria, such maintenance and recognition being incompatible with the fundamental principles of existing international obligations and with the good understanding between the two countries on which peace in the Far East depends.

It follows that, in adopting the present report, the Members of the League intend to abstain, particularly as regards the existing regime in Manchuria, from any act which might prejudice or delay the carrying out of the recommendations of the said report. They will continue not to recognise this regime either *de jure* or *de facto*. They intend to abstain from taking any isolated action with regard to the situation in Manchuria and to continue to concert their action among themselves as well as with the interested States not Members of the League. As regards the Members of the League who are signatories of the Nine-Power Treaty, it may be recalled that, in accordance with the provisions of that Treaty: "Whenever a situation arises which, in the opinion of any one of them, involves the application of the stipulations of the present Treaty and renders desirable discussion of such application, there shall be full and frank communication between the Contracting Powers concerned."

In order to facilitate as far as possible the establishment in the Far East of a situation in conformity with the recommendations of the present report, the Secretary-General is instructed to communicate a copy of this report to the States non-members of the League who are signatories of, or have acceded to, the Pact of Paris or of the Nine-Power Treaty, informing them of the Assembly's hope that they will associate themselves with the views expressed in the report, and that they will, if necessary, concert their action and their attitude with the Members of the League.

INDEX